Surviving
the Eighties

Strategies and Procedures
for Solving Fiscal
and Enrollment Problems

Lewis B. Mayhew

Surviving
the Eighties

Jossey-Bass Publishers
San Francisco • Washington • London • 1979

SURVIVING THE EIGHTIES
Strategies and Procedures for Solving Fiscal and Enrollment Problems
by Lewis B. Mayhew

Copyright © 1979 by: Jossey-Bass, Inc., Publishers
433 California Street
San Francisco, California 94104
&
Jossey-Bass Limited
28 Banner Street
London EC1Y 8QE

Library of Congress Catalogue Card Number LC 79-88773

International Standard Book Number ISBN 0-87589-428-3

Manufactured in the United States of America

JACKET DESIGN BY WILLI BAUM

FIRST EDITION

Code 7929

Preface

≈≈≈≈≈≈≈≈

Surviving the Eighties is essentially an extended consultation concerning the assorted perplexities that collegiate institutions must be prepared to face intensively during the 1980s and 1990s. The comments and advice contained herein are based on the belief that higher education in the United States, after a century of gradual and then rapid expansion, must now anticipate several decades of no growth or even decline. Some well-established institutions will adjust to this steady or declining state with only minor difficulty. But others, especially the privately controlled institutions, may experience such travail as to have their very existence seriously jeopardized. Whether comfortably situated or approaching mortal danger, all institutions will face new conditions and must arrange their affairs accordingly.

In a sense, over thirty years has been spent in the preparation of this book, for it rests largely on impressions gained from visiting or consulting with members of almost 700 collegiate institutions of all sorts since the early 1950s. To those impressions have been added fruits of the research of others and the gracious responses of many different institutions to requests for information regarding their status and the strategy and tactics they were using to ensure the healthy continuation of their institutions. This is clearly not a scientific monograph in the sense that every observation is based on experimentation that could be replicated. It does make use of some such information. It is, however, intended to be a serious reflection on how colleges and universities operate and how those operations can be made smoother or more effective and, when appropriate, more efficient.

This book is addressed specifically to individuals directly responsible for maintaining institutions. It is hoped that it can be read with value by members of boards of trustees, presidents, administrative associates, faculty members, and concerned laymen, who ultimately must provide the legitimacy and survival of each collegiate institution.

Appreciation and thanks go to many different people. Several hundred college presidents graciously responded to a questionnaire and several score allowed me to visit their institutions. Although the number of women entering the top levels of college administration is growing, most of those whom I saw in connection with this study were men, hence the use of *he* throughout the book. Partial funding was provided by the Spencer Foundation under the leadership of its president, H. Thomas James. As with other tasks, my secretary, Phyllis Anderson, has worked diligently to produce the manuscript and to maintain some order for the heavy flow of information. My research assistant, Nancy Kaible, has gone over this material endlessly, checked on details, and done some of the essential fieldwork. As always and forever, love and thanks go to my wife, Dorothy C. Mayhew, just because she is there.

Finally, this book is dedicated to my long-time friend, mentor, confidant, and collaborator, Paul L. Dressel, without whose help and encouragement this book and others may never have been written.

Stanford, California   Lewis B. Mayhew
August 1979

Contents

ㅈㅈㅈㅈㄷㄷㄷㄷ

The Author

⋈⋈⋈⋈⋈⋈⋈⋈

Lewis B. Mayhew is professor of education and chairman of the
Committee on Administration and Policy Analysis in the School of
Education, Stanford University. After five-and-one-half years in the
U.S. Army during World War II, he spent twelve years at Michigan
State University (1947–1958), three years at the University of
South Florida (1959–1962), and fifteen years at Stanford (1962–
present). For seventeen years (1957–1974) he served as part-time
director of research at Stephens College in Columbia, Missouri. He
received his bachelor's and master's degrees from the University of
Illinois (1938 and 1947, respectively) and his Ph.D. in history from
Michigan State University (1951).

He has written about many parts of higher education in the
United States (over 20 books and 200 articles), consulted widely
(over 500 institutions), and served on many different regional and
national committees, such as the Educational Testing Service Board
Committee on Test Development and the Senior Commission of the
Western College Association. He was consultant to the White House

Conference on Education during Lyndon B. Johnson's administration, president of the American Association for Higher Education, and rated one of the 44 most influential leaders in higher education in the *Change* magazine survey in 1974.

Lewis Mayhew has been married for forty years to Dorothy C. Mayhew, and has three children, Lewis B., Jr., Madeline, and Robert. In addition, he and his wife have informally adopted a second daughter, Trudy. The Mayhews live on the Stanford campus.

Surviving the Eighties

≋≋≋≋≋≋≋≋

Strategies and Procedures
for Solving Fiscal
and Enrollment Problems

Chapter 1

⋉⋉⋉⋉⋉⋉⋉⋉

Increasing the Chances
for Survival

A number of factors, some obvious and some not, appear to be
positively related to the survival and vitality of American colleges
and universities. When these factors are absent, the viability of an
institution can be seriously threatened. Although some circumstances
may be impossible to change, an institution facing increasing difficulties should nonetheless be aware of them. This opening chapter
points out the factors important to the longevity of an institution and
identifies the types of colleges and universities most likely to be in
serious danger during the 1980s. Several contrasting examples are
offered of how institutions are increasing or decreasing their chances
for survival.

1

Contributors to Viability

Among the factors contributing to longevity, being a public institution helps. States having a vested interest in their institutions simply do not allow them to die. They may undersupport them and they may require retrenchment but they do not kill them off, even when a rational analysis indicates—as in Minnesota, Montana, and Wisconsin—that these institutions are maintaining more campuses than are needed. In the past, some states have purchased or taken over struggling private institutions, as Missouri did with the University of Kansas City and New York did with the University of Buffalo. But few states are likely to take over marginal private institutions in the foreseeable future. Few private liberal arts colleges, for example, have enough capacity to provide real benefits for a state system, and building an entire new campus would be less expensive than expanding an older, small campus designed for 500 to 1,000 students. Moreover, existing public campuses may more than suffice to meet enrollment demands during the projected enrollment slump of the 1980s. Thus, the most that private institutions can expect from the states during the new decade is some financial aid, advice, and encouragement—but rarely a bail-out.

Almost as important to institutional viability as public sponsorship is the existence of a consistent constituency large enough to generate the needed students and resources essential for survival. Thus, Oral Roberts University in Oklahoma, Wheaton College in Illinois, and the colleges maintained by the Seventh-Day Adventist Church are in no danger of failing as long as the conservative, evangelical Protestant population in the country continues to grow and to insist that new generations be educated in Christian values and ethics. Any institution, private or public, with an equally dedicated and committed constituency has the potential of indefinite life. Others with an ill-defined, declining, or ambivalent base of support face critical problems.

Related to the factor of constituency is the location of an institution in a state or region that is heavily populated and growing. The survival of the University of South Florida in Tampa, for example, has never been in question, whereas Florida Atlantic University in Boca Raton was in jeopardy almost from the time it opened its doors. Perhaps the most important reason for this difference is the fact that Tampa has been a fast-growing region while Boca Raton has not. Although a few institutions have moved to more favorable sites—Carthage College moved from Illinois to Wisconsin, and Marymount moved to the Los Angeles campus of Loyola University from elsewhere in California—these are exceptions. Few established institutions can get rid of a physical plant and begin again in greener pastures.

Possession of a reasonable endowment is another obvious factor. Few institutions have significant endowments, however, and it appears doubtful that more than a few can realistically hope to raise one. In the past thirty years, only one well-endowed private institution has been created—Brandeis—and it was built with many gifts from one special constituency, the Jewish community. The first great period of institution building was in the late nineteenth century, when the land-grant universities and the private universities founded by major capitalists were started. But the days of the large gifts that produced such major institutions as the University of Chicago, Johns Hopkins, and Stanford seem past, except for adding to the large endowments already in existence. It seems equally true that the second great period of institution building—during the 1960s, when the states created their complex systems based on a core of existing institutions—has also come to an end. In both periods, a reasonable financial base was provided to see new institutions through to established respectability. Now, younger institutions lacking that financial core may never attain adolescence, much less mature adult status.

Indeed, longevity seems to produce still greater longevity. In recent times, no private institution over a hundred years old has died, whereas the vast majority of those that have succumbed have been under twenty years old. Among universities, a key to maintaining a viable undergraduate program that attracts able students willing to pay high tuition is the presence of a strong graduate faculty and strong professional schools. It is these that enhance the reputation of an institution. But few struggling colleges will have the option of launching graduate and professional schools—even if permitted to do so by their accrediting agencies—in order to attract more undergraduates.

And then there is luck, or the power of historical accident. At Nova University in Florida, for example, after an inauspicious start, a radical new program now seems destined to last because of a gift of $10 million for endowment. Once, at a private liberal arts college, I predicted with good reason its early death, unaware at the time that the local press was present. The headlines that a Stanford professor foresaw the college's demise produced, among other things, a substantial gift that has enabled it to continue to function. But such windfalls can prove false—as witness the difficulties of Colorado Women's College that stemmed from a presumed gift of $25 million.

Particularly Vulnerable Institutions

Four types of institutions will face the most serious problems during the 1980s, assuming the predicted drop of about a million students, and assuming the market for new students proves to be limited: (1) the small, little-known liberal arts college, (2) the private, single-sex two-year institution, (3) the small, recently created private institution designed to serve a quite specific clientele, and (4) the middle-level, private, urban universities and perhaps a few of the more remote state colleges located in regions experiencing sharp population declines. Their problems are likely to extend from maintaining a precarious existence produced by enrollment declines, rising costs, and tuitions that have come to be regarded as too high for values received, to a final death struggle characterized by exhausted reserves, no line of credit with banks, and a flow of cash so limited that bills cannot be paid. It is impossible, of course, to predict which specific institutions will fail. Even the indicators discussed here have, for the most part, proven too inexact or so open to manipulation that the future of any single institution is indeterminable. However, the broad characteristics of each type of institution and the central problems they face can be described.

The first group comprises the small, little-known liberal arts colleges with enrollments of 40 to 1,000, little or no endowment, and rather substantial debt service charges and financial aid provided out of operating budgets. Scores of these struggling, "invisible" private colleges exist, bearing the name either of their local community, of a long-dead benefactor, or, hyphenated, of their two or more institutional forebears that managed to survive at least in name. In the past, these institutions served the communities in which they were located, regional church constituencies, and some students from the largest metropolitan area in the state. During the 1960s, they were able to expand enrollment and to experience a degree of prosperity unknown in their histories. Faculties were enlarged and salaries were improved. Physical plants were expanded typically through various federal loan programs and moderately successful capital fund drives. When these colleges first experienced a deterioration of applications, they sought new markets out of state, typically in the East, in states having limited higher education capacity in the light of need. New York and New Jersey were prime recruiting grounds. By the mid-1970s, however, these sources for new students began to dry up and enrollments began to slip. During the late 1970s, these institutions began to use the generally accepted techniques to improve their positions. They postponed plant maintenance, froze wages and salaries, cut back on a variety of services, and conducted planning activities to develop new and more attractive programs. They sought to augment annual donations and increased the amount of student financial aid in the hopes of attracting students. From time to time, their situations would improve—for example, an unexpected increase in enrollment in one or two particular years. When enrollments would increase and when budgets would be in balance, there was general faith that the corner had been turned—hence, new programs could be started that would help continue the upward spiral. But then would come an unpredicted drop in enrollments. In such institutions, an enrollment drop of 30 students is serious and a drop of 100 is catastrophic. And so the pattern of belt tightening would begin again, this time including actual termination of faculty appointments. Meanwhile, the accumulated operating deficit would have reached a point that banks maintaining lines of credit had to rethink the validity of the college as an investment. As these institutions approach the 1980s, their leadership exhibits faith and hope based largely on the fact that their institutions have suffered adversity before and survived and will do so again.

The second group of vulnerable institutions consists of the private, single-sex two-year colleges that flourished from the 1920s on. The women's colleges were finishing schools that provided young women from moderately financially comfortable homes with a degree of high culture, some vocational preparation, and, typically, opportunity to meet eligible future husbands. The men's institutions met such needs as providing military discipline for young men whose parents believed it was good for character or who had been unable to cope with difficult sons. These institutions began to experience some problems as early as the 1960s as public junior colleges and new state colleges began to compete. A few, such as Stephens College and Colorado Women's College, sought to become four-year institutions. They next increased admissions efforts. By the 1970s, however, the adverse factors affecting all of higher education took their toll. In addition, the changing social values lessened demand for the unique purpose these institutions served. Thus they found themselves in a weak financial condition and suffering a loss of identity.

The third type of imperiled institution is quite different. It is the recently created private institution frequently designed to serve a unique clientele. These may be free-standing graduate or professional schools, liberal arts colleges stressing a particular vision of the liberal arts—great books or humanistic psychology or some combination of undergraduate and professional programs offered to the working adult. They typically are small, have few resources (often only rented physical plants), and represent the dream of a single individual who found himself or herself displeased with established higher education. They are tuition based and frequently compete with established higher education through generous granting of academic credit for a variety of life experiences. Typically, their critical need is to gain regional accreditation so that students with federal or state subsidy can enroll and public grants and contracts can be obtained. Their annual budgets are usually in the range of one to three million dollars, which, for those that are candidates for accreditation or are accredited, are really inflated. A substantial portion of these amounts are public funds that are simply conduited through the institution for tuition payment. Many of these institutions are absolutely dependent on such federal programs as veterans benefits or basic educational opportunity grants. Whenever there is talk of policy changes in Washington, their faculty (typically part time) and leadership shudders.

These institutions are particularly vulnerable from several different directions. Their typically small administrative staffs, widespread use of part-time faculty, and lack of owned physical plant and library resources attract suspicion from formal accreditation. It seems likely that accreditation dominated by established institutions will subject these new competitors to greater and greater scrutiny as the supply of talented students decreases in the 1980s. The new institutions face a real dilemma. If they increase administrative, faculty, and physical plant costs to conform to accepted standards, they will have to charge tuition comparable to that charged by existing institutions—and their reason for being would end. To keep costs low, they must run the risks of, at worst, loss of accreditation and, at best, constant public suspicion as to the quality of the programs they offer. Neither alternative promises long and healthy institutional life.

Much less precariously situated, although still in some danger, is the fourth group: the middle-level, private, urban universities and the smaller regional public colleges and universities, many of them carrying their community's name—whether Boston or San Francisco, Dayton or Denver. The former, in the past, served the youth of the cities in which they were located with relatively low-cost, open-access education. It will be recalled that a major mission of New York University was to serve New York youth who could not gain admission into the highly selective, no-tuition city colleges. The sharp rises in tuition during the 1960s priced these institutions out of their traditional markets and they were forced to recruit more broadly. However, the quest for a national clientele was begun after the truly national institutions had emerged and preempted the field of national appeal. The major task of these institutions is to find a position in between the distinguished national institution and their previously occupied position as streetcar colleges. The prognosis for doing so is difficult to gauge. Most who do find a tenable position for the 1980s will likely have a reduced undergraduate full-time enrollment and will make up the tuition difference through new off-campus enrollments consisting of older students who wish to combine work and the quest for a degree.

The chief dangers to this fourth group of institutions are: (1) an attempt at too many different income-producing programs without adequate administrative staff to monitor and maintain them, (2) an overreliance on state and federal programs of student support for scholarship purposes, (3) more intense competition from nearby public institutions, (4) state restrictions on the offering of academic credit courses by out-of-state institutions within state boundaries, (5) inflated costs of high-priced professional programs such as medicine becoming an extreme drain on total institutional resources, and (6) continued deterioration of urban areas making the campuses less and less desirable for students to attend. In coping with these situations, the chief strengths of such institutions are that they are large enough to warrant state takeover if they really began to fail and that they have a potential source of external support in the wealth of some urban residents. Additionally, since a large number of the urban universities are church related, there is always a reasonably sized and reasonably local constituency.

Examples of Success

These observations about particularly vulnerable types of institutions are not intended to be nihilistic. Institutions in these categories, as well as others likely to experience problems of survival, may find particular attributes of health closed to them, but they can then examine other factors and perhaps find a combination that will work. It seems inevitable that some institutions will die during the 1980s and 1990s because of finite resources and finite populations of potential students. Those that achieve even modest and undramatic improvement in their operations, however, may be around to see the twenty-first century, when conditions for colleges and universities may improve drastically once again.

As to how these institutions might change, some lessons may be learned from Bowdoin College in Maine and Dartmouth College in New Hampshire. One of the oldest institutions in the country, Bowdoin College has, through most of its history, stressed the primacy of the liberal arts and sciences. Until recently, enrollment was limited to men. In the 1950s, along with other institutions, Bowdoin conducted an institutional self-study under financial support from the Ford Foundation. Most of the studies produced recommendations for major changes, but not the one done at Bowdoin. Under the title *Education in the Conservative Tradition,* Bowdoin's report reviewed what the college was doing, found it good, and determined that no significant changes were needed. And so, during the 1960s, Bowdoin continued on its way, experiencing, however, along with other institutions, an increase in expenditures greater than the increasing rate of income. The severity of its condition became apparent during 1970–71 after the institution had faced and survived a half decade of real, if genteel, student protest and dissent. The seriousness of the problem was revealed when the first draft of the budget for 1972 projected an intolerable deficit of $780,000. As president Roser Howell, Jr. struggled to reduce that projection, he and his associates assumed that a variety of measures had to be taken, not just a reduction in expenses. They also determined (and this was probably the most remarkable example of vision) that the financial problem was not a temporary one and that, in the long run, the college should limit the things it would attempt to do. The institution would build on strength and restrict new departures.

During that year, Bowdoin undertook several important operational steps and one major substantive step. All units of the college reviewed their budgets and made cuts in them. All units undertook economies of operation. A faculty-student committee for budget review was created to advise the president and the board's committee on investment policy, with the aim of seeking greater yield from endowment. Then tuitions and fees were increased. The major substantive decision was twofold: to maintain the size of the existing faculty while, at the same time, increasing enrollment by becoming coeducational. Increased enrollment was to be secured through an even more intensified personalized admissions process symbolized, in part, by ending the requirement for college entrance examinations. The desired enrollment was secured.

By the next year, the situation at Bowdoin had brightened and a deficit-free budget was projected. As part of the process of achieving that condition, an external review of college management was undertaken and, as a result, some administrative changes were made. Two consortial arrangements were scrutinized, and one ended after being judged an unwarranted financial drain. But most importantly, the principle was reiterated that the college would not embark on the development of new and frequently attractive programs. Curricular patterns established earlier were maintained—such as Afro-American studies, a revised language program, and the free elective system—but their effectiveness was reviewed to determine if they were still affordable.

The financial good health with which Bowdoin entered 1972–73 was clearly the result of many forces and factors—chiefly the increase in coeducational enrollment while maintaining a constant faculty size. The chances for maintaining that health were to be ensured, in the short run, through authorization to increase tuition and fees as needed to meet expenses and, in the long run, through a major fund drive to increase endowment and to provide funds for faculty improvement. Institutions that have approached the 1980s with reasonable financial strength appear to have used different patterns for improving faculty and physical plant during the fifties, sixties, and seventies. Stanford University and Knox College elected to spend first for faculty; hence, in the late sixties and the seventies, they had to stress new construction. Bowdoin took a different tack. During the sixties, it built a beautiful physical plant and then, during the seventies, began to restore faculty compensation to levels competitive with other strong Eastern institutions. The new development program was also to generate designated funds for student financial aid to help offset the effects of the inevitable increases in enrollment and fees.

While the situation was judged good in 1972–73, the future remained uncertain. Attractive as Bowdoin appeared to students, soonor or later it would experience enrollment problems if for no other reason than its constantly increased costs. Further, the college would have to face at least the issues of unionization, federally funded programs and their influence on institutional autonomy, and the possibility of revised tax laws that could jeopardize philanthropic giving. And it had to accept the fact of life of inflation. What was not expected was the sudden inflation of the costs of energy and the deflation of the value of and income from securities which took place in 1973–74.

Inflation, energy costs, and endowment income decreases made the task of keeping a deficit-free budget especially difficult during 1974. It was accomplished, however, through careful management and faculty-administration cooperation and, especially, through severe limitation on increases in staff, faculty, and administrative compensation. Further economies were achieved through adhering to the policy of limiting new programs and activities and by developing a charter for living with a steady state. The chief danger of such measures is, of course, that they could very well produce a general sense of stagnation and a loss of educational and intellectual creativity. During the 1960s, when external funds were plentiful, a sense of development and creativity was fostered by incremental growth: more faculty, more students, new courses or whole new programs. The task for the remainder of the seventies would be to remain vigorous, but in the context of constrained resources.

Compared to many other institutions, Bowdoin College entered 1977–78 in a strong position. Its major fund drive had been successful and had contributed to a sizable endowment. Its application rates remained high, except for minority group students, and the budget was deficit free (although by only a slim margin). Although the future of an institution in such happy circumstances as Bowdoin is still uncertain, the prognosis for much more than survival seems reasonably good. That condition seems to rest on several major factors. First was the decision, after a decade of deficit financing, to maintain a balanced budget through stringent management and vigorous fund raising. This came about through early recognition by the president and board that the golden years for higher education were gone, possibly forever.

Second was the decision, made at the right time, to increase enrollment by admitting women but not to augment the size of the faculty. The combination of increasing enrollment by 450 students, raising tuition regularly, and keeping the faculty small produced the needed cash flow to maintain viability.

Third, although the president consulted widely with faculty about financial matters and sought its support, he himself maintained a clear vision as to what conditions were and what had to be done. When difficult decisions had to be made, he had the moral strength to insist on stringent economies, a freeze on faculty appointments, restrictions on library acquisitions, and tight controls on increased levels of faculty compensation.

Throughout this period of stabilization at Bowdoin, curricular changes, none radical or requiring substantial increases in expenditure, continued to take place. There was the movement to a free elective system, followed by a restudy of possibly new general education requirements. There were interdisciplinary courses and seminars, which were periodically reexamined. There was a steady pattern of adding new courses but, equally important, a pattern of dropping courses as well. There was experimentation with a number of the fads of the sixties and seventies, such as a new academic calendar, encouraging students to take leaves of absence for travel or other purposes, and greater use of independent study. And there were attempts to refine and make more effective the counseling and advising of students. But none of these changes was viewed as a panacea for the problems of the college or as a replacement for the academic core of the institution—the teaching of important courses in liberal arts and sciences by a highly qualified faculty. An important ingredient in maintaining that core and limiting experimentation was clearly the moratorium on faculty appointments. Given the values of a faculty such as would be attracted to Bowdoin, when forced to choose between major innovation or a reasonably traditional curriculum, the conclusion would never be in doubt.

A fourth important factor in the present strength of Bowdoin was the decision to mount a major development effort to secure the capital that the president and the board believed essential for future viability. This was to be a two-phased effort, with $14.5 million the goal for the first three years and a total goal of $38 million over a ten-year period. Adequate planning time was allowed and the needs for support sharply focused. The total amount sought was carefully tailored to the best estimates of what the natural Bowdoin constituencies could afford. Thus, a first estimate of a needed $80 million was rejected as being unrealistic.

Lastly, the importance of an active admissions program was recognized, and the admissions staff was provided the needed resources to ensure a large pool of qualified applicants. The institution, recognizing that the decision as to what college to attend is a personal one for each student and family, stressed a personal approach to admission in which each individual was helped to examine the pros and cons of Bowdoin for his—and eventually, her—individual needs.

This matter of coeducation for the previously single-sex institution is so potentially significant as to warrant further comment. The changing social values in the United States during the 1950s and 1960s, coupled with the changing financial situation for collegiate institutions by the late 1960s, tempted many institutions to consider becoming coeducational. Some that did so had remarkable success; others ended financially worse off than before. One broad survey suggests that the effects of going coeducational differ for men's and women's institutions. Women's colleges appear to gain enrollments at first after the change, but in time the institution's character changes and it becomes less appealing to its traditional clientele. Male institutions suffer much less deterioration of image.

Dartmouth College, like Bowdoin, became coeducational at the right time and in the right way, and the change produced an institution with great strength to face the future. Dartmouth became a truly national institution with respect to enrollment and national regard only during the 1960s when the then president, John Dickey, finally was able to replace one of the oldest faculties in the country with the well-prepared products of post-World War II graduate schools and was able to make the institution highly selective as demand for college exceeded capacity during the 1960s. However, intensive faculty appointing during the 1960s produced a large, young, tenured faculty which could restrict institutional quality as that faculty aged; at the same time, no new blood could be appointed.

The move to coeducation at Dartmouth seems to have been stimulated less by immediate financial problems than by a desire to make the institution attractive to high-quality students in the future, as coeducation became the prevailing mode of education in the country. Once the decision to become coeducational appeared likely, the question as to how became relevant. Alumni would consider coeducation only if the number of men was not reduced. The administration was unwilling to expand enrollment substantially if that required financing and building new residence halls and classrooms. One answer, which other institutions have tried and failed at, was to use the physical plant for year-round operation. Going to college in the summer has long been contrary to the style in this country, except for teachers and other vocational groups who have the summer free and need additional education for career purposes. Year-round operation was tried at the University of Pittsburgh and failed, as it also did at the public institutions in Florida and California. It did succeed at Parsons College, but only because attendance in summer was required for students on probation if they were to enroll the following fall. Since most Parsons' students were on probation and since being drafted was the alternative to being in college, the summer session, even in the not too salubrious Fairfield, Iowa, typically enrolled 85 percent of the normal fall enrollment.

The dynamics and processes by which Dartmouth reached its decision to accept women are instructive and may suggest to other institutions how to cope with politically sensitive issues. President John Kemeny (1975) well describes the problems involved:

> Coeducation was an issue on which men of good will who deeply loved the college could hold diametrically opposite views and firmly believe that they were right. They could—and they did.
>
> A majority of the alumni favored the education of women at Dartmouth *in some form*. On the other hand, no specific plan could come close to mustering majority support. Of the 40 percent of the alumni who were opposed to any form of coeducation, more than half had extremely strong feelings on the subject. Furthermore, the alumni classes were split according to when they graduated from the college. The classes in the '20s were firmly opposed, the classes of the '60s were strongly in favor, and there were all gradations between. . . . The constituency most strongly in favor of coeducation was the faculty, which came out nearly 10 to 1 in favor. The student body was also strongly in favor, but with a vocal minority in opposition. . . . In short, this was potentially the most divisive issue facing the college.

Kemeny goes on to tell of the "truly memorable Charter Day celebration" in December of 1969 when he presented the major report on coeducation to the alumni council. His fears of alienating the council proved groundless:

> I would never again judge the alumni so unfairly; I learned that if one faces a group of alumni and tells them honestly and frankly what the issues are, and why people feel one way or the other about the merits of the issues, one gains respect even from those who totally disagree.

Upon his election to the presidency of the college the following month, Kemeny prepared to meet the challenge of devising a plan that would be "in the best interests of the college" and would satisfy, as far as possible, the alumni and the board of trustees:

> From my discussions with the alumni council it became clear that even alumni who favored the admission of women would not accept a large reduction in male students. Yet I was reluctant to follow the examples of Yale and Princeton in enlarging the student body significantly. A thousand more students on campus would require the construction of very expensive facilities and would result in a degree of crowding that would have a highly negative effect on the educational process. I therefore began to think seriously about the idea that we increase the total student body without increasing the number on campus at a given time. The idea was to add a fourth term to the academic calendar and spread a larger student body out among four terms. While I had no more than the germ of an idea, and two separate faculty committees would eventually have to put in enormous amounts of work to design a practical plan, I do not believe that the trustees would have voted in favor of coeducation if it had not been coupled with the Dartmouth Plan.

Another major issue was the form of coeducation to be adopted. Although Kemeny was "prepared to compromise" on some form of "associated school" in order to gain wider alumni acceptance, the faculty voted overwhelmingly against such a plan.

In November of 1971, the board of trustees met for two days to decide the issue of coeducation at Dartmouth. Consultants presented their view that the "combined financial impact of coeducation and year-round operation" would be negligible, a forecast that has since proven accurate. The experiences of Yale and Princeton in going coeducational were reviewed, as was a survey indicating that high school students would, in considerable numbers, accept the plan for year-round operation. In addition, reports Kemeny:

> Two other developments might have had an effect on the board's decision. The possibility had been raised that new federal legislation would make it mandatory for the college to

become coeducational, and there was a fear that applications to Dartmouth might start declining as they had at other private single-sex colleges. The board was informed that neither of these two events had occurred, and therefore it was under no *compulsion* to act in favor of coeducation. . . .

The most fascinating part of the board's discussion centered on the question of the role of women in future American society. Several trustees expressed the conviction that women would play an increasingly important role in leadership positions in the country. Therefore, they argued, Dartmouth, which had traditionally prided itself on the training of leaders, should train women as well as men for leadership roles. It was also argued that if, in the future, our male graduates would work side by side with women, we would be providing an unreal learning atmosphere in an all-male college.

In a dramatic conclusion, Kemeny reports:

The board recessed late Saturday afternoon to give its members a chance to reflect overnight. I believe that none of us had much sleep that night. The Sunday morning session was a solemn one. All the arguments were over, and it was up to the board of trustees to decide the future of the college. Under the leadership of its chairman, Charles Zimmerman '23, the board passed two key votes. It voted unanimously to put the college on year-round operation. It then voted—by a substantial majority but not unanimously—to matriculate women as undergraduate students starting in the fall of 1972.

As Kemeny implies, the curricular device that Dartmouth used to ensure full enrollment in summer was the so-called Dartmouth Plan. Overly simplified, this involved reducing the number of terms of attendance needed for graduation from twelve to eleven and, at the same time, requiring each student to attend one summer session. Under this plan, students spent only ten fall, winter, and spring terms on campus, providing space for a 25 percent increase in the student body. It was this 25 percent that enabled women to make up the larger enrollment the institution needed to operate most effectively.

The presence of women on campus, the charm of rural New

England for a new generation of people seeking a more simple life, a uniquely rich summer session featuring for the most part upper-level elective courses, and the flexibility for students and faculty in having one less term in residence required—all these factors have made the use of the summer term a success at Dartmouth. The Dartmouth Plan has allowed the institution to grow from 3,200 to 4,000 students, resulting in a marked increase in net tuition received.

As of the spring of 1979, Dartmouth had no application or enrollment problems. It received 8,355 applications to fill just over a thousand spaces. Its year-round operation was working and it was enrolling about 1,000 women as a coeducational institution. However, it still faced financial problems—not of the extreme sort, but real. Its expenditures were increasing at a faster rate than its income for most of the well-known reasons: inflation, energy costs, enriched student services, declines in the stock market, and increased student financial aid. The institution has taken a number of steps to improve its situation.

First, it developed a computer-based model with which to examine various alternatives as far as five years in the future. It also changed its budget review by the board of trustees. Previously, the board acted on the budget for the next year in April. Now the board examines a four-year forecast in autumn, after which it establishes guidelines for the preparation of the next year's budget.

Second, it examined carefully the matters of faculty size and the proportion of faculty on tenure. Here the computer model proved invaluable in projecting consequences to the budget of various student/faculty ratios and the varying proportions of faculty holding tenure. After wide discussion, Dartmouth adopted what in essence is a quota system that allows each department to make 2 tenure appointments over a decade for each 10 department members. This could cause a transitory imbalance but within fifteen years should produce a steady 180 tenure appointments in a faculty of 300. The 120 nontenure appointments would include 30 temporary ones and 90 assistant professors.

Third, it examined the future of its previously unique two-year medical school, which had become impossible to operate as the four-year schools stopped accepting transfers. It decided to expand the school to degree-granting status but with a definite condition:

Enough new endowment must be raised within ten years with which to operate the school with no drain on the institution's other resources or the school would be closed. Everyone connected with the school realized this and knew the odds (about 50–50) for the school's continued existence.

To maintain the quality of Dartmouth's academic program, the board of trustees has approved a five-year use of higher-than-desirable endowment income, while at the same time the institution is mounting a $160 million campaign for new endowments. If the campaign succeeds and if the stock market improves, the end of five years should see larger endowment, larger reserves, and a return to an acceptable payout rate of endowment funds—typically 4 to 4.5 percent.

During the first year of Kemeny's new presidency, a gift from the alumni supported a full external-management study which helped the new president understand his situation and caused him to suggest a lean but somewhat different administrative structure. The new structure involved a vice-presidential arrangement with vice-presidents for the faculty, student affairs, administration, development, and investment. Another temporary vice-president was appointed for women's affairs. The new structure clarified responsibilities and has enabled the institution to reach decisions somewhat more rapidly and effectively than previously. It is hoped that it may eventually enable a reduction in a total administrative staff that has grown at a much faster rate than enrollment or faculty.

Dartmouth has had one of the most sophisticated computer systems in the country, with over 400 terminals on campus. Yet its record keeping was just as confused as that of the vast majority of colleges. With the help of a gift from an alumnus and some foundation support, a full management information system was developed which allows access to data from any terminal on campus. The president has one in his office and can quickly obtain specific information on such matters as faculty salaries, teaching loads, or progress of affirmative action programs. This management information system has allowed study of decisions such as those concerning the use of endowment, the desired size of the student body, and the matter of tenure.

In addition to creating a clearer administrative structure, Dartmouth tried to improve its governance arrangements. The institution consists of four faculties: arts and sciences, engineering, business, and medicine. These were highly independent entities with no faculty group having broad power over them. There was the General Faculty of Dartmouth College, but it had no power. A modified change gave the general faculty nonbinding power to vote on matters affecting the individual schools. More importantly, a steering committee of the general faculty was set up with the power to create committees and to set agendas for their consideration. This has led to the creation of such bodies as the Collegewide Council on Budgets and Priorities, which does have a major voice in financial affairs.

Under the leadership of President Kemeny, Dartmouth has taken major steps to strengthen itself and to prepare for the future. In order of importance, these steps appear to be: (1) initiating co-education and year-round operation, (2) creating of a sophisticated management information system, (3) setting up long-range budgets, (4) planning a major fund drive and improving alumni annual giving, and (5) clarifying the administrative and governance structure. These methods seem to have worked at Dartmouth but they might not work elsewhere—for several reasons. The Dartmouth saga is so strong that it could attract students with or without year-round operation. A less appealing place might well find that a summer requirement for all students would produce a decline in applications. Another proof of Dartmouth's strength is the ease with which women were assimilated into the institution without changing its character. Weaker institutions have found that going coeducational did, in the long run, change the environment in unfavorable ways. The management information system was quickly institutionalized, in part because of long experience with and high sophistication in the use of computers on the part of most of the faculty and key administrators. That technical capacity is typically not present in institutions that have been unable to use a management information system. A decision to increase payout from endowment was, of course, possible only because it was there and because the institution had the demonstrated capacity to raise more endowment. Substantial alumni giving

could be increased because Dartmouth alumni have sufficient resources to allow large donations. In short, Dartmouth seems to have
succeeded because it had succeeded.

But there may be lessons for less-advantaged places. Perhaps
the most important lesson is the need to reduce complex problems to
their critical elements, to state alternatives starkly, and then to reach
clear, unequivocal decisions. Thus, year-round operation was the
only way Dartmouth could afford to become coeducational and to
increase its size. A degree-granting medical school could be afforded
only if it quickly became self-supporting, and this could be discovered only through a real, but limited trial. Increased endowment
payout could be justified only for a limited time and with every
likelihood that funds used could be replaced. A faculty balanced
with respect to age could be achieved only through a definite and
effectively binding tenure policy. Such reduction to essentials can be
done in any institution in which there is intelligence and will.

Bowdoin and Dartmouth succeeded by correctly gauging the
future and by taking prudent steps to cope with it. Other institutions
have not been so fortunate, but their mistakes are also informative.

Portrait of Distress

A less encouraging example is New College in Sarasota,
Florida, which opened in 1964 with a self-proclaimed mission of becoming the first truly distinguished college in the South. New
College was to be a highly selective institution, recruiting the most
able students in the country and providing them with heavy financial
aid to pursue an individualized, intellectually potent curriculum. A
relatively young, but highly qualified faculty was recruited with the
incentives of high salaries, the excitement of starting a new institution, and, to some extent, the salubrious climate of the west coast of
Florida. The new institution was to occupy at first several buildings
of the Ringling estate, with students housed in nearby motels. Eventually, New College would acquire property across a main highway
and construct a main campus consisting of buildings intended to
express the new intellectual spirit that pervaded the undertaking. It
also acquired land along the coast to the north of the Ringling

estate, which would allow expansion or which could become part of a hoped-for substantial and essential endowment.

Motivations for creating New College were several. Florida, after World War II, became one of the fastest-growing states in the Union. It needed an expanded system of higher education to serve its culturally variegated population and to produce the professional work force needed to bring Florida into the mainstream of American economic and intellectual life. A state master plan called for creating as many as twenty-nine junior colleges and new bachelor's degree-granting institutions in Tampa, on the lower east coast, and in the Pensacola area, as well as expanding the three existing institutions located in the northern part of the state. There was competition among the various communities to have new institutions assigned to them. Sarasota leaders had hoped that the institution that was finally located in Tampa would be located in their community. When that did not happen, they became receptive to the creation of a new private institution there.

Sarasota leaders found that the educational leadership of the Congregational church was also interested in founding new liberal arts colleges that might eventually achieve as well as did the first Congregational effort—the creation of Yale University. The interest of the two groups of leaders merged in the chartering of New College. The new institution would express the educationally innovative ideas then current of reemphasis on the liberal arts and sciences, tutorial teaching and independent study, and an explicit concern for the intellectually gifted. These ideas were endemic in the higher education community at the time and were reflected in the rhetoric of a proposed new institution in Amherst, Massachusetts, a new campus of the University of California in Santa Cruz, a new branch of Michigan State University in Oakland, Michigan, and at Florida Presbyterian. This new intellectualism was especially pushed by the Ford Foundation's Fund for the Advancement of Education, whose president, Alvin C. Eurich, and his wife, Nell, were to play critical roles throughout the history of New College.

As the new institution began to take shape, a number of assumptions were made that would come to plague New College during all of its life as a private institution. The first of these was that the substantial and growing wealth in Florida could be exploited in a continuous way by the college to build a campus, produce operating funds, and establish an impressive endowment. The first president, having had business management experience at the University of Florida and development experience at New York University, was to exploit this wealth but he also felt compelled to open the college before adequate funds were at hand. Having claimed that at least $10 million should be available as a financial core, he, in fact, opened with well under half of that in actual cash. This was an especially dangerous decision since he and his associates elected to pay premium salaries to the first faculty and to pay premium awards of financial aid to get the intellectually apt students that he, the academic dean, and the director of admissions desired. Although a few residents of Sarasota contributed generously and continued to do so, New College never really established the stable financial base needed by a selective private liberal arts college. From 1964 to 1975, the college lived from one financial crisis to the next and probably would have died had not the concern of the Eurichs contributed to a timely grant of $600,000 from the Ford Foundation, enabling the college to meet its obligations.

A second faulty assumption was that the college would be dedicated both to traditional concepts of academic excellence and to innovation. In the American context these are almost antithetical, for academic excellence involves the liberal arts and sciences, intellectual rigor, and stringent intellectual discipline, whereas innovation has typically stressed loosened requirements, emphasis on affective concerns, interpersonal relations, and individual student goals rather than faculty-imposed goals. This effort to reconcile the irreconcilable contributed to tension on campus and the early departure of the first dean, several key faculty members, and finally, the board of trustees.

A third assumption, also erroneously made in several other new institutions, was that a cosmopolitan student body could be recruited and placed in a parochial and somewhat conservative community that had expected the new institution to serve its own sons and daughters but found it catering to children of the East and West coasts. Michigan State University at Oakland, the University of Wisconsin at Green Bay, and Evergreen State College in Olympia, Washington, all made the same mistake. In American higher education, institutions develop and prosper first by serving directly the community in which they are located, gradually building up a financial base and achieving some recognition in the broader region, and eventually, for a few, attracting a national or international clientele. Stanford first served the children of California and only much later was strong enough to serve the nation. But not all institutions can make the leap from serving communities and restricted regions. The University of Denver, Boston University, and New York University are still trying to accomplish the shift from regional to national orientation, and the University of Southern California continues to prosper by not really trying to do so.

In addition to these three crucial and faulty assumptions, New College also had to struggle with several critical administrative errors. The first of these may well have been the first presidential appointment. Although he had considerable financial experience, the first president seems to have had little understanding of the details of academic administration. For example, he set an enrollment goal of 1,200 high ability students without analyzing the composition of high school graduates and the appeal of established institutions to determine whether there were available that many qualified high school graduates whom New College could attract. Events revealed that only half that projected number would ever enroll at any one time. He spoke to many audiences about the new curriculum of New College without thinking through the logistics of how such a curriculum could be made operational. Colleges and universities need different kinds of people to serve as chief executives at different times. Thus, a builder may be needed at one time and a consolidator at another. Reflecting on the new institutions created during the 1960s that encountered difficulties and those that proceeded smoothly, it is possible to theorize that the first president needs a highly sophisticated knowledge of the actual operation of an academic program. The first president of the University of South Florida and the first chancellor of the University of California at Santa Cruz each knew academic programs as well as did the deans and faculties they appointed; hence they were not led toward impossible claims and expectations. The first president of New College lacked these insights.

A second administrative mistake may have been the staff and

faculty recruiting policy of the original key faculty and administration. Of the provost, division deans, and director of admissions at New College, only one was a Southerner, and the faculty they recruited came largely from the Ivy League and the flagship state universities of the West and Midwest. Now although Florida is claimed to be, and may indeed be, more cosmopolitan than other Southern states, it is still the South, still regionally oriented and somewhat suspicious of the "snowbirds." Thus, any real hope for close relationships with the social and economic elites of Florida, which were necessary if the institution was to gain genuine and lasting local support, may have been jeopardized by recruiting a Northern and liberal faculty and administration. This point is difficult to prove, but a more prudential recruitment policy might have been 50 percent Southern and 50 percent from outside the South.

Perhaps the most serious mistake was the failure to keep the academic program and financial resources in equilibrium. The entire curriculum consisted of the most expensive modes of instruction: tutorials, seminars, no survey courses, comprehensive examinations, and independent research requirements. Now these may be tolerated if there are a number of low-cost activities that can help subsidize the high-cost ones. For example, a great virtue of large freshman and sophomore survey courses is that they generate enough income to subsidize upper-division small classes and seminars. Or expensive educational programs can be undertaken if there is a large enough endowment to support them. Neither of these conditions prevailed at New College. Indeed, it is difficult to conceive of a set of factors more likely to produce economic disaster for an institution than those that obtained as New College opened its doors. High-salaried faculty, heavy financial subsidy for students, labor-intensive modes of instruction, no financial reserves, and an unrealistic anticipation of major philanthropic support were all factors that operated to move the institution close to bankruptcy before the end of its first decade.

New College, of course, made efforts to survive. It changed administration and sought external funding. It exploited its ties with foundations and obtained several life-saving grants. It allowed salaries to deteriorate, as well as plant maintenance. And it intensified student recruitment. None of these worked, and the institution turned to a more radical solution. Under the leadership of its third full-time president, it sought and accomplished a merger with the state-supported University of South Florida, which had opened in 1960 and had grown, as originally anticipated, from a first class of 1,500 to over 20,000 students. The University of South Florida, for the most part, had been well planned and operated, and its original plans had always anticipated several branch campuses along the west coast of Florida. Thus, when the idea of a merger was seriously suggested, the president of the University of South Florida was willing and began the delicate negotiations with the board of regents and the legislature to enable the university to absorb New College but to do so without destroying it. It should be noted, however, that the legislature was persuaded to appropriate the funds by the argument that the merger was really a good real estate investment.

The final arrangement is unique in the history of American higher education. In 1975, the State of Florida purchased New College and all of its property for something in excess of $4 million and assigned it as part of the University of South Florida. The Board of Trustees of New College was, of course, disbanded but, at the same time, chartered as the board of a new foundation whose purpose was support of the New College program. The contract of purchase specified that the new foundation board would raise approximately $750,000 each year to underwrite the difference between the high cost of the New College program and the cost of instruction at the University of South Florida. Students are charged only the regular in-state or out-of-state tuition charged by all public institutions in the state. Should the foundation board fail to produce its annual contribution, the University of South Florida can eliminate the program of New College as an entity and use the property in whatever way is consistent with the academic mission of the university. At the time of the merger, the university began offering a variety of upper-division courses and programs on the Sarasota campus in addition to the New College program. These will be expanded as needed.

Although the faculty and students of New College felt betrayed and feared a loss of identity, events have revealed a reasonably satisfying result. The New College program operates as it had in the past, and enrollments continue to be small but highly selective.

The first year after merger saw the departure of about a fifth of the faculty, but the faculty that remains and those newly appointed seem satisfied that their academic program can continue. The foundation board has managed to raise almost the full toll each year, and the chief administrative officers of the University of South Florida have been supportive of the institution both in word and deed. Administratively, the Sarasota campus is under a dean of regional campuses to whom the provost of New College, who is in charge only of the academic program, reports. The incumbent dean believes in New College as an educational alternative for undergraduate students and hopes that it will continue.

As of the fall of 1978, the merged arrangement has been in existence for three years. The faculty and students of New College of the University of South Florida exhibit a stoic faith that their institutional program will continue as it has survived serious crises in the past. The administration of the University of South Florida expects that New College will survive, but there are some problems. First, there is concern that the foundation board may have difficulty in continuing to raise its share of funding. Second, since the state is limiting growth of expenditures for higher education, it is possible that the relatively modest state expense to maintain the small enclave of high-cost instruction will be eliminated. If the foundation board can find ways to maintain its obligation and gives evidence of intent to continue its philanthropic role, and if the new president of the University of South Florida does not face serious budgetary problems, and if the non-New College programs on the Sarasota campus continue to expand, the arrangement may work. Change any one of these variables, and the New College idea may well end.

The significant question here is, What can other private institutions learn from the merger that could help their own struggles for survival? The answer seems to be, not much. A great deal can be learned as to what not to do in creating a new private institution in the United States. Examining New College and other relatively traditionally colleges created during the 1960s suggests that the effort will likely fail. Few, if any, of those created are in stable or good financial condition. As to merger as a way of saving identity within a public system, the record provides little hope that it can be accomplished. Kansas City and Buffalo have become just other public institutions. Pittsburgh and Temple have been able to maintain some elements of private universities despite their state-affiliated status, but they were really not distinctly different from state universities even when they were completely private.

Steps for Survival

Why have some institutions succeeded and others failed? In the chapters that follow, one central argument emerges: *Institutional vitality, viability, and even survival depend on the timely interaction of established and tested procedures and processes, wise human skills and abilities, and fortunate vagaries of history.*

Established procedures and processes can produce favorable results for an institution if adopted and adapted by skilled institutional leaders. But if they are ignored institutional difficulties typically mount. Thus, the first step toward gaining, regaining, or retaining institutional vitality is the establishment of an administrative structure that preserves for central administration the needed prerogatives of implementing effective policies and assuring that subordinate units of the institution behave in fiscally responsible ways, while at the same time allowing for orderly consultation with all members of the academic community. Chapter Two explains this needed administrative structure.

An essential second step is the assumption of administrative leadership. Both public and private institutions must adjust to past decisions made on the basis of euphoric assumptions of the 1960s when continued growth was generally taken for granted. During this period, new residence halls were constructed with borrowed funds in full confidence that revenues would more than pay off the obligations; the proportion of faculty on tenure was allowed to rise from under 50 percent to 70 or 80 percent in full confidence that continued enrollment increases would allow for continued additions to the faculty; teaching loads were reduced in the belief that continued increases in finances would be available to pay for the qualitative improvement in instruction that these reduced loads were presumed to produce; new programs were started with external funding under the assumption that increased institutional funds would permit their continuation; and, especially in institutions oriented toward graduate and professional schools, research was built into the normal expectation of faculty responsibilities with confidence that external support of research would continue and even increase. The question of how to live and cope with these decisions in a period of limited funds and steady or declining enrollment presents administrators with a cluster of problems that must be solved without tested guidelines or techniques. Chapter Three examines the leadership skills and abilities needed to face and overcome these problems.

A key to more effective leadership is the creation of accurate systems of information, the development of various monitoring devices to ensure the most effective use of institutional resources, and the wise application of established principles of planning. One small example involves cash flow. In the majority of private institutions with no or modest endowment, the biggest proportion of income is received twice or three times a year as tuition is collected at the start of each semester or term. If the institution has been running operating deficits for several years and has not offset them by using reserves, endowment, or gift income (as is the rule), it has accumulated considerable long- and short-term debts and probably a substantial amount of accounts-payable obligations. Prior to the 1970s, the typical pattern was for the institution to borrow from banks in midsummer to pay obligations due between then and September when tuition funds would allow loan repayment as well as operation. But by the mid 1970s, borrowing typically took place earlier and more frequently, and the business office was faced with choices of paying bank loans, obligations to vendors, or salaries and wages. Thus, a new kind of financial management came to be required to order the priorities of payments in such a way as to maintain minimum credit and, at the same time, have funds available for emergencies and the constant recurrence of the payroll. What was true of financial management was true in all administrative areas: More accurate information, management systems, and planning were needed. Chapter Four describes new approaches to management information and systems to meet this need, and Chapter Five discusses new approaches to planning.

In regard to planning, possibly the most significant long-run administrative problem for an institution is to develop a clear mission and image that will attract the students it wishes to serve and the support it needs to survive. Almost without exception, each institution that faced and solved enrollment and financial difficulties in the early 1970s projected a distinctive image that enabled it to compete successfully against other institutions vying for the same students and support. How to assure a distinctive mission and a competitive position of visibility among other institutions is the subject of Chapter Six.

Through planning, institutions can better understand the future toward which they are moving and can anticipate the needed enrollment and financing necessary for their survival. More accurate and focused information will undoubtedly reveal that enrollment and tuition income is the most important ingredient of financial stability. Hence, solving enrollment problems is likely to be given the highest priority. As enrollments have begun to slow, many institutions have created new programs, a number of them off campus and frequently nontraditional, to attract new students. But these efforts have produced new sorts of administrative problems, ranging from finding a balance between new and old programs to monitoring the new programs adequately to assure maintenance of quality. Chapter Seven examines ways to continue to attract traditional college-age youth and to recruit new kinds of students to replace any decline in traditional enrollments.

In addition to more active recruitment, enrollment can be aided by retaining more students through the completion of their programs. Research has shown that students select particular colleges and elect to remain at them for a longer time not so much because of a specific kind of curriculum but rather as a result of the impact of the institution as a whole. Curriculum revision and improvement of instruction are important to maintain intellectual vitality and to retain existing students, but of equal and often more immediate significance is the orchestration of the many components of college life that affect students, such as counseling and extracurricular activities. Chapter Eight explores ways in which the total educational program of an institution can be improved.

Clearly related is the issue of faculty improvement, including development, redeployment, increased responsibility, retrenchment through attrition, and even termination. Few issues generate more intensity of emotion, but few are as crucial to the health of an institution. Efforts here involve persuading faculty members to redirect their professional interests and lives, add to already heavy workloads and duties, and face realistically the termination of appointments. Chapter Nine discusses how to increase faculty resources, and Chapter Ten analyzes ways of cutting faculty costs.

These various ideas and suggestions for survival provide a context for viewing the most significant elements. The vital, viable institution is likely to be one that has remained reasonably true to its traditions and whose innovations and reforms are built on well-developed and entrenched strengths. Radical change in institutional practice and orientation generally leads to problems or reflects them. Additionally, the healthy institution needs a well-understood and smoothly functioning administration. Perhaps the large majority of serious institutional pathologies stem from administrative failure. Through a healthy administration, faculties can improve themselves and make the institution a place that students will find interesting and enjoyable. Chapter Eleven elaborates these points, especially the need for effective administration, one of the major theses of this book.

Further Readings

It is almost impossible to pick up a book or article dealing with higher education in the United States since 1970 without finding analyses of its difficulties and suggestions for restoring and ensuring institutional vitality. In one way or another, most of the publications of The Carnegie Council on Policy Studies in Higher Education deal with those matters. In those statements and in other writings, the suggestions range from the gloom and doom predictions that nothing can really be done to save large numbers of private institutions to the happy contention that things are really not bad and that if institutions have faith and keep on doing what they are doing they will survive and even prosper. Froomkin sees perhaps hundreds of institutions closing, with only a radical change in public policy saving even quite strong institutions, whereas Gollattscheck and his associates see major enrollment increases if only institutions will cater to a large, part-time adult market. Mayhew, however, sees considerable danger in that latter approach and suggests that adherence to traditional academic values is the only reasonable road to salvation. A reasonably good sample of the suggestions made are contained in the following documents.

ANDREW, L. D., AND FRIEDMAN, B. D. *A Study of the Causes for the Demise of Certain Small Private Liberal Arts Colleges in the United States.* Blacksburg: Virginia Polytechnic Institute and State University, 1976.

ASKEW, T. A. *The Small College: A Bibliographic Handbook.* Washington, D.C.: Council for the Advancement of Small Colleges, n.d.

Carnegie Council on Policy Studies in Higher Education. *The States and Private Higher Education: Problems and Policies in a New Era.* San Francisco: Jossey-Bass, 1977.

Carnegie Foundation for the Advancement of Teaching. *More Than Survival: Prospects for Higher Education in a Period of Uncertainty.* San Francisco: Jossey-Bass, 1975.

CHEIT, E. F. *The New Depression in Higher Education.* New York: McGraw-Hill, 1971.

FROOMKIN, J. *Needed: A New Federal Policy for Higher Education.* Washington, D.C.: Institute for Educational Leadership, 1978.

GOLLATTSCHECK, J. F., AND OTHERS. *College Leadership for Community Renewal: Beyond Community-Based Education.* San Francisco: Jossey-Bass, 1976.

JONSEN, R. W. *Small Liberal Arts Colleges: Diversity at the Crossroads.* Washington, D.C.: American Association for Higher Education, 1978.

MAYHEW, L. B. *Legacy of the Seventies: Experiment, Economy, Equality, and Expediency in American Higher Education.* San Francisco: Jossey-Bass, 1977.

MINTER, W. J., AND BOWEN, H. R. *Independent Higher Education.* Washington, D.C.: National Association of Independent Colleges and Universities, 1978.

SHULMAN, C. H. *Private Colleges: Present Conditions and Future Prospects.* Washington, D.C.: American Association for Higher Education, 1974.

WORMLEY, W. M. "Factors Related to the Ability of Certain Small Private Liberal Arts Colleges to Cope with the New Depression in Higher Education." Unpublished doctoral dissertation, Stanford University, 1978.

Chapter 2

ᔕᔕᔕᔕᔕᔕᔕᔕ

Improving Administrative Structures and Policies

The number of problems and issues faced by an institution attempting to survive in the 1980s is enormous. Ways must be found to increase endowments and to cultivate federal funding agencies. Student protests, such as those over investment policies, must be dealt with. Decisions must be made on restoring or rebuilding obsolete facilities and on continuing or dropping intercollegiate athletics. The average age of faculty members will rise, at least during the 1980s, and faculties must be helped to renew themselves intellectually. A growing public disenchantment with education must be counteracted. Similarly, demands for accountability must be satisfied, but with the awareness that evidence regarding the outcomes of education is ambiguous and that an assessment in clear and understandable terms of the real purposes of education may not be possible. This ambiguity is reflected in the need to respond to egalitarian sentiments in the society while at the same time holding on to traditional academic values of rigor, excellence, quality, and merit.

The task is to develop administrative structures and processes that can most effectively solve such problems. Some have argued that a quest for administrative models is likely to be fruitless, either because collegiate institutions are organized anarchies responsive to no predictable laws or because they are organizations that inexorably follow certain paths regardless of intervention by individuals. It is the position taken here that although there are ambiguities in collegiate institutions regarding goals, technologies, and techniques of evaluation, there is, nonetheless, enough clarity of purpose and enough tested technique to suggest likely successful and unsuccessful administrative organization.

Common Administrative Weaknesses

The need for an effort to develop a sound administrative structure is revealed in some frequently encountered administrative failures.

Centralization of Authority. One common failure involves the matter of centralization and decentralization of authority. Centralization of a great deal of power in a chief executive may produce dramatically effective decisions but is as likely to produce dramatically bad ones. However, if the power to make major decisions is decentralized to departments or to a faculty as a whole, such diverse interests may be so juxtaposed as to prevent decisions being reached. Consider this example of a liberal arts college faced with the need to reduce faculty because of enrollment drops: The full faculty was informed of the crisis and asked to develop guidelines for terminating faculty and actually to recommend who should be terminated. Six months after the charge was given, the faculty was still unable to come to grips with a problem whose solution was so painful. Eventually, the president himself had to make the decisions. At the other extreme is another university whose president, faced with similar conditions, decided to notify a substantial number of faculty of termination and actually sent the notices, hoping that some of them could be rescinded if financing improved. This seemingly arbitrary action of central administration precipitated a crisis that led directly to the formation of a faculty union and indirectly to the termination of the president's appointment.

Obviously, what is needed is some balance between centralized authority that must ultimately be exercised and decentralized consideration of the various complexities of the issues. In the case of the liberal arts college, an actual structure such as a faculty personnel committee, with definite processes, could have deliberated the matter in a responsible way and provided the president with several possible alternatives. A similar device at the financially troubled university would have slowed the decision making and again given the president options, each having been examined in a decentralized way.

Administrative Misalignment. Another fairly common failure is the improper location of an administrative office—for example, a planning office administratively so lodged that the data it generates are typically not available to those who need them. Another fairly typical misplacement is that of the admissions office in institutions that exist almost exclusively on tuition. The president must rely so much on enrollments in such institutions that the director of admissions should always report directly to him so that he can keep close track of shifts in the application and admissions situation. From time to time, some unusual administrative arrangements may be tolerated—for example, three people, each charged with some aspect of a student-life program, reporting directly to the president because none of the three would agree to supervision by one of the others and each had but a short time until retirement. But as a general rule, considerable attention should be given to placing administrative positions according to function rather than because of individual personality or personal relations.

Confused Communication. Related to the foregoing problem is the matter of confused channels of communication frequently produced by confused administrative roles. Collegiate institutions typically are rather flexible bureaucracies tolerant of violation of channels of authority and communication, but they are bureaucracies nonetheless. Certain offices are responsible for certain activities and that responsibility must be generally recognized. However, all too frequently a president may feel entitled to decide expenditure questions, student-discipline questions, or teaching-load questions, whereas, at other times, he may expect the business manager, dean of students, or dean of faculty to decide. When this becomes a pattern, confusion reigns and critical matters are left undecided or are poorly decided. Especially in times of adversity, when rumor spreads quickly, it is essential that all know who is responsible for doing what and why it has to be done.

Misunderstood Senate Roles. A variation of the problem of communication and responsibility, which has become particular vexing since the late 1960s, is that of making clear the faculty or faculty senate role in financial matters. As faculties have consolidated their de facto control over academic matters through the creation of senates operating under charters approved by the board of trustees, they have also expressed desire to have a voice in budgetary matters. And in some institutions, provisions have been made for some faculty participation, chiefly in an advisory way. But it is all too easy for faculty groups to misunderstand their role and to equate advice with decision. Such a misunderstanding can quickly produce confrontation and ill feeling if faculty advice is not taken regarding serious budget matters. In one Kansas institution, low faculty morale was plunged even deeper when the elected faculty committee on the budget recommended administrative cuts as a means of balancing the budget but the president elected faculty and staff cuts instead.

Administrative Overload. One problem that is serious in its own right but also contributes to other problems is the excessive workload frequently placed on or assumed by key administrators. In one liberal arts college, for example, a single individual occupied the positions of dean of the college of liberal arts and academic dean, as well as holding membership on twenty-one different committees. Such an overload prevented a reasonable flow of administrative action, especially program action with major financial implications. Administrators in American collegiate institutions tend to accept heavy workloads consisting of meetings, talking with people, preparing reports and memoranda, and making some decisions. In part this is because of tradition, in part because institutions have become more complex and the sheer act of coordinating various posts requires more communication, and in part because activity itself is used as evidence of individual effectiveness. Especially when faculties have become more critical of increasing the numbers and cost of administrators, principal administrative officers are tempted to add responsibilities to their own portfolios rather than face additional faculty criticism for adding administrative staff. Thus, at a time when managers must cope with such delicate matters as faculty retrenchment, requiring enormous expenditures of time, they may find themselves overloaded with details and functions that could better be done by others or even left undone.

Inadequate Preparation of Administrators. Another problem is the lack of administrative specialists and staff people with the background and training needed by educational institutions. Modern colleges and universities are complex organizations that require people who understand financial matters and who know how to accumulate and use large amounts of statistical data, generate funds, plan buildings, deal with state and federal government, plan land use, manage investments, and deal with faculty and students. Yet the route to administration is typically through the academic ranks and on-the-job preparation after appointment to this or that administrative post. Although there are academic programs designed to prepare academic administrators, they typically prepare generalists instead of the needed specialists and turn out people who are chiefly acceptable in limited numbers and types of institutions. Thus, it is all too possible for highly specialized positions to be filled by individuals who really do not understand the needed technology or who do not understand the application of a known technology to an educational institution. Twenty years as comptroller for Boeing may ill equip a person to become comptroller of a liberal arts college, as may twenty years of teaching home economics ill equip a person to be a director of institutional research.

Uncoordinated Program and Budget Responsibility. A major violation of workable administrative procedure is the failure to link program responsibility with budget responsibility. The normal system in American institutions is to assign budget responsibility to the president, the deans and, in some institutions, the department heads. At the same time, there is a tendency to encourage program development along side of that structure, but without assigning budgets and budget control to heads of institutes, centers, and special curricular programs. Not only does failure to make specific budgetary provisions for a special activity make failure of the activity likely, but it may also conceal hidden costs that can undermine the financial base of an institution. This is particularly probable and dangerous as financial decline approaches. When enrollments begin to sag, institutions tend to create new programs to attract students. Yet all too frequently, programs are created without full awareness of both immediate and ultimate cost. The only way to avoid that danger is to make specific short- and long-range budget provisions for every new program created and to indicate the source of funds to be used. If it were required that the full cost of a new testing program, a new program in general education, a new affirmative action program, or a new internship or cooperative-work program be specified, as well as the source of funds, one has the strong suspicion that new program development would slow considerably.

Ineffective Boards of Trustees. Boards of trustees in American institutions serve a number of critical roles. They are the technique used to assign legitimacy to the institution and what it does. No officer, for example, can serve the institution except through a formal action of the board. The board serves as a device to mediate between the institution and the larger society and seeks to interpret each to the other. It represents a major check in a system of checks and balances that maintains institutional stability. It ensures that neither the administration nor the faculty nor any other group gains excessive power. As the board of trustees is so central, its failures can be especially destructive. Thus, a board that selects the wrong president can harm an institution, sometimes irreparably. A board that does not require strict presidential accounting can allow an institution to drift into serious difficulties, whereas one that intervenes in administration below the presidential level can limit the presidents power to govern. Finally, a board that does not assume its responsibilities to help finance an institution can limit institutional flexibility.

A Case of Poor Administrative Organization

There are, of course, many other kinds of administrative failures. For example, in small institutions organized by departments, academic deans may attempt administrative supervision of too many

subordinates. In large institutions, central administration may become so concerned with external affairs as to lose contact with the
internal realities of the institution. Rather than continuing to
enumerate such failures, let us consider their significance in aggregate for institutional survival as illustrated by the following composite case study.

Consider a reasonably typical Midwestern liberal arts college. Its enrollment during the 1960s grew from 600 to 1,200, its
faculty from 50 to 120, and its budget from $1.2 million to $5 million. Its physical plant expanded by the addition of two new residence halls, a new library, and a new science building, and its endowment increased from $200,000 to $2 million. The institution had
been church affiliated until the 1970s when it became independent,
although the catalogue still claims that it stands in the liberal Protestant Christian tradition. It is located in a state having a declining
population of six million and a reasonably diversified economy, with
agriculture, heavy industry, and transportation the major elements.

The incumbent president is a clergyman who also holds a
Doctor of Education degree in student personnel work and who
previously had been vice-president for student affairs at a state university. He has been in office for four years and is assisted by vice-
presidents for academic affairs and for development who had served
with the president in his previous position. The business manager is
in his late fifties, has been in his position for ten years, and had been
associate comptroller of a rubber company prior to joining the staff
of the college. He is a close personal friend of most of the members
of the board of trustees, who selected him for this post in order to
improve the financial management of the institution. He also is a
member of the board of trustees and is its treasurer. As treasurer,
he maintains absolute control over the budget and shares its details
only with the board.

The academic program is conducted by twenty-one departments, ranging in size from one person to fifteen, with the average
being five. Department heads are appointed by and report to the
academic vice-president. They request annual operating budgets but
are never given a final budget indicating what funds have been
granted them. Wages and salaries are not part of the budget of departments, the library, the various student affairs offices, or the

other administrative subunits on campus. Personnel costs are budgeted directly by the business manager.

The dean of student affairs has a religious background as a lay worker in the conservative wing of the church that originally had operated the institution. He believes that the college is as responsible for developing Christian character in students as for developing their intellectual powers and preparing them for vocations. He maintains tight supervision over three counselors, two directors of activities, a director of testing, the campus nurse, and the director of the student union. He also pays great personal attention to the residence halls and their directors.

The faculty, which includes teachers, counselors, and all other professional staff members, meets once each month as a whole and maintains committees on academic affairs, student affairs, and the library. It votes on course changes, graduation requirements, rules of student conduct, and membership on the three standing committees. There is a small local chapter of the American Association of University Professors whose members have long urged the creation of a faculty senate, but the central administration has remained convinced that the existing governance structure is adequate.

The admissions staff consists of a director who has strong church contacts and good contacts with high schools in several large urban parts of the state. He is aided by three admissions officers, all relatively young recent graduates of the institution. Two live close to campus and one lives 200 miles away in a part of the state strongly supportive of the institution, especially as interpreted by the dean of students.

In 1970, there was a sudden drop in new student application rates. This was judged to be of scant significance because attrition rates had also dropped, leaving enrollments stable. The following year, however, application and enrollment rates of new students continued to fall and there was also a net loss of thirty full-time equivalent (FTE) students, producing a deficit of $70,000—the first deficit in the seventy-five-year history of the institution. Since the amount was small and since the deficit was finally made up through increased gifts, the board of trustees did not concern itself with the matter. The trend continued, however, so that by 1976 enrollment had dropped to 800 students, the annual deficit had increased to

$250,000, and an accumulated operating deficit had grown to $1 million. In an effort to slow the annual deficit growth, the institution allowed the faculty to drop in size to ninety. A salary raise of 5 percent was granted in 1970, 6 percent in 1973, and 3 percent in 1976. Faculty travel was eliminated, and secretarial and maintenance staffs reduced. One residence hall was closed and left uncared for, and meals provided students in residence halls were reduced from twenty to eighteen per week.

In the fall of 1976, the board of trustees ordered an end to deficit budgeting and an elimination of accumulated deficit through liquidation of a part of the endowment. In addition, it called for an increase in the academic ability of new students. It also set a target of an enrollment of 1,000 to be achieved in four years, the additional students to be attracted by new programs to be created. The president, academic vice-president, and dean of students were each asked to prepare plans to be submitted to the board to achieve these goals. At the same time, the vice-president for development was asked to mount a major drive to raise $5 million, half of which was to go to endowment and half to retire capital debt.

These were, of course, impossible demands. It is conceivable they might have been met by an institution better organized. But the structure and style of administration and organization of this particular institution made success impossible. Consider these problems —and these are endemic in such institutions throughout the country:

1. The president was held responsible for the institution, yet could not obtain full financial information from the business manager.
2. The total faculty was too large and the departments too small to plan attractive new programs—besides which, neither faculty nor departments could know what funds would or would not be available to support new programs.
3. The board was clearly being supplied poor information regarding enrollment trends, which led to the impossible demand for enrollment increases together with increases in student academic ability.
4. The fact that the board ordered vice-presidents and deans to report directly to the board revealed a confused system of control

and communication, as well as an obvious distrust of the president himself.

5. It also seems likely that there was or could well be a split in the central administrative group—with the academic vice-president and dean of students linked to the president, the business manager to the board of trustees, and the vice-president for development basically a solitary factor.

In times of slow or no growth combined with low expectations, colleges and universities could and did function with such poorly contrived administrative and organization structures as the one just described. Efficient organization and administrative structures were also relatively unimportant during periods of rapid growth, affluence, and fairly high expectations. However, such casual arrangements will not be effective in situations of high expectations conditioned by the immediate past, coupled with enrollment and financial slowdowns. It is argued here that while some variation, institution to institution, is possible, indeed demonstrable, there are reasonably well documented and accepted administrative principles, often violated or ignored, that represent good administrative practice in general and absolutely essential practice in times of adversity. These principles involve: a limited number of administrative officers whose duties are clearly specified and understood; a limited number of standing committees, commissions, or boards including both faculty members and administrators and having clearly defined domains or spheres of influence; and written and generally understood processes and procedures.

Unitary Administration

The first of these desirable arrangements is the unitary system of administrative responsibility, which makes the president alone responsible and accountable to the board of trustees. In the last part of the nineteenth century, as businessmen and lawyers began to replace clergymen on boards of trustees, some institutions adopted a dual structure, with the president and chief financial officer both responsible to the board of trustees. At Stanford, for example, the president was responsible for the academic program and the business manager for financial affairs. Gradually, the dual structure was abolished in most institutions. However, in some institutions, some elements of the dual system remained, and in still others, duality began to reappear as conditions changed.

In some liberal arts colleges, the business manager is ex officio a member of the board of trustees and serves as treasurer of the institution. It is he who proposes the budget for board approval and who defends it. The president may or may not know the financial condition of the institution. In one institution, a three-way split of responsibility was adopted, with the business manager, the president, and the provost each responsible to the board of trustees, respectively, for finances, external affairs, and internal affairs. In some of the recently created private institutions that emphasize strong egalitarianism, multiple forms of administrative responsibility have been urged. The Antioch Law School in Washington, D.C., for example, was created by a husband-and-wife team and both are responsible to the board and are expected to divide duties as they see fit. The University Without Walls in Berkeley, California, assigned administrative responsibility to the executive committee of the board of trustees, with no particular portfolio assigned to each member. So confused did conditions become in that institution that major misallocations of federal funds took place with no single officer aware of what was happening. And even in well-established institutions, the external demands on the time of the chief executive officer have produced a situation in which authority for on-campus affairs simply devolved upon the vice-president-provost. This can be tolerable if the president and vice-president can work together and recognize the line beyond which the provost will not exercise power. But with a less congenial relationship, the division of authority can impede essential flow of information, place the board in a position of adjudicating differences between the president and provost, and actually divide the campus into antagonistic camps.

Without exception, the president should be the only officer who reports directly to the board of trustees. Other administrative officers should meet with the board only upon the express invitation of the president to discuss only specific items on the agenda. The president's office should prepare agendas and distribute documents to the board and should be the only channel through which documents from other administrative officers reach the board of trustees. This in no way limits the power of the board to request advice from subordinate officers, but such requests should be to the president, unless the board is considering removal of the president from office. The power to conduct the institution that resides in the board of trustees may be delegated but should be delegated through the president. Thus, if some power or discretion is granted a faculty senate, it is granted because the president requests it and with a clear statement of presidential right to overturn *any* decision of the senate.

This stark doctrine of presidential power and discretion is essential if institutions are to cope with rapidly changing conditions. The president must be privy to all financial information and have the power to act quickly (with safeguards to individual rights, of course) in event of unexpected events or a crisis. During the energy crisis of 1973, for example, and the simultaneous downturn of the stock market, institutional budgets approved in June proved to be out of balance by the following March. Presidents had to act quickly not only to offset immediate budget shortfalls but also to initiate plans to correct the longer-term shortfalls that derived from the crisis.

Periodically during the 1970s, tuition-dependent private institutions experienced a large and unexpected enrollment drop in September. In such a contingency, the president needs the authority to place an immediate moratorium on expenditures, to reallocate budget items so as best to overcome the unanticipated income loss, and to take immediate steps regarding staff and faculty appointments as insurance against a possible second year of large enrollment drops. This does not imply that the chief executive should act without consultation—indeed, not to consult broadly would lead to serious problems of morale and even litigation. But it does imply that after consultation and consistent with fair play and approximation of legal due process, the president must have the authority to send letters of intent to terminate faculty and staff appointments and to cancel budget appropriations. If the institution has a unionized faculty and a negotiated contract, the right of the president so to act should be recognized with only the processes of consultation as part of the contract.

This concept of presidential power seems so elementary as to question why it is belabored. The fact is that erosion of this basic characteristic of the American college presidency has contributed to serious inability of institutions to respond to crises.

Cabinet System of Administration

Consistent with the concept of unitary administration is the concept of a cabinet system of administrative coordination. The president typically has several principal administrative subordinates: officers in charge of academic affairs, financial affairs, student affairs, public relations, development, and admissions. These officers should be organized into a consultative, deliberative, and decision-making body that meets regularly, recognizes its collective responsibilities, and is recognized by all campus constituencies as one of the major policy-forming agencies of the institution. Figure 1 illustrates such as administrative cabinet, parallel to the executive committee of the faculty.

Figure 1. Suggested Administrative Organization.

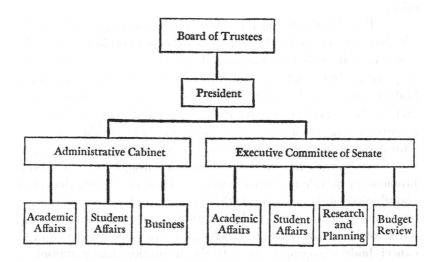

In some institutions without an administrative cabinet, the president has attempted to coordinate the work of his subordinates through individual consultation. This method is time-consuming, prevents the airing of many different points of view, and does not allow for all principal officers to be kept informed. In other institutions, the president has feared to declare his subordinates a cabinet with policy-forming and decision-making powers because of faculty suspicions or student criticism of the establishment. In still other institutions, the president has not created a cabinet because of lack of esteem for the qualities of his chief administrative associates or because of his belief in his own judgment. And in a few places, personality differences between various individuals have made group meetings so emotional and distasteful that cabinet-style adminstration has been allowed to disappear.

None of those situations, however, can be rectified by the chief executive's merely possessing judgment and moral courage, terminating impossible subordinates, or meeting criticism of an administrative oligarchy by creating other bodies to discuss and recommend policy. To be effective, administrative leaders must themselves meet regularly to coordinate their priorities and efforts.

As indicated in Figure 1, the administrative cabinet would be set up alongside a faculty organization in such a way as to ensure great interaction, a reasonably smooth flow of problems and issues, and fairly quick solutions or decisions. For example, if it became apparent that the institution was not attracting enough new students to fill residence halls or not holding an adequate number until graduation, there would be standing committees of both faculty and administration that could examine the problem, consider various alternatives as solutions, and then gain approval and support from the various relevant constituencies. This, of course, sounds much more simple than it really is. Serious decisions are reached through a great deal of discussion and consultation, reeducation, and political manipulation, as well as through bureaucratic processes. But structure can facilitate those time-consuming efforts. Thus, the president's cabinet might begin discussion of the problem and elaborate its implications. The matter might then be referred to a standing senate committee charged with research and long-range planning. The senate committee would discuss the matter, consult with faculty, and ponder alternative solutions. It might, for example, judge the matter so critical as to recommend that discussion of the problem be given first priority by all divisions, departments, and offices and that proposals be produced within a three-month period. It has been demonstrated that if a problem or issue is shown to be serious enough, a properly constructed organization can act promptly.

Faculty Participation in Decisions

As a counterforce to administration, the faculty should be so organized that its judgment may be expressed on all issues and decisions made on those matters that come within its purview—namely, curriculum, faculty membership, entrance and graduation requirements, and some matters of student life. Faculty advice should be available with respect to institutional purpose, priorities, including financial ones, and any other matters involving the entire institution. In far too many institutions in trouble, there is no clear faculty structure and no clear understanding of faculty powers and prerogatives. Typically, there is a formal faculty, which meets monthly and debates issues and which has standing committees with no real understanding of what their powers are. No clear and legitimate way is provided to bring together the opinions of administration and faculty so as to produce prudent decisions. One of the first pieces of advice that should be given an institution in trouble is to create an effective and formal faculty structure. This, it should be noted, should apply to all institutions. When Columbia University faced outbreaks of student protest in the 1960s, it was discovered that there was no formal instrument that could engage the full faculty in considering the troubles of the institution.

As shown in Figure 1, a structure can be envisioned with two major policy-making agencies—the administrative cabinet and the executive committee of the senate—each reporting to the president and each responsible for specific categories of deliberation. The executive committee and the four major committees of the senate—academic affairs, student affairs, research and planning, and budget review—would be elected by the faculty senate, with the relevant administrative officer serving ex officio as chairman. Thus, the academic dean and the dean of student affairs would chair their two committees, the business manager would chair the budget review committee, and the president would chair the executive committee and the committee on research and planning.

Under normal circumstances, matters would be referred back and forth between the administration side and the senate side, with considerable freedom and flexibility. Thus, the administrative cabinet might wish faculty discussion of a shift in institutional emphasis toward soliciting greater support from the conservative wing of the church with which the institution is affiliated. It would ask the executive committee to request the committee on research and planning to discuss the matter and to make recommendations. Or the committee on academic affairs might ask the president and administrative cabinet to examine the possibilities of financing a new ethnic studies program.

This model may seem overly rigid and bureaucratic but, ideally, it should prove to be flexible and reasonably efficient in operation. Its possibilities may be stressed by comparing it with other structures, such as one emphasizing the separation of the senate and its committees from administration. In such a structure, administrators do not sit on committees and the chairmen are elected from the faculty. Actions are taken or recommendations are made to the administration, which then is put in the position of accepting or rejecting but with little opportunity for modification. Since administrative offices maintain the files of information needed for recommendations, this separate structure either encourages debate without information or places a burden on administrative officers to supply information, frequently in unusual or sophisticated form.

The particular administrative structure suggested here is based on the belief that in American collegiate institutions, faculty and administration operate from different premises regarding educational and institutional matters. Faculty members tend to be fairly conservative with respect to educational change and innovation. They have long been socialized concerning academic and educational content, processes, and techniques. Disciplines represent the keystone, the integrity of which is safeguarded by academic departments. Courses are taught in lectures, seminars, and laboratories and represent the major way faculty members express their scholarship and expertise. The disciplinary department and traditional procedures are carefully guarded, and suggested changes are typically perceived as threats to them—as indeed they are. Consider the frequently suggested reforms of interdisciplinary courses, using educational technology, team teaching, or independent study. All challenge the traditional role of a faculty member as one who knows and will tell but only under his or her own conditions.

Administration, on the contrary, although its members were faculty at one time, tends to be dynamic and concerned with institutionwide interests, which are frequently seen as different from and even in conflict with departmental interests. From the institution point of view, for example, staff-taught, interdisciplinary general education courses may have strong appeal as being less expensive to offer and possibly attractive to students. But they compete with department courses and hence are resisted by faculty.

Now both of these postures are valuable. Conserving academic traditions is important, but so is modifying them as changing times dictate. However, an institution can be so traditional as to atrophy or it can change so fast as to lose all sense of purpose. What is needed are techniques that can keep the conservatism of the faculty and the dynamism of the administration in a kind of creative tension. The dynamic urges of presidents and deans encounter the resistance of the faculty, and out of this interaction comes the ordered change that is needed.

Such tension and ordered change is especially significant during periods of decline. Faculty, operating through department, will tend to defend existing courses, requirements, and patterns of courses, regardless of changes in course enrollments. The defense will be made in the intellectual terms of protecting the integrity of essential disciplines. Central administration, however, will seek to keep the institution responsive to changing preferences and demands of students and will encourage new experimental courses, redeployment of faculty time, and new occupational programs. For institutional health there should be change—but not too much. And there should be adherence to tradition—but not too much.

To produce this needed creative tension, there should be a clear assignment of responsibility to faculty and to administration, subject to specific checks and balances and, of course, ultimately to the power of the board of trustees. Faculty, as indicated earlier, should be generally responsible for the content of the curriculum, the qualifications of its own membership, and the conditions of student entrance into and exit from the institution, and should have

general purview over conditions of student life. Central administration and each major subordinate level of administration should have
power over the acquisition and expenditure of funds, appointment
of administrative officers, setting of major agendas, and execution
of the policy established by legitimate bodies, whether board, faculty, or administrative.

To demonstrate application of these powers, a faculty (college, school, or department) could decide what courses to offer, but
the department head, dean, or president could decide whether to
provide the needed finances. A faculty could refuse to approve an
appointment recommended by administration, but the administration could also reject a faculty request for funds for a faculty position. Such checks and balances could produce an impasse that could
be resolved only by the board of trustees. The likelihood of this can
be avoided if there is continuous faculty-administration legitimate
interaction regarding all such matters. This may be most clearly illustrated by examining two ways for granting tenure.

One method of granting tenure is for the faculty member to
request consideration for tenure or for a department to elect to consider someone for tenure. Once the faculty of the department or
school approves the recommendation, it is forwarded to an elected
faculty tenure committee. This committee may consult with administrators but is not bound to do so. If the recommendation is
approved by the committee, it is sent to the president, who has only
the options of accepting or rejecting it. This, of course, is a situation
with high potential for producing confrontation. A more cumbersome method is for the department or school faculty each to recommend regarding tenure. Both recommendations are then reviewed
by the next higher administrative authority (council of deans, provost staff, or the like). It may accept or reject the recommendation.
If it accepts, it sends the recommendation to an elected committee
of the faculty. If the committee accepts, the recommendation is then
forwarded to the president, who may submit or not submit it to the
board of trustees. This faculty and administrative involvement at all
levels allows various interests to be expressed and needed compromises to be reached. Central administration can thus express the
need to limit the number of faculty granted tenure, and the department can express the need to fill specific disciplinary requirements.

Similarly, routine annual budgets would originate at the departmental level within guidelines developed by the business manager and president and approved by the administrative cabinet. In its semifinal form, the budget would be reviewed by the senate budget review committee and their suggestions made in a joint meeting of the committee and the administrative cabinet.

A nonroutine matter, such as a crisis precipitated by a sudden drop in enrollment, might move differently. This problem might move from the administrative cabinet to the committee on research and planning, to joint meetings with the cabinets of the vice-presidents for academic and student affairs, to the faculty senate, to joint meetings between the senate and the cabinet, and finally to the president and board of trustees.

In reality, of course things do not move so smoothly. It is difficult to schedule meetings regularly enough to enable progress toward a solution. Extraneous matters will arise deliberately or by accident that distract from consideration of the central problem. Individuals and groups each have hidden agendas that must be satisfied before progress can be made. Essential information may be lacking. Problems, issues, and solutions may become mixed so that a solution adopted might or might not be a rational response to a particular problem. Solutions proposed may be impossible to put into effect because of a variety of constraints. Finally, the system may become so clogged with normal activities in addition to crisis matters as to come to a standstill.

A further complication is that the model used is that of a small institution. Will such procedures work in larger, more complex institutions consisting, for example, of 7 schools, 100 departments and institutes, and 20,000 students, and having large investments and budgets of $50 million a year or more? In general, it is believed that the same principles apply, although they may operate somewhat differently because more people are involved and major decisions are arrived at more slowly. Large institutions really consist of smaller institutions, and they clearly can operate along the lines of the small-institution model. But total institutional concerns can be handled best by: (1) following the principles of unitary administration; (2) making administrators responsible not only for their programs but for the budgets as well; (3) limiting the number of administrative specialties to demonstrated needs, be they substantive or cosmetic; (4) including faculty and administration in legislative and policy-discussing bodies; and (5) specifying duties, responsibilities, and procedures in written and well-distributed form.

Decentralization of Budget Preparation and Administration

Financial problems represent a central focus of this book. Sound financial decisions can be reached efficiently by using the insights of both faculty and administration. Consider the following example of an important but frequently ignored budgeting system.

In September, the central administration prepares and distributes a broad set of budget guidelines indicating, to the best of its ability, the likely income and possible categories of expenditure that might be expected for the next academic year. These are sent to schools and departments and to the academic senate for discussion and development of school or department budgetary needs. The chief academic officer visits with each school or department to interpret the intent of the guidelines, obtain reactions, and hear of specific problems. These meetings are followed by discussions with deans and department heads as each seeks to maximize the support for his or her unit. From these meetings emerge very specific budget guidelines, including the amount and kind of salary changes that would be acceptable. Deans and department heads then prepare their detailed-budget requests, which are consolidated and refined prior to submission to the board of trustees for approval. Once the budget requests are approved, the deans and department heads are notified so that they can plan during the summer and know, with reasonable certainty, what funds they will have during the next academic year.

The essential elements in such a system are early and open discussion of budgetary needs by subordinate units within the broad guidelines first established by central administration and its final budget decisions. There is opportunity for faculty discussion and great sharing of information, but final decisions are made centrally.

A significant element of budget preparation and budget administration is determining the administrative level at which direct budget administration should be placed. In many private liberal arts colleges, budgets are administered centrally or departments are given knowledge of and authority over only small operating budgets for the purchase of supplies and a few services. Control over travel, operating capital purchases (microscopes, for example), communications, and salaries rests with the business manager. Even when funds have been budgeted for supplies to departments or divisions, many of these institutions require a second approval by the business office. The reason given for such practices is that the central administration must retain complete budgetary control if the institution is to have the flexibility to meet sudden shifts in income as, for example, when there is an unexpected drop in enrollment. It is also argued that departments in liberal arts colleges are typically small and that decentralized information about salaries would mean that everyone would quickly know the exact salaries of everyone else. In addition, until the actual income can be known, following fall registration, there is unwillingness to make final budget allocations that actually alllow subordinate units to spend.

Such practices represent incorrect application of the principle of unitary administration and appropriate centralization. As a general rule, the administrator responsible for specific programs should also be responsible for administering the full budget needed for those programs. It is true that many departments in small institutions are really too small to be effective as administrative units. In those situations, a divisional structure seems warranted with the division responsible for the programs in several related fields of study. The head of each administrative unit should be expected to prepare full budget requests, including funds for professional salaries, staff salaries, capital outlay, travel, communications, and operating expenses. Once the budget has been approved, those units should be sent approved budgets and given freedom to expend funds or to expend subject to final approval given after fall registration.

This decentralized system of budget preparation and administration has several clear advantages. First, it forces recognition of the full cost of various programs, which in turn allows cost-benefit decisions to be made. Thus, when the full humanities division budget is examined and compared to other divisions in the light of enrollment trends, information becomes available upon which program decisions can be made. Those institutions that centralize budget administration have difficulty knowing specific program costs since the major expense items are shown only in aggregate. Second, it forces the heads of administrative units to assume full reponsibility for their units. If salaries, for example, are not the affair of division heads, they are not inclined to think of alternative ways of delivering educational services. They simply ask for the faculty they think they need. But with responsibility for salary, they can examine such alternatives to full-time professional positions as part-time positions, teaching assistants, or an increase in staff size. A science division head can insist that laboratory sections never exceed twenty—on difficult-to-challenge educational grounds—but with salary responsibility, he or she is forced to examine the relative merits of larger sections and larger salary increases for faculty versus larger faculty, smaller sections, and smaller salary increments.

Presidents, academic deans, and business managers of small institutions, and even some larger ones, are likely to resist such decentralization in the belief that only they have the information and the broad view necessary to manage institutional funds. It is strange that presidents will urge decentralization of decisions about the central activities of a college or university, such as the content of the curriculum, yet will fear that subordinate administrators responsible for academic programs do not have the competence to manage money. It is an attitude akin to the nineteenth-century belief of boards of trustees that the management of an institution's finances could not be entrusted to academic leaders, but only to someone with business experience.

Clarification of Administrative Duties

The position of the previous section—that heads of schools, divisions, centers, institutes, and departments should have responsibility for the budgets needed to operate their units—is related to the belief that collegiate administrators of programs should typically be expected to perform several quite specific duties. One of the major weaknesses of collegiate administration is that the roles and duties of administrators at the second, third, and fourth levels have been so ambiguous. Thus, department heads may be senior or junior faculty members, may be expected to serve one year or three years or indefinitely, and may be expected to attend to only administrative chores or to be closely involved in personnel decisions.

With varying degrees of emphasis, according to level of administration and type of institution, academic administrators from president down to department heads should be expected to perform a number of different duties.

- *Faculty and staff development.* A first essential is to facilitate the professional development of faculty. This duty would include reviewing student evaluations of faculty and faculty professional activities, counseling with individual faculty members, and making judgments regarding them that will affect their professional careers. It would also include setting up in-service training programs and other activities for the development of faculty. With regular attention to such matters, there would be little need for new offices of professional development to be created.
- *Budget preparation and budget control.* Budgets are really statements of educational purpose phrased in fiscal terms. Thus, budget and program responsibility should always go together.
- *Advocacy.* A department or division head, dean of a school, or even the president should be an advocate of the unit he or she represents and should work to achieve adequate resources for it. A good test of the effectiveness of a department head would be the changes in budget appropriations for the department made during his or her incumbency.
- *Titular Representation.* There are many different occasions when a unit must be represented by someone for both substantive and symbolic reasons. Deans sit on the platform at commencement, and department heads hold receptions for new students and faculty in the fall. When visitors or prospective students wish to find out about a program, it is the titular head to whom they go. This role not only ensures that reasonably accurate information is provided but also other faculty members are not bothered.
- *Facilitation.* An important duty of the heads of units is to facilitate conditions most favorable to the effectiveness of the unit. This includes taking definite steps to develop a sense of community and ensuring that faculty members have adequate offices.
- *Communication.* Each administrator is, in effect, a direct com-

munication link between his or her unit and other units in the institution. Thus, department heads, meeting as part of the dean's cabinet, can report to their colleagues concerning their own units and the activities of other departments.

- *Execution of policies.* Administrators spend considerable time just carrying out policies developed by their faculties or at higher levels of administration. This duty ranges from acting on student requests to answering correspondence and preparing reports.
- *Financial development.* In institutions such as research universities, even department heads are expected to search for funds for the department members to carry on needed or desired activities. Indeed, in some institutions, the "every tub stands on its own bottom" doctrine extends down to departments in the expectation that each department will earn enough tuition and secure enough external funds to maintain its faculty and other expenses.

Such specific duties assigned to each academic administrator are especially significant for institutional survival in approaching times of trouble. If division heads are held responsible for maintaining enrollments, they can be expected to encourage faculty and program improvement to attract and hold students. If held accountable for operating within a budget, they can be expected to consider alternative ways to expend money to gain greater benefits. If held responsible for the morale of the members of their divisions, they can be expected to advocate their courses strongly at higher administrative levels.

Limitation of Administrative Staff

There is a tendency in all organizations for the number of managers and staff to increase, especially if the external environment grows more complex and demanding. This tendency has been especially pronounced as collegiate institutions expanded during the sixties, faced greater external regulations during the seventies, and anticipated the difficulties of the eighties. Thus, the 1960s saw the rise of deans of sponsored research and contracts, directors of institutional research, and assistants to the president. During the 1970s, there were such new positions as affirmative action officer, full-time legal counsel, and director of federal and state relations. To cope with the 1980s, institutions are urged to create new positions, such as director of faculty development, director of institutional management, facilitator of budget adjustment, and local coordinator for consortial arrangements. The need for and value of these new administrative roles is, for the most part, a matter for each institution to decide in the light of what it wants, needs, and can afford. However, it is possible to comment on a number of different roles in the light of experience and theory and to differentiate between the essential and the possibly nonessential.

At the outset, two fundamental principles can be advanced. The first follows from the recommendation in the preceding sections that program responsibility, fiscal responsibility, and facilitative responsibility should be kept together: Planning, data analysis, staff development, and other functions should be the obligation of the administrator responsible for the program and budget of a unit and should not be set apart in some special office. The second principle is that if an administrative role or specialty is worth maintaining, it should be filled by a full-time incumbent. The tendency to have part-time administrators—whether directors of institutional research, associate deans, or directors of planning—should be resisted.

From these principles, the basis of an administrative structure can be recommended, whether the institution be large or small. First, the number of administrators should be kept as small as possible and should not include administrative specialists unless they are mandated by law or unless a clear economic case can be made for each position adopted. And second, the specifications for each of the limited number of administrative positions authorized should accommodate all of the essential administrative functions. For example, the position of division head should be full time with no required teaching responsibilities. The role should be so specified as to include faculty development, placement of graduates, and the maintenance of divisional records in such a way that they can be aggregated in the office of the academic vice-president. There thus would be no special placement office unless there was persuasive evidence that the availability of an active placement effort increased or maintained enrollments and tuition sufficiently to support the office. There would similarly be no associate deans or an office of institutional research unless a convincing economic case could be made.

As an illustration of this recommended structure, let us consider the case cited earlier of the liberal arts college that suffered rather serious enrollment and budget setbacks during the mid 1970s. For such an institution, there are some essential line and staff administrative roles which, if they cannot be filled with full-time appointments, the institution should consider eliminating. A list of these positions follows:

- President
- Academic vice-president
    Five division heads
    Librarian
    Registrar
    Director of religion (where relevant)
- Vice-president of finance
    Director of physical plant
    Comptroller
    Director of housing
- Vice-president for development
- Essential staff
    Director of admissions
    Director of public relations
    Chief negotiator for collective bargaining (where relevant)
- Vice-president for student affairs
    Director of student activities
    Director of counseling
    Director of athletics (where relevant)

This is a parsimonious list. Institutions have been urged to increase administrative staffs to accommodate various additional activities. And many of the suggested additional roles may be appropriate—if the institution can afford them. For an institution facing a severe question as to survival, however, the wisdom of the existence of a number of administrative roles, such as the following, can be questioned:

- *Director of institutional research.* The values of a discrete position here have not been proven: After twenty years, only about 20 percent of all institutions have such a position. The responsibility for generating data can be assigned to each of the basic administrative units.
- *Assistant to the president.* This would seem to be a luxury, with the incumbent either assigned chores that could be left undone or expected to create a role composed of possibly desirable but non-essential activities.
- *Director of faculty development.* As indicated earlier, this should be one of the chief duties of the academic vice-president and the five division heads.
- *Director of financial aid.* Financial aid can properly be assigned to the director of admissions.
- *Director of evaluation services.* This position too would seem to be a luxury. The institution could not afford more than one professional for the role, and the amount of evaluation that a single person could perform is so limited as to be of little value.
- *Director of investments.* For smaller institutions, a contract with a bank or investment firm would seem to be more economical and more effective.
- *Assistant or associate deans in academic affairs and student affairs.* These positions are also luxuries. The incumbents, like assistants to the president, must carve out roles for themselves that will usually not be essential.

In larger institutions, of course, there are needs for more administrative staff positions. However, some positions that have been urged can also be questioned:

- *Dean of undergraduate education.* This is basically a redundant position with duties overlapping those of deans of the various schools that offer undergraduate programs.
- *Director of the center for the improvement of instruction.* A close examination of such centers suggests very little overall impact on the institution, although some have helped a few individuals enormously.
- *Director of long-range planning.* Planning should be a major chief

administrative activity and should be assigned to the heads of the various administrative units. There can, of course, be specialists—land development, budget planning, and the like—but pulling together the elements that have been produced by specialists is the responsibility of chief executives of institutions or subunits.

These arguments may suggest an overconcern for economic considerations and a neglect of more qualitative considerations. But the position is adopted in the belief that the assertions of qualitative values of a number of administrative specializations have been based on inflated judgments. For example, the position of vice-president for educational development is created to stimulate innovation and to generate external funds for program development. Unless there are clearly demonstrated increases in innovative efforts and equally clear increases in external funding that contribute overhead sufficient to offset the cost of the office and the increased costs that the office actually produces, the office should be eliminated or not created. Similarly, offices of institutional research have been urged on the grounds that they conduct a needed continuing internal audit of the ongoing educational program of the institution. Differences between those institutions that do and do not maintain such offices have yet to be demonstrated.

Written Policies

A characteristic of administration of American higher education until the late 1950s was the absence of detailed written policies, procedures, bylaws, and constitutions. Such matters as possession of tenure, faculty conduct, administrative responsibility, and procedures for faculty appointment or dismissal were governed by oral tradition or simple broad statements of value. As the decade of the sixties wore on, however, and as institutions grew larger and more complex, they were forced to create written and detailed statements governing a variety of matters. Detailed conditions regarding granting of tenure were prepared, and faculty members who had long considered themselves to have tenure were notified in writing that indeed they did. Senates were created and their duties specified and given formal approval by the board of trustees. Faculty duties were finally put into written form and disciplinary procedures developed, together with levels of punishment. Faculty, student, and administrative handbooks became more detailed, as did the written statements of qualifications needed for various kinds of appointments.

There can be no retreat from this formalism and specificity. Nor should there be. Indeed, as institutions face the uncertain future through the decades of the eighties and nineties, greater attention must be focused on formal administrative arrangements. Thus, the total administrative organization should be clearly described in handbooks and bylaws so that every person in the institution knows the processes to be followed and the responsibilities of the various offices and committees. Such documents can make especially clear the duties of administrative officers and the kinds of activities that particular committees are expected to undertake.

Summary

This chapter has attempted to describe administrative systems which, if properly used, can maintain institutional health, detect problems as they appear, and allow for prompt remedial actions. The components of an effective administrative structure are not new; they are just, unfortunately, too often disregarded. The key elements of that structure are: an active and concerned board of trustees, a president who is alone responsible and accountable to the board, and a predictable council of heads of major administrative units that meets regularly with the president and has generally recognized policy-developing powers. In addition, there will be a formal faculty senate or similar organization with delegated powers and with a committee structure that includes faculty and relevant administrative officers. Such an organization will serve as one check on administration, just as the board of trustees serves as another. The heads of subordinate administrative units, including academic departments and divisions, will be considered and will consider themselves as administrators and will be provided budget and program responsibilities for their units. This decentralization will allow a form of management by objectives to function. The number of special administrative services staff officers will be kept severely limited, and these positions will be authorized only when strong and persuasive economic consideration warrants it. Throughout the institution, there will be an active system of communication that will allow all constituencies to know in detail the exact status of the institution, the problems to be faced, and their likely prognosis. Finally, consistent with this concept of wide diffusion of information will be the policy of requiring written and detailed statements for every major matter, ranging from processes for gaining tenure to conditions and sanctions of faculty discipline.

Further Readings

The literature regarding administration is large, although the portion that addresses itself to the actual practice of administration and discusses effective and ineffective structures and practices is relatively small. The Knowles *Handbook* presents a wealth of information, and Stroup comes out strongly in favor of a bureaucratic structure. Eble's readable book comes perhaps closest to the point of view of this chapter, although much of its underlying rationale is comparable to Corson.

BALDRIDGE, J. V., AND OTHERS. *Policy Making and Effective Leadership: A National Study of Academic Management.* San Francisco: Jossey-Bass, 1978.

BLAU, P. *The Organization of Academic Work.* New York: Wiley, 1973.

Carnegie Commission on Higher Education. *Governance of Higher Education: Six Priority Problems.* New York: McGraw-Hill, 1973.

CORSON, J. J. *Governance of Colleges and Universities.* (rev. ed.) New York: McGraw-Hill, 1975.

DILL, D. D. *Case Studies in University Governance.* Washington, D.C.: National Association of State Universities and Land Grant Colleges, 1971.

DRESSEL, P. L. *Handbook of Academic Evaluation: Assessing Institutional Effectiveness, Student Progress, and Professional Performance for Decision Making in Higher Education.* San Francisco: Jossey-Bass, 1976.

DRESSEL, P. L., AND ASSOCIATES. *Institutional Research in the University: A Handbook.* San Francisco: Jossey-Bass, 1971.

DRESSEL, P. L., AND FARICY, W. H. *Return to Responsibility: Constraints on Autonomy in Higher Education*. San Francisco: Jossey-Bass, 1972.

EBLE, K. E. *The Art of Administration: A Guide for Academic Administrators*. San Francisco: Jossey-Bass, 1978.

GREEN, J. L., JR. *A New Approach to Budgeting in Higher Education*. Detroit, Mich.: Business and Finance Office, Wayne State University, 1972.

HARKNESS, C. A. *College Staff Personnel Administration*. Urbana, Ill.: College and University Personnel Association, 1965.

HEILBRON, L. H. *The College and University Trustee: A View from the Board Room*. San Francisco: Jossey-Bass, 1973.

KNOWLES, A. S. (Ed.). *Handbook of College and University Administration*. New York: McGraw-Hill, 1970.

MC CONNELL, T. R. *The Redistribution of Power in Higher Education*. Berkeley, Calif.: Center for Research and Development in Higher Education, 1971.

MC HENRY, D. E., AND ASSOCIATES. *Academic Departments: Problems, Variations, and Alternatives*. San Francisco: Jossey-Bass, 1977.

MILLETT, J. D. *New Structures of Campus Power: Success and Failures of Emerging Forms of Institutional Governance*. San Francisco: Jossey-Bass, 1978.

MORTIMER, K. P., AND MC CONNELL, T. R. *Sharing Authority Effectively: Participation, Interaction, and Discretion*. San Francisco: Jossey-Bass, 1978.

NASON, J. W. *The Future of Trusteeship*. Washington, D.C.: Association of Governing Boards of Universities and Colleges, 1974.

RICHMAN, B. M., AND FARMER, R. N. *Leadership, Goals, and Power in Higher Education: A Contingency and Open-Systems Approach to Effective Management*. San Francisco: Jossey-Bass, 1974.

SCOTT, R. A. *Lords, Squires and Yeomen: Collegiate Middle Managers and Their Organization*. Washington, D.C.: American Association for Higher Education, 1978.

STROUP, H. *Bureaucracy in Higher Education*. New York: Free Press, 1966.

Chapter 3

≽≽≽≽≼≼≼≼

Enhancing
Administrative Leadership

This chapter is a kind of primer of academic administration. Why such a chapter in a book on institutional survival? The reason is that a violation of basic administrative concepts seems to have been directly involved in producing most, if not all, institutional problems. Rectifying administrative deficiency may not solve serious institutional problems, but not doing so will likely ensure continuation of serious difficulty.

Problems of Leadership

All organizations respond to the interaction of many different factors and forces, so it is difficult to isolate a single factor as being chiefly responsible for subsequent events. However, in addition to the weaknesses of administrative structure that encourage confrontation, discussed in Chapter Two, it is possible to enumerate a number of administrative practices that appear to have contributed to unfavorable conditions on many campuses. Changing these practices might have produced significantly different and better consequences. The evidence for this claim is based largely on case material and is open to challenge, but some validity perhaps can be inferred when similar administrative practices appear in large numbers of institutions in difficulty:

- Failure to use simple systems of monitoring and accounting for managing income and expenditure
- Presidential decision, without consultation, to terminate faculty appointments
- Board-of-trustee unwillingness to grant the president authority needed to govern, and even encouragement of faculty to approach members of the board directly or even the board itself
- Presidential unwillingness to delegate responsibility to administrative associates
- Presidential decision to foster expansion without consultation and without full information
- Mutual lack of confidence between the president and immediate subordinates
- Lack of proper checks by the board and faculty on presidential power
- Presidential failure to understand budgets and systems of financial accounting and reporting
- Presidential ignorance of academic life
- Lack of a mechanism to control program expansion

The likelihood of colleges making such mistakes is linked unfortunately to several recently emerged problems of higher education.

Three new and major phenomena affecting higher education stress the significance of better presidential and administrative leadership.

Adjustment to Decline. The first of these circumstances concerns the psychological impact of the need to administer decline.

During expansion, leaders can use the sheer fact of expansion as evidence of success. It is a happy time when each year the various administrative associates can report more applications, higher SAT scores, higher proportion of faculty with Ph.D. degrees, larger budgets, greater reserves, new buildings started or completed, larger and more varied library holdings, and improved book value of endowment. But with stability and decline, the joy of progress disappears as does the usual evidence of success. Reporting annual deficits to boards of trustees, salary moratoriums to faculty, and decreases in service to students are painful acts. Even the creation of new programs, which apparently went on throughout most of the 1970s, requires the tortured rationalization of giving while taking away.

Unionization of Faculty. A second and much more tangible problem is the threat or actuality of a unionized faculty, staff, and even student body. The presence of a union and contract does make the management of stability and decline different and probably more cumbersome. Unions quite properly seek to protect the economic interests of faculty, which may, at least for the short run, be antithetical to the economic well-being of the institution.

Supracampus Structures. The third complexity may be only circumstantially related to the facts of stability or decline. However, the acceleration of centralization of state higher education authority and changing financial conditions makes inference of causation plausible. This third factor is the development and expansion of supracampus boards and administrative staffs and the imposition of new state and federal requirements. Between 1957 and 1967, the various states moved toward creating systems of institutions and systems of coordination in order to produce a more orderly expansion of higher education at a reasonable increase in cost. In the 1970s, there was a steady growth of interest in increasing the powers of systemwide administrative structures and the numbers of statewide boards of control for all of public higher education (as was done in Rhode Island, Wisconsin, and North Carolina) and even the creation of such agencies in some private institutions.

To these three specific aspects of the difficult new environment for administration must be added other broader, yet relevant matters. The first of these is the impersonal and seemingly irreversible fact of inflation. Second, there is the steady growth in bureaucratic procedure and litigation which increases the complexity of reaching needed decisions. There are regulations regarding affirmative action, freedom of information, and protection of the physically handicapped, the environment, and individual privacy—all aimed at commendable social goals but all limiting flexibility. The third pervasive element of the climate in which administration must conduct itself is a return to interinstitutional competition, but in a much more rigorous and even cut-throat manner than in the past. Throughout most of the history of American higher education, institutions have had to compete with each other for students and financial resources. The one major exception is the period roughly from 1958 to 1970, when demand for higher education exceeded capacity. Since 1970, however, competition has become the rule again—but in a sharper, more frenzied, and more varied way. In order to maintain the institutional standard of living of the 1960s in the face of mounting inflation, new programs for new students have been created, time required to complete degrees reduced, and standards sharply cut in return for dollars, institutions have established cut-rate centers near the home campuses of other institutions even a continent away, and operating funds have been used in increasing proportions to attract students. These trends pose new problems for administration.

Examples of Ineptitude

A classic example of gross administrative ineptitude is Parsons College in Fairfield, Iowa, which shifted from being a small church-related college in the late 1950s to a large second- or third-chance college in the late 1960s to a defunct institution in the 1970s. Under the leadership of Millard R. Roberts, the institution undertook a series of innovations that were intended to revitalize a college almost ready to close its doors and to ensure its economic viability. President Roberts argued that these procedures had never before been attempted and that through them Parsons College might actually be operated at a profit. Essentially, what he proposed was a restricted curriculum of large-sized survey courses and smaller upper division courses as a way of balancing the high costs of the latter with the low costs of the former. The survey courses would be taught by highly paid professors on the grounds that their abilities and experience could make the largely lecture courses interesting to students. To keep capital outlay under control, president Roberts proposed to build relatively inexpensive new buildings to be paid for and replaced within ten to twenty years. Through a centralized administration, tight management controls would be imposed and decisions quickly reached. A well-trained corps of admissions officers would actively recruit students, and an equally qualified group of tutors and counselors on campus would help students to adjust and would cut down on attrition.

Now none of these proposals was particularly new, and all had been tested and found to work well. The general education program at Michigan State University had established that well-taught lower-division, required courses, offered to consistently large classes (thirty to sixty students), could generate income to support a major entry of the institution into graduate work. In the 1920s, James Madison Woods created an admissions staff that covered the entire country and provided the students to make Stephens College in Columbia, Missouri, which was absolutely dependent on tuition, into a viable institution. Across the country, the World War II veteran enrollments were educated in Army surplus buildings with no appreciable weakening of the education they received. Earl J. McGrath, Beardsly Ruml, and Donald Morrison all demonstrated in theory and from data the close positive relationship between a restricted curriculum and higher faculty salaries.

Parsons College failed, not because of the basic ideas and procedures but because of gross and continuous mismanagement. President Roberts consistently made large expenditures not provided for in his budget. He seriously overestimated future enrollments and made commitments based upon those estimates. He paid high faculty salaries, but these did not attract the truly distinguished professors who could make the curriculum come alive. He built not just inexpensive buildings but shabby ones that began to deteriorate even before completion. His admissions hard sell produced not capable students but warm bodies seeking to avoid the draft. And his centralized decision-making process denied the checks and balances so necessary for prudent as well as rapid decisions.

More recently, several different private colleges in other parts of the country that were suddenly faced with growing competition from the public sector compounded their educational and financial difficulties through presidential inadequacy. Most academic institutions typically select as presidents former professors and deans who well understand the functioning of institutions of higher education, but these institutions during the 1960s selected for their presidents individuals judged to be highly imaginative, innovative, and charismatic, and unburdened with loyalty to established ways of collegiate institutions. The idea was to bring in new blood who could lead their institutions into better ways of education and administration and could make them more competitive with the growing public sector. A very aggressive public school superintendent or a dynamic associate minister in a large church or a medical doctor would illustrate the range of such appointments. These appointments were made by boards of trustees that would issue a mandate to produce substantial experimentation, innovation, and change. The president would be assured that he was expected to run the institution without particular reference to the board of trustees, so long as what was attempted accomplished the goal of enhancing institutional vitality and competitiveness.

In these several institutions, the innovations followed quite similar patterns. First of all, perhaps assimilating the corporate world doctrine of diversification through the creation of conglomerates, these presidents initiated programs to create satellite campuses throughout the nation and, in some situations, in foreign countries as well. The motivation for doing so undoubtedly was complex, but a major intention was to create satellite campuses that would not only be self-sustaining but would also in time produce enough revenue to help support the home campus. It should be pointed out that these institutions were not affluent. They typically had no endowment and had to struggle each year to maintain balanced budgets or budgets generating quite modest surpluses. The move to diversification was seen almost as a kind of endowment, much in the way that at one time Catholic women's religious orders that operated both hospitals and schools viewed the hospitals as an endowment generating revenue to make up for deficits experienced by the schools and colleges.

As to where and in what kind of facilities satellites would be located, practice varied. Some institutions purchased existing campus sites with relatively low down payments in the expectation that when the satellite became fully operational it would generate enough tuition to provide debt service, reduction of principal, operating costs, and a surplus to be returned to the general operating funds of the home campus. Others rented space, and a few were able to use space in public schools or military bases without cost.

Students were expected to be attracted to satellite campuses by programs judged to be unique, whether because of a definite international flavor produced by location in a foreign country or through explicit concern for the needs and interests of specific localities in the United States. These unique programs were to be taught by professors recruited from the locality in which the satellite campus was located, but overseen by officials from the home campus.

In most of the cases, there was presumed to be a functional and organic relationship between the home campus and the satellite campuses. For example, it was assumed that the academic programs at home and at satellite locations would be highly articulated so that many if not most students could plan on taking some academic work on a satellite campus with other work taken on a home campus. Thus, in one situation, students normally might be expected to take one or two years on a foreign campus and two or three years on the home campus. Or other students would be expected to take part of their degree work in an urban situation and part in the more rural setting of the parent institution. Decisions as to the feasibility of this interchange of students were made largely through intuition and with no hard market research evidence indicating that students would behave as expected. As an adjunct and stimulus for the interchange of students, most institutions of this sort sought also to create a definite, unique, and intricate curriculum structure. This curriculum would be coordinated from the home campus and would require specific and complicated systems of student evaluation, common instructional materials, and even common approaches to instruction.

The planning for these programs was accomplished largely by the central administration of the home campus, frequently without serious consultation with the faculty of the home campus. This, at first, was not generally perceived as at all unusual, for in most of the situations examined, there was no clearly defined faculty organization possessing mechanisms and instrumentalities to question or oppose presidential recommendation and decision. This lack of a faculty mechanism or control was aggravated by the locally recruited faculties of the satellite campuses. These faculty members were frequently part time and, in any event, did not feel that they had power or responsibility to govern the destinies of the satellite campus. Thus, in each of a half-dozen or more campuses, a situation developed in which the president was urged to be aggressive and innovative, with neither the board of trustees nor the faculty being able effectively to check or modify presidential decision. Thus, if a president believed that further expansion would be appropriate, further expansion typically took place.

A highly significant common feature of these institutions was their limited administrative strength and ability to coordinate a complex and far-flung educational corporation. As these institutions did not have strong financial bases, and for economic reasons, it was judged wise to limit the size and cost of administrative superstructures. For example, one institution sought to coordinate as many as eighteen to twenty off-campus locations with a basic administrative structure appropriate for a moderate-sized, single-campus institution. This was, of course, insufficient for even sheer physical and personnel activities and proved to be totally inadequate for supervising, maintaining, and expediting the operation of extremely complicated educational programs.

Very quickly after diversification was inaugurated, common problems began to develop. Enrollments, hence tuition income, did not reach projected size. Therefore, the satellites (with few exceptions) were not able to sustain themselves, much less contribute funds to the home campus. Maintaining satellite campuses proved to be a financial drain on the institution's resources, which generally were not strong to begin with. As expansion continued, a downward financial spiral began in which each satellite campus added to the financial strain. This situation very shortly produced a pattern of deficit spending that persisted over time and resulted in rather substantial accumulated operating deficits. The problem was compounded for those institutions that had actually purchased property through mortgages, culminating in increased accumulated capital deficits as new campuses and activities were begun.

Within a very few years, a common phenomenon could be observed. The creation of satellite campuses, rather than producing surpluses, caused a financial drain that began to limit activities on the home campus. In the face of tight resources, morale among faculty and junior administrators began to deteriorate, generating a tattoo of criticism aimed at a leadership that had produced an empire but one that could quickly approach bankruptcy.

As the difficulties incident to the diversification mounted, central administration was typically forced to take rather extreme measures to sustain the operation, fiscally as well as intellectually. Thus, home and satellite campus physical plant maintenance was deferred. Payments to vendors were delayed and the length of the delay increased year after year as the debt-service load mounted. Contributions for fringe benefits were reduced and institutional payments into those funds delayed, as were payments for other services. Then came drastic reduction—first among the faculties of the satellite campuses and then among the faculties of the home campus. When this still proved insufficient, the payment of salaries was delayed and all but the most essential services terminated. All of this was accompanied by the use of lines of credit at banks—lines that finally would be limited under pain of some kind of bank supervision of management activities and the ultimate possibility of bank foreclosure.

The debilitation of the institutions produced by this pattern left them without resources to respond to major, unexpected problems, difficulties, or crises. Although the unexpected was different in each of the institutions, it is revealing of the power of chance that each experienced one or more serious accidents. In one Midwestern complex, the crisis was removal of accreditation. In another institution, the crisis was a federal government demand for repayment of $1.5 million which the government charged had been erroneously paid to and spent by the institution. In still another situation, the crisis was the demand on the part of lending agencies to reduce short-term indebtedness within a matter of a relatively few weeks.

Misfortune generated additional misfortune. Campus and

satellite morale dropped still further, and in some situations faculties threatened open revolt. The press, picking up rumors of institutional difficulties, spread word of the problems. Disgruntled individuals began to appeal to accrediting agencies, the federal government, or whatever agency the individuals believed might help ease their situation. As these events occurred, the institutions found themselves in intense crisis conditions and began to take even more extreme action. Gradually, they began to dismantle their dispersed systems and to concentrate energies on a few or even one campus effort. In several of the institutions, the board of trustees finally changed the chief executive officer and began to monitor administrative activities much more closely, and central administration began, as it has in most institutions finding themselves in financial straits, to exercise much tighter managerial and budget control.

These several institutions exhibit a cluster of factors that in aggregate could be expected to contribute to failure. First among these was the intent on the part of relatively financially weak institutions to solve anticipated enrollment and fiscal problems through expansion and diversification. In the American business world during the 1950s and 1960s, there emerged a pattern of diversification and the creation of conglomerates consisting of many different kinds of industries and businesses. Such procedures may have been appropriate for business enterprises, although the weight of evidence is not clear on this point. However, diversification in educational institutions has not proven to be a valid solution for private institutions that rely on tuition. And there can be some serious question as to whether, in the long run, diversification is even wise for public institutions. Antioch College in Ohio expanded during the late 1960s and created a number of new centers and campuses. By 1977, the home campus faced serious financial problems and the future of the off-campus locations was, as of 1979, in considerable doubt.

A second factor contributing to failure was the adoption of very specific and complicated academic programs without real information as to their likely appeal and without financial and administrative resources to put them into effect. It was not known, for example, whether students would, in any significant numbers, spend appreciable parts of their academic careers on different campuses, in different parts of the country or in foreign countries. Certainly,

the experience of the most successful consortia, in which large numbers of students move periodically from one member campus to
another, has not suggested that this is likely to be a mass phenomenon. Even had there been large markets for such programs, the educational and physical logistics of constantly moving students, faculty,
and materials would require administrative staffs larger than financial resources provided chiefly through tuition could possibly support. Further, when specific systems of instruction, such as extensive
use of educational technology, are adopted as a means of significant
financial savings without hard evidence that such savings could
result, institutions are really living dangerously.

The third factor in all cases was administrative. In each situation, a condition developed in which the president, without deep
experience in academic affairs, could make major decisions free of
real checks by either the faculty or the board of trustees or both. It
is the intricate system of checks and balances that enables American
institutions to be dynamic and responsive to changing conditions,
yet to remain reasonably stable. Had strong, experienced faculties
been able to question some of the financial or academic decisions,
and competent boards been able to monitor fiscal policy, these institutions might have been kept out of serious trouble.

Other institutions have also exhibited mismanagement of
such magnitude as to threaten their viability. In one, the president's
drinking, coupled with board reluctance to oversee decisions, allowed the institution to drift into a serious deficit-spending situation.
In another, a new president accepted and acted upon a report of
the business manager that an $800,000 anticipated deficit (after
five years of deficit spending) had been reduced to $80,000 in one
year, although there had been no significant increase in income.
Making commitments on the basis of the optimistic report put the
institution in a situation of such severity that banks refused essential
credit. In still another institution, the president so alienated major
elements of the faculty that every issue became a personal confrontation and essential decisions could not be made. Enrollments
dropped, debt mounted, and faculty and student morale declined
as student attrition increased. Only the retirement of the president,
for health reasons, saved the institution from drifting into a mori-
bund condition. And in yet another institution, lack of board super-

vision allowed chief administrative officers so to mishandle federal funds as to cause first an audit, then impounding of funds, and finally the closing of the institution for lack of funds.

The major types of serious mismanagement in these institutions can be quickly summarized:

1. Serious and continued overestimation of enrollments and the making of major financial commitments based on those estimates
2. Use of budgeting and accounting procedures that conceal deteriorating financial conditions, for example, failure to reveal the full cost of new programs created to generate cash flow
3. Administrative failure to consult widely as to the long-range implications of critical decisions, for example, a decision to deny student use for political purposes of campus land historically used for such purposes
4. Failure to verify all details of major financial transactions, for example, the true yield of a gift on the basis of which an institution would change its name
5. Presidential failure to keep informed of major policy decisions made by subordinate administrators, for example, the faculty recruitment policy of an academic dean
6. Failure to determine full costs of a series of educational reforms, for example, the full cost of a new tutorial system of instruction, a new system of media-based instruction, or a far-reaching open-admissions policy
7. Failure to reveal that an important part of income came from reserves and that what is shown as a balanced operating budget is actually a deficit situation.

An Example of Effective Leadership

In this chapter, an attempt will be made to describe administrative practices that, if properly followed, could prevent the mistakes just enumerated. A major criterion for all administrative behavior is a blend of academic management and academic leadership. Management means bringing all relevant information together concerning an issue, reflecting on it in rational ways, and making judgments and plans about the issues. Chapters Four and Five describe such a process and indicate what happens in its absence. Administrative leadership is the presence of an enlightened vision of what an institution is and can become and the ability to persuade others to accept that vision and to act responsibly to achieve it.

In the United States, academic administrators have always played a unique and significant leadership role, different and more powerful than their counterparts in collegiate institutions in other developed nations. Presidents and their administrative associates typically have and exercise legitimate power or discretion which in western European nations, for example, is distributed between the faculties and the centralized state government. With obvious individual or institutional exceptions and some differences at different historical periods, central collegiate administration in the United States has typically been dynamic and innovative, optimistic about the future, somewhat paternalistic in a benevolent sort of way, and able to allocate those resources (few though they be at some periods) that were not obligated by long-term contracts.

In spite of some changes in the presidential role that came about during the 1960s, such as the evolution of faculty senates and admission of students into deliberative and sometimes decision-making roles, presidents and their colleagues on most American campuses still represent the most powerful constituency of the institution. (On this point, see March, 1974). They still are chiefly responsible for securing necessary funding, personifying and representing the institution, and resolving those conflicts that inevitably appear in organizations. But they must now do so in a situation new to the history of American higher education—the anticipation of actual decline in the coming decades.

A clear example of strong administrative leadership, with its advantages and drawbacks, is Boston University. Boston University was a Methodist-related streetcar university that had long provided liberal arts, vocational, and professional education for the youth of the greater Boston area. It had, during its history, moved quickly from an early moment of affluence to financial adversity following the Boston fire of 1872, in which its initial endowment was decimated, to a comfortable middle-income existence during the 1950s and 1960s. In that time, the university had grown in size with little effort and had accumulated comparatively adequate reserves, accomplishing this with scant attention to student recruitment, cultivation of alumni, or even sophisticated financial accounting or planning. As late as 1967, its financial records seemed to be maintained in pen and ink in schoolboy notebooks. The cautious thrift of the place was well revealed by its maintaining balances of several million dollars in non-interest-gathering checking accounts, with the business manager pleased that the bank did not charge for checks written. The university was one of the most decentralized in the nation, with the deans of the sixteen schools free to do pretty much as they wished, so long as they maintained enrollments and caused no public trouble.

But Boston University began to experience the same problems as other city-based private institutions. During the 1950s and 1960s, when the pressure for admission was great and the SAT scores of entering classes were increasing, tuition was kept unrealistically low. This shortsightedness left the administration of President Silber with the task of rapidly raising tuition to reasonable levels in the 1970s when the national demand for admission had leveled off. Thus, Boston University moved into competition with leading colleges and universities without the advantage of low tuition and before its growing academic reputation had been generally recognized. The presence across the Charles River of Harvard and M.I.T. was an additional burden for the morale of the institution. As the drift toward problems began, the long and benign administration of Harold Case ended and a new president, Arland Christ-Janer, was appointed. Christ-Janer's administrative track record may imply an unusual approach: Within fifteen years, he was president of Cornell College (1961–67), Boston University (1967–70), the College Entrance Examination Board (1970–73), New College-Florida (1973–75) and Stephens College (1975 to the present). He remained at Boston for three years, unaware of the deteriorating financial condition of the university but much disturbed over the growing student protest of the late 1960s. His ignorance of the financial condition was caused by the business manager's practice of balancing each year's budget with funds taken from reserves but treated as fresh income. The full financial picture, including the condition of fund balances, was evidently not understood. The impact of that confusion is revealed by the fact that a year before the institution was to face a possible $8 million deficit, the president could tell the candidate who was to succeed him that although Boston University might have problems, finances were not among them. The institution had operated and would continue to operate in the black.

When Christ-Janer resigned, disillusioned over student conduct, a pleasant dean became acting president. The former dean gave promise of a continuation of the comfortable style of decentralized administration in which the deans were allowed to run their own affairs without financial worry. There was little awareness that the annual balanced budgets, including adequate salary increases, were exhausting the reserves and might soon cut into endowment.

It was into this scene that the new president, John R. Silber, was injected in 1971. Silber was a man of intense convictions, high intelligence, and great knowledge, with a personality that could as quickly attract intense love and respect as dislike. He had been a talented but controversial philosophy professor at the University of Texas, then dean at the same institution, and an emerging spokesman on the national scene for a return to academic rigor and high and demanding standards. Silber was selected as president in part because some few members of the faculty and a number of the members of the board of trustees had sensed that sleepy Boston University needed help and that he could provide it.

John Silber arrived, managed to alienate some, scare others, but convince most that drastic changes were needed and would be forthcoming, including the appointment of some new faculty members to aid Boston University in an intensified quest for excellence. As part of his appointment, he was given permission to deficit spend for a few years so as to appoint outstanding faculty members and new, more capable administrators. During his first full year, he asked that the budget provide $1.5 million for faculty improvement and was informed that, even with this new expenditure, the budget was still in balance. Only after repeated probing did he discover that the balance was produced by withdrawal from reserves and that a display of the full financial condition revealed a likely deficit of $8 million rather than a budget in balance. Silber's response was immediate, stringent, and designed to achieve his goals for the university. He instituted a line-by-line review of the budget, ordering cuts in both administrative and academic areas where these could be made without endangering academic excellence. At the same time, he authorized the appointment of strong new faculty members and development of modern techniques of management and budgeting on which he believed the vitality of the institution would rest. Despite decanal and professorial grumbling, the various economies, coupled with new appointments, reduced the anticipated deficit from $8 million to $2 million and added faculty strength upon which the university would build in the future. With the emergency finally understood and at least partly contained, the president then set about improving the quality of faculty and administrators to the fullest extent possible. He began the active recruiting of strong deans and key central administrative people who could carry out his mandate for fiscal responsibility and academic excellence. And he also began to make his presence known in the larger society by questioning the expansion of low-priced state higher education, student use of the tactic of disruption over social ills, and the unethical "business" of selling term papers, and by affirming the values of a Jeffersonian elite based on talent and virtue.

An important ingredient in the saga of John Silber and Boston University is the personality of John Silber and his dealings with people. He can appear to be hard and abrasive, can use profanity when appropriate, and is quite prepared to pit his own judgment against even a majority. He forms strong opinions and does not suffer fools gladly. From some who left the institution a constant stream of, for the most part, disproven stories emerged. As examples of this campaign of vilification, he is said to have thrown papers into the face of a young faculty member, insulted the intelligence of a dean, reviled the work of the student press, and told key administrators to do something or else be fired and that he, the president, would prefer the latter. It should be noted that, at the same time, he participated actively in the recruitment of outstanding professors and deans, increased staff and faculty salaries, and created a vibrant intellectual climate in which serious debate over important issues was encouraged. Since 1971, President Silber has seen the formation by the local chapter of the American Association of University Professors of a faculty union among 880 of the university's 2,200 faculty members, an effort on the part of a small group of board members to remove him as president, and an expression of no confidence by some of the deans (in part generated by that same small group of board members). But he has also seen marked increases in contract research, faculty productivity, and the quality of students. Feelings on the part of the minority of faculty, deans, and board members who resented him led to a variety of unsubstantiated charges. When such charges were fully explored by the board of trustees and proven to be false, the board gave him a resounding vote of confidence with his needed presidential prerogatives endorsed.

University reserves have been restored, endowment and annual giving increased, and research funds greatly augmented. In addition, application rates and the quality of students have gone up, major new programs have been created that became immediate successes, and the overall reputation of the faculty has been enhanced. In 1967, the university had no plan—except a draft of next year's budget. In 1979, it has plans to occupy a position of distinction in many areas, with special emphasis on those not preempted by Harvard or M.I.T. These plans include a wide-ranging and continuing education program (budget $8 million) and a concentration on developmental economics and the fine arts. Boston University now has a new approach to student recruitment and, for the first time in its history, a well-developed alumni program. And there is no evidence whatsoever that the educational program suffers or that students and faculty are not doing their essential jobs.

Boston University is clearly in a stable condition in 1979 and seems reasonably likely to remain so for the short run. For the long pull, its future will be determined in part by state policy regarding portable scholarships, inflation, and energy, and by what the state does with respect to expanding capacity in the state sector.

Different people will draw different lessons from the Boston

University experience. Some see Silber's administration as having destroyed morale on the Boston campus and the careers of academics with whom the president disagreed. Such a point of view is nonsense. What the episode really demonstrates is the need, in critical times, for someone to take decisive action. The Boston faculty appears to have been like so many other faculties—quite comfortable and enjoying the good academic life, with the added factor that the sheer existence of Harvard and M.I.T. so near provided a good excuse for not striving to make the institution into something different. The faculty's reaction when informed of financial problems was disbelief, followed by the conviction that the new president was engaging in scare tactics to create an emergency that would allow him to act against individuals. As remedial action was taken and even more stringent action anticipated, the faculty moved to unionize to protect its financial position. On so many campuses that are surviving nicely, a similar pattern appears. Each fall as budgets are planned, based on anticipated enrollments and other income, a deficit is forecast and the president, if responsible, informs the community of that fact. Then, during the year, the president works at raising the extra funds needed to balance the budget. If the president is successful for several years, the faculty becomes convinced that there really is no problem and that the president cries wolf as one device to manipulate the faculty.

Now strong leadership need not be abrasive, and there can be no question but that President Silber can and does irritate some people. But it can be argued that strong, even abrasive presidential leadership is better than kindly, genteel nonleadership. In many of the institutions that are in serious financial difficulty, conditions might improve if the president cared less about being loved and more about restoring the institution to health. More John Silbers might help enormously.

All of this is not to argue for presidential authoritarianism. There must be strong checks and institutional ways for various constituencies to have influence. In Boston University, there were the checks of a largely informed board, a group of strong deans, largely selected by the president, and what appears to have been a technically competent service administration. The checks and balances mechanism broke down once, when a minority of the board encouraged the deans' revolt. When that revolt ended, however, the mechanism was restored and, by the spring of 1978, the institution was once more dynamic.

Conclusions

Without entering into a debate as to the nature of academic leadership, the actual behaviors of successful and unsuccessful presidents can be enumerated. As a general rule, presidents who have contributed to increased institutional strength have these characteristics:

1. They make strong appointments to the chief subordinate administrative offices and to deanships. They appear to be able to put aside personal likes or dislikes and appoint, or influence the appointment of, individuals to whom they can entrust major elements of the institution. They appear to be willing to remove people from office, in spite of length of tenure, and replace them with people of better, or at least different, competencies.
2. They devote considerable time to the details of management so that they know the precise financial situation of the institution, the exact enrollment situation, the way in which various offices function or do not function, and the relative strengths and weaknesses of the faculty. They appear to conceptualize how institutions behave and seek to make decisions consonant with their concepts. Invariably, presidents of colleges in trouble talk only in generalities as to how the various parts of the institution interact, while presidents of stronger institutions are able to read the score and describe how they propose to orchestrate the entire ensemble.
3. They appear to have a highly developed intuition for finances. While they may not have been trained to make or use a budget, they seem to sense when figures are fuzzy or when gaps appear. And if their instincts say something is wrong, they keep questioning until they do fully understand a financial condition. Thus, in the case of Boston University just discussed, President Silber knew that he could not add $1.5 million to his budget without

putting it out of balance, despite the assurances of his business officer. Silber kept on questioning until he finally discovered that reserves were being used to balance the budget.

4. They are able to establish priorities for their own agendas and concentrate on those, leaving to others matters which, while possibly interesting, do not demand presidential time and energy. And they are able to discuss what those priorities are and why they are so arranged. Thus, as illustrated in Chapter One, president Kemeny of Dartmouth knew the significance of coeducation and year-round operation and so concentrated on those matters, leaving to the dean of faculty the details of the academic program and the stimulation of educational innovation.

5. They are able to value and trust their faculties but, at the same time, resist faculty efforts to intrude on prerogatives essential to the governing of the institution. Thus, president Lyman at Stanford devised techniques by which faculty opinion about finances could be expressed but resisted efforts of the same faculty to exercise a reviewing and sanctioning power over the budget. President Kemeny of Dartmouth was quite happy for faculty to suggest different plans than his own to control tenured appointments, so long as his prerogative of controlling tenure was not abrogated.

6. Lastly, successful presidents know the fundamental nature of higher education and what things will not work. In short, they are the masters of the enterprise over which they preside.

Further Readings

Writings about educational leadership, especially that of college and university presidents, has for the most part been autobiographical, descriptive, or exhortative. This book assigns considerable insight to the presidency with respect to institutional health and survival, a position elaborated by Brown and by Dodds. Cohen and March properly should be read for a different point of view. Although they grant that presidents have more power than anyone else on campus, they feel that, with respect to most fundamental activities, presidents can scarcely affect events that happen as a result of a dynamic of the events themselves. These additional readings seem to cover reasonably well the potentiality of leadership and some of the contraints upon it.

BENNIS, W. *The Leaning Ivory Tower*. San Francisco: Jossey-Bass, 1973.

BERDAHL, R. O. *Statewide Coordination of Higher Education*. Washington, D.C.: American Council on Education, 1971.

BERDAHL, R. O. (Ed.). *New Directions for Institutional Research: Evaluating Statewide Boards*, No. 5. San Francisco: Jossey-Bass, 1975.

BROWN, J. D. *The Liberal University*. New York: McGraw-Hill, 1969.

COHEN, M. D., AND MARCH, J. G. *Leadership and Ambiguity*. New York: McGraw-Hill, 1974.

DODDS, H. W. *The Academic President—Educator or Caretaker*. New York: McGraw-Hill, 1962.

HELSABECK, R. E. *The Compound System: A Conceptual Framework for Effective Decision Making in Colleges and Universities*. Berkeley: Center for Research and Development in Higher Education, University of California, 1973.

KAUFFMAN, J. F. *The Selection of College and University Presidents*. Washington, D.C.: Association of American Colleges, 1974.

LEE, E. C., AND BOWEN, F. M. *The Multicampus University*. New York: McGraw-Hill, 1971.

MAYHEW, L. B. (Ed.). *Educational Leadership and Declining Enrollments*. Berkeley, Calif.: McCutchan, 1974.

MILLETT, J. D. *The Multiple Roles of College and University Presidents*. Washington, D.C.: Americn Council on Education, 1976.

NESS, F. W. *An Uncertain Glory: Letters of Cautious but Sound Advice to Stanley, a Dean-in-Waiting, from C. F. Coltswood, a President-at-Large*. San Francisco: Jossey-Bass, 1971.

PERKINS, J. A., AND ISRAEL, B. B. (Eds.). *Higher Education: From Autonomy to Systems*. New York: International Council for Educational Development, 1972.

Chapter 4

❧❧❧❧❦❦❦❦

Managing Crisis
and Developing
Management Systems

Approaches to institutional management vary according to the situation. For institutions in crisis, elaborate long-range plans, data systems, or complex budget procedures are clearly inappropriate. When enrollments are down, cash flow limited, and even bank credit precarious, one sort of intervention is necessary. For other institutions, such as Dartmouth, which have reasonable resources to respond to even quite destructive changes in the environment, other management policies and procedures can be used. And for those institutions that are currently in a stable condition but are

84

facing clouds on the horizon, still other tactics and strategies are needed. This chapter examines these different approaches.

Management of Crisis

For the institution in extreme crisis, the goals are few and painfully clear. Enrollment decline must be stopped, expenditures reduced, cash flow improved, credit restored, stability achieved, and, if only for morale reasons, a time set for achieving a turnaround situation. This does not mean that such an institution can ignore the sound principles of planning. Indeed, several are crucial: a clear statement of goals based on the best evidence available, formulation of a definite plan with individuals assigned precise responsibilities, and creation of an information system that will reveal changes in key indicators. It does mean, however, that the techniques used are relatively few and are applied differently than they would be in a less critical situation.

Management of crisis must be centralized in the hands of the president, who must be aware of the problems to be faced. The president must assume personal responsibility for solving the few most critical problems and must be willing to delegate full responsibility for other areas, even such highly important ones as curriculum and instruction. This delegation of responsibility in times of trouble is one of the hardest lessons a president must learn. People become college presidents for many reasons, the most important one being a concern for education and an interest in academic matters. Even in situations of extreme financial difficulty, many college presidents have directly concerned themselves with such matters as curriculum reform or have attempted to exert educational leadership.

Management of crisis requires, first of all, ensuring that the core activities of the institution—curriculum, teaching, advising, and student activities—continue in as stable a manner as possible. No new ventures should be attempted, and someone, typically the academic dean, should be given full responsibility to maintain the status quo.

The central administration should be streamlined to allow maximum energy and resources to be developed on the most serious matters. The president, director of admissions, director of development, and chief financial officer might compose the forward command post, to use a military metaphor, while the academic dean, dean of students, and others concerned with programs, would be the rear command post. There obviously should be communication between the two, but the educational program should not be a particular worry of the forward group.

The individuals most responsible for survival should each determine a few highly specific but realistic objectives and a realistic plan by which they propose to achieve them. Thus, the director of admissions might develop a goal of an increase of fifty students for the next year and a definite plan to obtain them. The business manager might set a goal of some specific sum by which expenditures are to be reduced and a second goal of converting some nonfluid resources into cash, for example, by the sale of property or securities. And the president and development officer might set a goal of producing a specific amount of money to be used for operating purposes. Such a goal should not be contaminated by other sorts of development activity, such as a capital campaign or a program of deferred giving. Those are luxuries that the seriously troubled institution cannot afford.

It is often said that successful fund raising for colleges and universities requires first an educational idea that can attract the interest of potential givers. And this is true. However, the institution in crisis is stuck with what it has. There is no time to decide on some new appealing ideal. A college that attempts to shift its image as an act of desperation may divert energies in that effort from more critical activities and may confuse conditions rather than clarify them. Institutions, especially those of considerable longevity, have a tradition and an image, and that is what should determine both the development and the student recruitment effort. If a new image is desired, the time to consider it is later, when the crisis has abated a bit.

The key elements of crisis management bear repeating. They are: (1) identify the essential problems and focus all available resources on them; (2) assign clear and full responsibility to major administrative officers and let them function, especially the academic dean who, in a crisis, really becomes the chief on-campus administrator; (3) set a few critical goals for each major area of concern and develop a specific plan, including needed cost to achieve them; (4) set up a few reliable indexes that can record daily or weekly progress toward those goals; and (5) assume that the core activities of the institution can continue without significant change for at least a few years. There likely will be some increase in faculty and student complaints, which simply must be tolerated—unless, of course, students begin to drop out in unacceptable numbers or the faculty goes on strike. In such events, crisis management would be extended to these areas.

An important question is, When has a crisis ended and sufficient stability been achieved to begin longer-range planning? In Chapter Ten, some conditions indicating financial difficulties are mentioned. Generally, when all of those conditions have been improved, the crisis may be judged over. But a smaller number of indexes might be based upon a projected enrollment large enough to support a minimum viable educational program. They key indicators would be:

- Applications increase three years in a row.
- Matriculation rates increase three years in a row.
- Projected gift receipts are actually obtained three years in a row.
- The operating budget is in balance three years in a row.
- A three-year line of credit equal to one third of annual operating expenditures is made available without bank audit of budgets and expenditures.
- Tuition rates equal to the mean of those charged in comparable institutions are imposed with no adverse effects on enrollment.
- Faculty salary increases equal to increases in the consumer price index are made two years in a row.
- The budget contains items equal to double the amount normally needed for plant maintenance for three years in a row.
- The budget contains an item for improvement of quality equal to 1 percent of the operating budget for three years in a row.

An Example of Crisis Management

At times, unfortunately, even the most level-headed, realistic crisis management fails to save an institution. An example of this during recent years is Cushing Junior College in Bryn Mawr, Pennsylvania. Cushing stemmed from the almost century-old Baptist Institute for Christian Workers, which, during most of its existence, had trained missionaries, Christian-education directors, and other professional churchwomen. By the early 1960s, such church institutes found themselves with enrollment and financial troubles as the education required for professional church workers more and more frequently became graduate-level seminary work. Thus, the Baptist Institute for Christian Workers sought a new mission and decided to become a two-year coeducational, liberal arts college, designed specifically to prepare middle- to low-ability students for transfer to senior college. It changed its name to Cushing Junior College, after the founder of the institute, and between 1965 and 1969 (its golden years) it functioned effectively, hitting its peak enrollment in the academic year 1968–69 with 189 students. But then decline set in and, by 1974, enrollments had dropped to just over 100 students.

In October of 1974, a new president was appointed and charged with making the institution viable. For several years, financing improved through liquidation of some property, acquisition of some additional physical plant, and an increase in fund raising from $600,000 to $1.2 million in a two-year period. However, enrollment problems continued and the institution could not reach a break-even level of 150 students, much less an optimum enrollment of 200. Contributing to its enrollment problems was the difficulty in securing regional accreditation for its new liberal arts program. Visitors to the campus typically were complimentary regarding progress with respect to clear statement of purpose, increase in library holdings, and the like, but withheld accreditation because of the lack of sufficient enrollment to provide adequate cash flow.

Faced with this chicken-and-egg situation, the institution undertook the logical steps of strengthening the admissions office, redesigning the layout of publicity materials, and participating in the College Entrance Examination Board Search program. It asked for names of prospective students in Pennsylvania and New Jersey having combined SAT scores under 800, a C– average in high school, and other characteristics that would fit the Cushing model. From contacts with 4,500 such students, fewer than 60 replies were received, and a follow-up indicated that most of those middle- to lower-ability students had been accepted at four-year institutions. Clearly, by the late 1970s, many institutions had become significantly less selective than they had been during the 1960s. Compounding this low yield from admissions efforts was Cushing's high attrition rate. The institution was planned on the basis of expecting students to stay two years. Typically, however, they stayed one year and then transferred to a bachelor's degree institution.

By 1978, it had become apparent that a snowball effect was taking place. Without enrollment, the college could not receive accreditation or even candidacy status. Without accreditation, it was shut out from federal funds and foundation sources. Without at least candidacy status, its students were ineligible for Pennsylvania State scholarship grants or guaranteed loans. These factors negatively influenced development efforts, with potential donors feeling that their benefaction would be wasted since the longevity of the institution was seriously in doubt. One prospective donor, asked to contribute $250,000 for a library to be named in his honor, responded that, much as he would have liked to have his name on such a building, he feared that neither the building nor the institution would be in existence within five years.

By April of 1978, institutional leadership decided to set an enrollment goal which, if missed, would signal the need to close the institution. It was at this time that the institution took a number of precautionary steps to ensure that if it did close it would do so with dignity, safeguarding insofar as possible the rights and welfare of all individuals associated with the institution. The following steps were taken:

1. The president's council was fully informed of the circumstances but its members asked not to comment about it to others.
2. The seven members of the president's council agreed to participate actively in an admissions effort and to seek ways to reduce attrition.
3. Faculty members were notified that contracts for the following year would not be issued until after the May meeting of the board of trustees, when a new budget would be adopted.
4. The president developed an alternate plan for closing that in-

cluded finding transitional funding to pay creditors, meet contractual obligations, and operate the physical plant until it could be sold. In addition, a plan was developed to protect student records.

5. The executive committee of the board of trustees was provided all information to ensure that every alternative was thoughtfully considered and the committee also set the date on which decisions would be made.

6. The spring meeting of the board of trustees, normally held in May during commencement activities, was postponed until June 3rd, two days after the date set for final decision. During the ten days preceding that meeting, the president talked with each board member and discussed the full range of alternatives.

7. At the board meeting, after full discussion, a resolution for closing the institution was prepared, discussed in small groups, and finally approved by the full board.

8. The board met on a Saturday and over the weekend several critical steps were taken. These included a carefully worded news release, a letter to creditors assuring them that they would be paid, arrangements with a sister institution to become custodian of student records, letters to present students, and the calling of a faculty and staff meeting for early Monday morning.

As a result of the planning, a line of credit was established so that all creditors could be paid in full and in an orderly manner. These funds also enabled the institution to continue payment to faculty whose salary had been distributed over twelve months and to pay staff for a two-week notice and administrators for a thirty-day notice. All individuals entitled to vacation pay were paid in full, and premiums for the health plan were paid through the third quarter of that year. Funds also allowed the maintenance of a skeleton staff to operate the physical plant and to negotiate the sale of the campus and its equipment. This skeleton staff also notified the various relevant state and federal agencies and facilitated the completion of the paper work on such things as the National Defense Student Loan program. The physical plant and various items of equipment were appraised and asking prices set somewhat lower than the fair market value in order to facilitate sale. Because the market value of the campus and equipment far exceeded liabilities, the institution avoided bankruptcy.

The example of this particular institution suggests some important generalizations. For one, it demonstrates how difficult it is for an institution to change its mission radically in order to cope with deteriorating fiancial conditions. In retrospect, it might have been better for the Baptist Institute for Chrisian Workers to close when its viability became unclear than to attempt to change character at a time when competition from other institutions was on the increase. But, second, the demise of Cushing shows that if an institution must close, careful planning can ensure closing with dignity and without undue recriminations. This example contrasts markedly with the closing of Parsons College, which left a residue of bitterness in the town of Fairfield, Iowa, and in the hearts of many faculty members who had tried to restore the institution after the debacle of the Millard Roberts regime.

An interesting insight came to President Robert E. Davis of Cushing, who administered the closing. Remarking on the tendency of college presidents to identify so closely with their institutions that trouble to the institution is for them personal travail, he recalled that a previous president had said, "If anything happens to this place I will die too." But Davis, while caring for the institution, kept his esteem for himself as a person distinct from his role as president of the college. "I might die," he said, "but the college need not; or it might die but I need not die" (Davis, 1978).

Management Information Systems

Institutions in crisis conditions have resources for only the most urgent matters—enrollment, cash flow, and reduction of expenditures. Planning for the long run may not be possible in such situations. If an institution can gain a few years of reasonable stability, however, it can then use more sophisticated approaches to management. Chapter Five describes in detail the techniques of planning possible for an institution, but planning as envisioned there requires reasonably precise information. Unfortunately, the availability of such information has not always been characteristic of American higher education.

The need for better information on which to base decisions began seriously to be expressed in the mid 1950s with the appearance of the concept of institutional research. There had been some institutional research efforts earlier at Ohio State, Illinois, and Minnesota, but only after about 1955 (when people first became aware that a rapid expansion of higher education was likely) did institutional research become an important tool for planning. Institutional research sought to obtain more, better, more consistent, and more utilitarian data concerning all aspects of an institution to provide a sounder base for decisions.

The idea of institutional research spread quickly at first as college and university leaders sought to expand their institutions in an orderly and efficient way. However, only about 25 percent of all institutions finally created offices of institutional research. The rest failed to do so for a variety of reasons. Good institutional research was expensive, and there were relatively few people qualified to do it. Faculty were suspicious of research into the dynamics of academic life. In addition, much research reporting presented masses of data but without focus or interpretation. A busy dean would tend to trust his instincts rather than seek meaning in a 300-page report consisting largely of raw data. Nevertheless, enough successful efforts did develop to maintain the promise of effective use of institutional research.

By the mid 1960s, a related concept appeared: management information systems. This concept was produced in part by the growing state and federal interest in long-range planning based on comprehensive data, and in part by the introduction of computers into the administrative practice of institutions. The perceived values of management information systems were enhanced as institutions began to encounter financial difficulties starting in 1970. Administrators needed to know how they had drifted into deficit situations and what steps might safely be taken to rectify conditions. Stanford reflects a typical pattern. In the late 1950s, its long-range planning was based upon data the provost kept in his desk or in his head. But by the early 1970s, when the rate of increase of expenditure began to outstrip the rate of increase of income, more detailed data were needed. And when a first effort to end deficit spending at Stanford failed, a still more sophisticated data system was generated.

"Management information systems" is a phrase that is much misunderstood. In most institutions, it refers to the maintenance, either manually or by machine, of simple data banks. Simple data banks are filled with information about students, courses, faculty, finances, and physical space. The adjective "simple" is misleading, however. For a data bank to be usable, a number of vexing problems must be solved, even if a bank is to be used in a single institution: First, definitions must be standardized so that all offices collect data that is compatible with data from other offices. Second, the data must be traceable for subsequent verification. Third, information must be condensed and focused so that the results have meaning and can truly clarify a problem or illuminate a solution. And fourth, the assumption behind the data must be explicit and clearly understood.

A well-designed data system, for which information has been carefully collected and verified, can be of enormous help, even if it just provides straight answers to such questions as enrollments by course and the percentage of use of instructional space. It can be especially useful in providing for a variety of ratios that reveal the institution's situation. For example, the following ratios, maintained over time, can tell a good deal about the health of the institution:

1. Students

$$\frac{\text{Number of new-student applications this year}}{\text{Number of new-student applications last year}}$$

$$\frac{\text{Number of accepted students}}{\text{Number of applicants}}$$

$$\frac{\text{Number of enrolled students}}{\text{Number of accepted students}}$$

$$\frac{\text{Number of enrolled students}}{\text{Number of applicants}}$$

$$\frac{\text{Full-time students}}{\text{Part-time students}}$$

$$\frac{\text{SAT-ACT of new students this year}}{\text{SAT-ACT of new students last year}}$$

$$\frac{\text{Number of sophomores who entered as freshmen (year N)}}{\text{Number of freshmen who entered (year N)}}$$

$$\frac{\text{Number of sophomores (year N)}}{\text{Number of freshmen (year N)}}$$

$$\frac{\text{Number of graduating students}}{\text{Number of students entering 2 or 4 years earlier}}$$

$$\frac{\text{Number of graduates}}{\text{Number of majors offered}}$$

$$\frac{\text{Number of students}}{\text{Number of majors offered}}$$

$$\frac{\text{Number of students}}{\text{Number of courses offered}}$$

2. Faculty

$$\frac{\text{FTE students}}{\text{FTE faculty}}$$

$$\frac{\text{Full-time faculty}}{\text{Part-time faculty}}$$

$$\frac{\text{FTE faculty}}{\text{Part-time faculty}}$$

$$\frac{\text{Majors}}{\text{FTE faculty}}$$

$$\frac{\text{Courses}}{\text{FTE faculty}}$$

$$\frac{\text{Total course credit hours}}{\text{FTE faculty}}$$

$$\frac{\text{Total student credit hours}}{\text{FTE faculty}}$$

$$\frac{\text{Total student credit hours (year N)}}{\text{Total student credit hours (year X)}}$$

$$\frac{\text{Total tenured faculty}}{\text{Total faculty}}$$

$$\frac{\text{Faculty with terminal degree}}{\text{Total faculty}}$$

3. Administration

$$\frac{\text{FTE students}}{\text{FTE administration}}$$

$$\frac{\text{FTE students}}{\text{FTE staff}}$$

$$\frac{\text{FTE faculty}}{\text{FTE administration}}$$

$$\frac{\text{FTE faculty}}{\text{FTE staff}}$$

4. Facilities

$$\frac{\text{Dormitory occupancy}}{\text{Dormitory capacity}}$$

$$\frac{\text{Total enrollment}}{\text{Number of classroom seats}}$$

$$\frac{\text{Total library volumes (year N)}}{\text{Total library volumes (year X)}}$$

It is entirely possible that simple data systems may be all many institutions need to find out about themselves and to suggest directions for decisions. There are, however, more advanced management information systems that allow for simulation of the likely behavior of an institution under a variety of conditions. These not only show where an institution is but also what will likely happen under each of several eventualities. Simulation systems are seen to have several distinct advantages. They force users to pay attention to interactions within an institution. They allow study of a wide variety of alternatives and help alleviate uncertainty by showing what will likely happen if certain events take place.

There are several different advanced systems that have been

used: resource allocation models that are based on enrollments and enable study of various cost factors, student flow models, faculty flow models, and space utilization models. While each of these has potential value, some version of a resource allocation model would seem to have the greatest utility for institutions trying to plan. The CAMPUS model, developed by the Systems Research Group in Toronto, Canada, provides considerable flexibility in simulation but at a cost of greater requirements for data. The System for Evaluating Alternative Commitments in Higher Education (SEARCH) was developed by Peat, Marwick, and Mitchell, and was intended for smaller institutions.

By far the most widely publicized system is the federally financed Resource Requirements and Prediction Model, made available by the National Center for Higher Education Management Systems (NCHEMS) in Boulder, Colorado. It is part of a series of programs that are interrelated, but elements may also be used independently. The series is called the Costing and Data Management System, and the two parts are the Data Management Module and the Resource Requirements and Prediction Model. The Data Management Module includes student data, faculty activities, personnel data, student outcomes, and a device that allows each of these to be interrelated. The module can either prepare straight, independent descriptive reports or can interact with the Resource Requirements and Prediction Model to allow simulation of the effects of various changes in enrollment or staffing configuration on the budget. The RRPM is intended to provide predictive cost information.

The NCHEMS system is intended to enable institutions to conduct cost studies, allow comparisons between institutions, facilitate federal reporting, and help planners to make better decisions through simulated study of implications of possible alternative conditions. Perhaps its chief advantages are the standardization of terms and data over time, which allows an institution to compare itself to others, and the fact that the basic unit is the smallest academic unit—the department or program. These features allow quite refined internal comparisons within an institution and force the department head to reach considered judgments. They also allow for an examination of trade-offs among competing programs. Because the developmental work on the system was subsidized, the cost of the materials was relatively modest. And the system seems applicable to both public and private institutions.

However, the system may be overelaborate for many institutions, especially those facing serious problems of survival. Although the cost of the actual computer programs is low, the cost of maintaining and updating information is a drain on institutional resources. Also, wise use of the model requires considerable technical skill, which may well not exist on a given campus and which is too expensive to purchase. Then too, those who must finally make decisions must be sympathetic to the use of models and be competent to know the capabilities and limitations of resultant data. It is no accident that in two institutions that have used modeling widely and wisely, the president of one and the vice-president of the other were computer scientists.

Consistent with estimates as to the effectiveness of the NCHEMS system is an assessment of the various management information systems sponsored in forty-four institutions by the EXXON Education Foundation starting in 1973. The foundation made grants to help institutions improve management and eliminate the crisis and opportunistic styles of reaching decisions. In 1974, the foundation asked the Higher Education Research Institute to study the projects sponsored and to evaluate their effects on institutional practice. Using a multifaceted research strategy, the institute reached a number of conclusions (see Baldridge and Tierney, 1979). Most of the projects consisted of creating or updating data bank systems, with a few of those being advanced management information systems. Some of the institutions tried simultaneously to develop information systems on programs of improved or modified management systems.

Overall, the research seemed to support the judgment that about half the projects were successfully completed, about a fourth clear failures, and about a fourth uncompleted at the time the research was conducted. Success was defined as the presence of more and better data after the project, evidence of basing decisions on those data, and changes in the financial conditions of the institution.

In general, successful institutions reduced cost variations between departments, decreased somewhat per-student cost, developed greater variety in strategies to increase income, and experimented with a greater variety of techniques to reduce costs than did institutions not developing management information systems. Several of these matters were of sufficient magnitude to suggest that management information systems and a related managerial structure might be appropriate for institutions facing serious financial difficulties. However, before urging such a step, it may be well to examine the characteristics of those institutions that developed successful projects. In general, the central administration was supportive of the project, had selected a competent staff for it, and had enough financial resources of its own to institutionalize the system after foundation funding ended.

Wesleyan University in Connecticut illustrates ideal conditions. It was a highly selective, well-endowed liberal arts college that offered a few graduate programs. Its enrollment had risen from about 1,000 in the late 1940s to 2,350 in the mid 1970s. For a time, Wesleyan had one of the highest per-student endowment rates in the country. However, it began to experience budget deficits and realized that it was cutting into endowment for operating expenses at an intolerable 8 to 9 percent annually. It had, as had comparable institutions, made five- and ten-year projections that all too frequently had proven inaccurate. Thus, it was seeking some more sophisticated method by means of which it might cope with its financial situation. With EXXON funds, Wesleyan selected the SEARCH model information system, which allowed aggregation of data by schools or large programs of students, faculty, program, faculties, and finance. For each of these, the present situation, internal variables—such as changes in enrollment—and external variables—such as inflation—could be interrelated. In practice, the model allowed study of ten critical variables: enrollment, faculty size and salaries, research support, support services, financial aid, inflation, endowment return, tuition, gifts and grants, and capital expenditure and debt service.

Once the basic data were obtained and the computer software operational, the leadership of the institution made several critical decisions. The outputs of analysis would be reviewed by an administrative responsibility that could not be delegated. Faculty reactions would be obtained through discussion of the four reports that were to be prepared and circulated. These reports concerned background data, alternatives open to the institution, and the administration's recommendations for decisions. These suggested, with documentation, an increase in student-faculty ratios from 10 to 1 to 12 or 13 to 1, an increase in enrollment by 100—consisting mostly of special students ineligible for financial aid—a slight over-admission of freshmen each year, and a reduction of faculty by 40, mostly through normal attrition. The reports also recommended a slowdown of faculty salary increases from the previous average of 7 percent annually to 4 percent, after consideration of such other alternatives as a one-year moratorium on salary increases. Also suggested was a cap on student financial aid taken from operating funds.

These recommendations were, with some modification, put into effect, and the use of the model was adopted as an essential ongoing part of budget making. This seems to have been made possible because the president believed in the effort, was able to employ competent consulting services from an agency that knew and understood the institution, and was able to locate a highly competent staff. Equally important, the institution was in strong enough financial condition that significant changes could be made without seriously affecting essential programs, faculty salaries, or the attractiveness of the university to students. Wesleyan did not face a problem of survival—thus it had the slack resources to effect change, once a desirable direction was identified.

There can be little doubt that the information base of collegiate institutions can be improved and that there are refined computer programs that can interrelate various sorts of information so as to point to problems, imbalances, and possible remedies. It is possible through simple data bases to discover substantial differences in expenditure by different departments, the sources of student applications and the programs desired, the effects on a salary budget of various policies regarding salary increases, and the amounts of operating funds being used for student financial aid. And through advanced management information systems, it is possible to study quickly the likely results of adopting any of several policy alternatives.

The question is, Are there conditions that warrant investment in management information systems in some institutions in difficulty but not in others? In general, development of a reasonably sophisticated management information system should be a high-priority item for institutions having most of these characteristics:

1. A president who has some knowledge of what can come from a system and a clear desire to put a system into operation.

2. Enough financial resources to maintain a system out of institutional funds and to put into effect major changes suggested by analysis. An institution whose bank credit is blocked and that has difficulty meeting payrolls each month has other things to do than create a management information system.

3. The availability of competent individuals to operate a system and to relate it to the decision-making apparatus of the institution.

4. A large enough administrative staff willing to be trained to use data, so that a system does not break down because one individual dies or leaves an institution.

5. A reasonably high faculty morale that can tolerate suggestions of major change and exposure of the fundamental institutional condition.

6. A reasonably clear and stable administrative structure staffed by people who generally understand their jobs and how administration functions.

7. A recent institutional history of reasonably stable changes and decisions. An institution with a recent history of almost frantic, trial-and-error changes is not one that should use time and resources to create a management information system.

8. A board of trustees whose members clearly understand their role and who are actively concerned with and involved in major policy and administrative decisions. This means that the board should be quite willing and able to confront a president and make important demands on him.

In brief, institutions in highly precarious crisis situations should not look to refined information systems for immediate help.

Decision Making

Another important management concept is the use of various new techniques or approaches to management and decision making, such as program planning and budgeting systems, management by objectives, open-system approach to management, contingency approach to management, or some combination of these. Most of the currently popular new styles and nomenclature have come from government, the military, and business, where varying degrees of success have been claimed for them. These should now be examined to determine what, if any, promise they might have for management and decision making in collegiate institutions.

One of the earliest suggested changes was to adopt a program planning and budgeting system (PPBS). This concept seems to have originated in the Department of Defense and to have spread throughout the federal government when President Johnson ordered all departments to shift to the new system. In essence, it seeks to budget for specific programs, such as academic departments, rather than through categories of expenses, such as salaries, supplies and services, and the like. It further seeks to relate the cost of these various programs to specific outputs, such as the number of people graduated with a bachelor's degree. In theory, examining costs by program can force decision makers to compare the benefits and costs of several possible programs and decide which to select.

There is an impressive literature trying to describe PPBS, and a growing literature seeking to discredit it. However, much of the pro-literature is virtually unintelligible, using language which when finally translated reveals either common sense—for example, it is good to examine alternatives before reaching a decision—or nonsense. However, assuming some theoretical validity for the concept of PPBS, it still has virtually no relevance for institutions of higher education. The preparation of a new system of budgeting that allows sophisticated techniques of analysis would require enormous expenditure of funds. The Department of Defense (the only agency really to claim success with the system), with its multi-billion-dollar budget, had the requisite resources. No collegiate institution has similar resources. In addition, the system is based on identification of precise outcomes, but the outcomes of education are difficult to discover except in quite superficial terms, such as the number of degrees awarded. Further, no single unit is responsible for a single output or a collection of outputs. The physics department is only one contributor to the output of a degree in physics. English, mathematics, and even art may make important, but impossible to measure, contributions.

The one value of PPBS for management of collegiate institutions is a symbolic one. Its literature points out the need to consider costs of specific programs in planning rather than the traditional, line-item budget elements of salaries, operating expenses, and operating capital outlay. This typically has not been done in the past. It should be done in the future, but it does not require the elaborate system of PPBS. It can be accomplished by the simple expedient of requiring all programs—departments, centers, institutes, or libraries—to prepare full budgets and to consider aternative uses of funds. Then, higher administrative levels can compare program costs and make whatever decisions such comparison suggests.

Management by Objectives

The essential element of PPBS is also central to another popular managerial concept—management by objectives. This also is represented by a growing technical literature. However, the essential element is that each subordinate unit—departments, admissions officers, counseling centers, and the like—is charged with developing its own objectives and converting them into budget requests and eventually into budget management. Management by objectives is an attempt to decentralize planning and budget preparation and to hold administrative officers more responsible for their units. Such a concept is a radical departure in higher education, in which, by tradition, administrative officers below the level of president and dean are not granted full administrative responsibility for the units over which they preside. In typical divisions or departments, directors and chairmen are responsible for relatively modest operating budgets, chiefly for supplies. They are not expected to consider such matters as salaries and the cost of physical plants in thinking about the mission of their units. Those matters are the concern of central administration. Further, subordinate academic administrators tend not to think of themselves as administrators but as academics who do some administrative chores.

Management by objectives requires as a first step that department heads and other subordinate administrators be regarded as responsible officers. They are asked to lead the members of their units to think about purposes, goals, and program objectives, to consider ways of achieving those, and to decide on the cost of doing so. The planning of subordinate units, then, becomes the basis for the planning of higher units and ultimately of the entire institution.

In theory, each department would be expected to develop both short- and long-range objectives in the light of financial and mission guidelines established for the entire institution. Each department would know the broad financial resources that would likely be available to it, including salary money. The final short- or long-range plans would indicate quite specific goals and the cost of achieving them. These plans would then be refined through interaction between administration at all levels until a final acceptable institutional plan was created, a budget approved, and the plan put into operation.

An administrative structure appropriate for management by objectives is described earlier in Chapter Two. That structure posits that subordinate administrators assume the full range of administrative duties, including program leadership, budget preparation, and budget management. And that structure can be urged as a goal. It should be recognized, however, that the achievement of that goal is a long-term affair requiring five to ten years to educate people, establish tradition and procedures, and create evaluation techniques. An institution in a crisis situation will find little help in adopting a management-by-objectives system. Asking a demoralized faculty to do rational program planning when there is no assurance that the institution will be in existence the following fall is asking the impossible. An institution in crisis must use palliatives and emergency measures to stabilize conditions. It must identify the critical points—enrollment, cash flow, bank credit—and concentrate on them. Only with reasonable stability can a more rational system be adopted. However, for institutions in reasonably stable condition in the 1970s, but which can expect problems in the 1980s, evolving a management-by-objectives system would seem to be a worthwhile venture.

Applying New Management Systems

The possibilities and limitations of long-range planning, management information systems, management by objectives, and complex analyses are well illustrated by Stanford University, which, in a relatively few years, moved from being a strong regional university to a position among the top several national institutions. This transition began with a major long-range plan developed by the president and a few associates during the 1950s. During those years too, the institution created a highly effective development system which resulted in one of the nation's highest annual gift incomes and, in the 1970s, the completion of the largest fund drive ($300 million) ever attempted by an American university. However, in spite of those achievements, in 1969 the university began to operate at a deficit, which gave promise of increasing each year. The university response was a four-year budget adjustment program intended to remove $6 million from the budget base and to bring rates of expenditure and income into balance. These were to be accomplished through two changes in budgeting procedure: The traditional incremental system of percentage increases to little-examined budgets was discontinued, and a five-year budget goal was created. The cuts in the base budget were to be made selectively by each school, institute, or department after it had defined its program and determined how best to function with decreased resources. However, before the goal of the $6 million reduction in budget base could be achieved, a declining stock market, exceptionally high inflation rates, and an energy crisis came to pass and made the effort impossible. By 1974–75, the university again faced over a million-dollar deficit.

This deficit stimulated a new attempt to bring the budget into balance and to keep it there. The new effort was led and made possible by a highly talented group of administrators serving the provost who were conversant with advanced management techniques as well as the functioning and history of Stanford University. The "budget equilibrium program" they devised was based on a detailed five-year financial forecast and sophisticated dynamic equilibrium modeling. The five-year financial forecast was accomplished by the various schools, departments, and activities in the university as though no budget-balancing program were applied, but on the assumption of a stable enrollment and related matters and reasonably stable increases in consumer price indexes. These forecasts were then placed in a model that allowed study of the effects on them of varying sets of assumptions, such as various levels of energy costs or tuition levels. Aggregating these forecasts and extrapolating from them led to a profile of a widening gap between income and expenditure by 1979–80. This profile was then examined and various interventions simulated to determine how best to achieve a real budgetary equilibrium. Such an examination was made possible through a second model used to find dynamic equilibrium. This model allowed the examination of many different trade-offs that could be attempted, as, for example, what tuition rates would be needed to support 1 percent of the budget being used for improvement.

The dynamic equilibrium model could demonstrate gross effects but could not make specific suggestions to administrators regarding the necessary decisions to be made to achieve actual budgetary balance. Thus, a third model was developed, called the "transition of equilibrium" model, which linked expenditures, income, deficits, budget reduction, and cash flow in and out of endowment. Key parameters in the model could be manipulated to see the impact of such things as different payouts on endowment.

After considerable work with the models, the central administration adopted a strategy of reducing expenditure by $10.2 million over a three-year period—a goal that was achieved during 1977–78—and a balanced budget was projected. As to the future, the university has adopted still a fourth model, called "trades." This allows for forecasting of income and expenses, defining equilibrium, assessing effects of trade-offs, and testing alternative tactics or strategies when problem areas appear. It allows for consideration, for example, of what would happen if either the best or the worst utility costs came true, or of how low faculty salary increases would drop if tuition were reduced. By 1979, the modeling has worked for Stanford. The university has a network of communications, a cadre of sophisticated planners, and an administration with the ability and moral strength to make decisions. However, there are problems as to the adaptability of such a system elsewhere, especially in institutions seeking to survive. Improperly used and interpreted, the models can produce mistrust and divisiveness within the institution. Everyone must know about the models and feel that his or her opinions are considered. Further, the models assume a fairly substantial endowment and reasonably stable conditions and are thus not appropriate for institutions in crisis or with widely fluctuating enrollment patterns.

More important to effective decision making are the processes that modeling generates. It can almost be claimed that if a number of processes could be ensured by other means, sophisticated information and modeling could be eliminated. Further, while many institutions cannot develop and use the Stanford system of quantitative planning, many could adopt its processes for reaching decisions. Decision making at Stanford, as elsewhere, is an imperfect art. It produces decisions with which many will disagree. However, an effective set of processes will produce acceptance of decisions in the faith that they were arrived at by rational thought and were based on informed judgment. At Stanford, the processes and criteria for decision making have two purposes: the administration and implementation of academic policy, and the derivation of educational policy.

There are four major processes that culminate in institutional policy: (1) academic planning and budgeting, (2) development of a faculty manpower and an appointment and promotion process, (3) facility planning and capital budgeting, and (4) development of academic priorities and plans for fund raising. Each of these processes (which should involve large numbers of people) yields long-range forecasts, budget guidelines and budgets, future manpower needs, future facilities needs, and clear-cut plans for fund raising based upon well thought-out priorities. The stress at Stanford is on processes—that is, protracted discussion by all interested groups before plans are made final. There is, of course, some danger that emphasis on processes will produce no decisions. However, if the processes are well structured, danger can be avoided.

To illustrate how these processes operate, consider the academic planning and budgeting process. The first essential need is for academic leadership to make clear the institution's academic priorities. In determining which academic programs to create, maintain, increase, decrease, or eliminate, four criteria are applied: (1) Is there now and will there be student interest? (2) Can the university be outstanding in the program? (3) Is the area academically important? (4) Can the needed funds be secured? For a program to be seriously considered for support, affirmative answers should be made with respect to each of the four. In arriving at those answers, all concerned elements in the university must have a voice, although the ultimate decision must rest with the academic leadership—that is, the president. This decision will have credibility only if all elements know that all possible evidence has been considered. In years past, Stanford did make critical decisions, such as eliminating architecture, which were criticized because certain elements felt themselves to have been ignored. The present posture is to lean over backwards to avoid that charge.

Examined in greater detail, this process presents much that is adaptable to other institutions. The academic planning and budgeting process is both year-round and two-way. The central administration of Stanford communicates considerations, constraints, and issues in schools and departments, which in turn communicate programs, considerations, needs, and judgments to the central administration. Typically the board of trustees in its March meeting discusses, evaluates, and eventually approves the operating-budget guidelines for the following academic year beginning on September 1. Next the central administration begins to flesh-out the budget guidelines, evaluate data on the previous year, and plan for subsequent analytical work that will be carried out during the summer. The analytical work involves research and analyses of programs, enrollments, faculty needs, financial-aid issues, and—on the institutional level—planning issues. At the same time, efforts are made to produce a long-range financial forecast and anticipate likely changes in the economy. Knowledge of detailed economic

factors that will impinge on the institution allows for several different projections regarding the institution under each of a variety of
different assumptions. By the end of the summer, a long-range
financial forecast is normally available and is reviewed by the
faculty senate and the board of trustees in October and November.
This forecast provides the context for all subsequent discussions regarding the operating budget.

In September or October, the central administration develops a set of documents called "budget protocols," which are
distributed to the various subordinate units in the university. These
protocols indicate the constraints and criteria that have been developed independently to other processes, and they solicit data and
judgment about program needs and academic direction. The budget
protocols then become the basis for extended discussions between
the central administration and the deans of the schools and the
heads of departments, as well as with various faculty oversight committees. From these conversations many decisions are made; some
are small and do not require a lot of machinery to examine, but
some major decisions require protracted conversation. After these
discussions, the subordinate units write responses to the budget
protocol, and these documents are then collected, collated, and
evaluated by the central administration.

To ensure widespread understanding of the evolving budget,
the provost and his staff make presentations, both to the board of
trustees and to the faculty senate. Each year the provost usually
makes three major presentations to the senate: the first is the long-
range financial forecast, the second is a preview of the following
year's budget parameters, and the third presentation concerns the
operating budget guidelines prior to review by the board of trustees.
Three similar presentations are made to the board. This process of
widespread consultation has proven invaluable because it permits
the institution to develop informed judgments based on various
data and studies, as well as on judgments of assorted peer groups.
This satisfaction is reflected in the words of the vice-president and
provost, William F. Miller, who contends that "We have sufficient
leeway to prevent the system from becoming inertia-bound and developing a life of its own, and at the same time the process is sufficiently systematic so that people have confidence that the judgments

are not whimsical. These processes have permitted us to undertake two rather major budget adjustment programs when the institution foresaw a financial crisis, and at the same time these processes made it possible for us to reevaluate and shift resources and develop new programs within the schools and between the schools" (1978).

Further Readings

One major development during the 1970s was the enormous interest in applying principles of management to colleges and universities. Perhaps more than any other category of the literature, that concerned with management contains considerable sense but a great deal of nonsense, as when inappropriate theories from the business or military are applied to higher education. Millett's many writings about the subject seem to be the best reasoned and reflect an awareness of the realities of higher education and the limitations of borrowing from other fields.

American Council on Education. *College and University Business Administration*. Washington, D.C.: American Council on Education, 1968.

BALDERSTON, F. E. *Managing Today's University*. San Francisco: Jossey-Bass, 1974.

BALDRIDGE, J. V., AND TIERNEY, M. L. *New Approaches to Management: Creating Practical Systems of Management Information and Management by Objectives*. San Francisco: Jossey-Bass, 1979.

BOLEN, J. G. *Management Information for College Administrators*. Athens, Ga.: Institute of Higher Education, 1971.

BUDIG, G. A. *Dollars and Sense: Budgeting for Today's Campus*. Chicago: College and University Business Press, 1972.

Carnegie Commission on Higher Education. *Papers on Efficiency in Management of Higher Education*. New York: McGraw-Hill, 1972.

Committee on Economic Development. *The Management and Financing of Colleges*. New York: Committee on Economic Development, 1973.

DEEGAN, A. X., AND FRITZ, R. *MBO Goes to College*. Boulder, Colo.:

Division of Continuing Education, Bureau of Independent Study, 1975.

HEATON, C. P. (Ed.). *Management by Objectives in Higher Education*. Durham, N.C.: National Laboratory for Higher Education, 1975.

Higher Education Research Institute. *National Conference on Academic Planning*. Los Angeles: Higher Education Research Institutes, 1978.

IVANCEVICH, J. M. "Longitudinal Assessment of Management by Objectives." *Administrative Science Quarterly,* 1972, *17* (1), 126–138.

JELLEMA, W. W. (Ed.). *Efficient College Management*. San Francisco: Jossey-Bass, 1972.

LAHTI, R. E. *Innovative College Management: Implementing Proven Organizational Practice*. San Francisco: Jossey-Bass, 1973.

LAWRENCE, B. G., AND SEVICE, A. L. *Quantitative Approaches to Higher Education Management*. Washington, D.C.: American Association for Higher Education, 1977.

MICHALAK, C. L. (Ed.). *Managing Tomorrow's University*. Proceedings of the University of California Academic Business Officers Conference, Berkeley, September 1977.

MILLETT, J. D. *Allocation Decisions in Higher Education*. New York: Academy for Educational Development, n.d.

MILLETT, J. D. "Higher Education Management Versus Business Management." *Educational Record,* 1975, *56,* 221.

RAIA, A. P. *Management by Objectives*. Glenview, Ill.: Scott, Foresman, 1974.

WEATHERSBY, G. B., AND JACOBS, F. *Institutional Goals and Student Costs*. Washington, D.C.: American Association for Higher Education, 1977.

WILLIAMS, H. *Planning for Effective Resource Allocation in Universities*. Washington, D.C.: American Council on Education, 1966.

Chapter 5

꙰꙰꙰꙰꙰꙰꙰꙰

Anticipating and Planning for the Future

Perhaps the most widely urged activity for administrators of collegiate institutions to undertake is planning. Prior to the 1960s, most institutions were created and grew with no real plan other than a generally shared ideal as to what a collegiate institution should be. They simply reacted to the period of rapid expansion of higher education as best they could—which turned out to be remarkably successful. Buildings were built (although some were temporary), faculties were enlarged (albeit with some dilution of quality, for example, a temporary drop in the proportion of Ph.D.'s), and scholars were quickly trained for the research made possible by increasing federal support. The sheer magnitude of growth concealed the effects of lack of planning. If a new program

111

proved unworkable, no matter: There were always more funds with which to create new programs. If there were a slight slip in annual giving, no matter: A quick grant from a friendly foundation would take care of things. From the end of World War II until the late 1960s—with the exception of the brief period from 1952 to 1958—growth, affluence, and optimism prevailed. Since all indexes were positive, leadership found no reason for close monitoring. Then, in the late 1960s, all of those indexes suddenly turned down.

The Need for Planning

When the "new depression" in higher education burst upon colleges and universities during the late 1960s, institutions made some significant discoveries—among them that administrators did not know very much about how their institutions were actually functioning, lacked tools to control the various elements of the institutions, and had no clear plan for the institutions to follow. Presidents discovered that their institutions had used up reserves without really knowing it, had begun to eat into endowment, had begun to lose desired students for reasons that had quietly developed over time, or had acquired a larger tenured faculty than could wisely be used if enrollment increases ever slowed. As recently as the early 1970s, large universities could be found with no other plans than the next year's budget and architectural models of a possible future physical plant which the president kept on display in his office. Even presidents who were aware of changes—as, for example, depletion of reserves and a growing accumulation of deficit—seemed unaware that their institutions were entering a new era and that recouping losses would be difficult, if not impossible.

When the severity of the depression was finally perceived, institutions typically took several actions. They reduced expenditures and they developed and put into place various sorts of management techniques and controls. They initiated better and more frequent budget reports, sought better-trained chief financial officers, and considered and frequently created offices of institutional research to provide the information they sought concerning applications and enrollments. In one institution, an extensive system for monitoring and controlling budgets, especially for certain auxiliary enterprises, was put into effect. Another institution adopted a new fund accounting system that revealed hidden outflows of cash, whereas still another appointed new personnel in financial management to bring accounting and expenditures under control.

Many institutions were able to stabilize their condition simply through the imposition of some rather primitive management and information systems. As of 1976, Bowen and Minter (1976, p. 2) could report that, overall, the financial condition of private institutions had held steady or improved, few institutions had experienced chronic operating deficits, and few had been forced to make drastic program cuts. As institutions move into the 1980s, however, improved management will require not only more elaborate and precise information systems and better ways to arrive at prudent and effective decisions but also long-range and short-range planning.

An Example of Poor Planning

The effects of poor planning can be illustrated by the case of a public comprehensive university that was created in the 1960s as part of a growing state system of higher education designed to serve a rapidly changing and industrializing state. Because of political considerations, the university probably will not die; but since its founding, it has demonstrated a cluster of traits that clearly are not benign.

This university was planned as an institution serving the largest city and the largest county in the state. It was linked to the public junior college system because it was an institution into which junior college graduates could transfer with great ease. Since it was a public institution, it was expected to maintain costs per student at the same levels as did other four-year institutions. However, other four-year institutions enrolled large numbers of lower-division students, whose lower costs helped defray the accepted higher costs of the upper division students. To compensate for this imbalance, the new university was expected to reduce the costs of upper-division students through massive uses of educational technology such as language laboratories, closed circuit television, and eventually computer-based instruction.

Unfortunately, the planners here as in several other states made some seriously mistaken assumptions. First, it was assumed that students would drive 140 miles each day along a toll road from a large metropolitan area to the donated campus site. This its potential clientele of first-generation college-attending students would not do, and the institution never was able even closely to approximate its enrollment goals. Indeed, in time, the state was forced to create still another institution to serve those students. Second, it was assumed that cost-per-student credit hour produced could be significantly reduced through the use of educational technology. At that time, there was no evidence that such savings could be achieved, although some media proponents argued eloquently that they could. Subsequent research has suggested that actual economies through the use of technology have rarely been achieved, and when all costs are considered—development of hardware and software, space, technical services, and equipment replacement— have never been achieved.

These two faulty assumptions were aggravated by administrative error. If technology is to be widely used, the faculty must be sympathetic and trained to use it. This suggests that a special kind of faculty should be recruited and brought on the job early enough to prepare for intensive use of equipment. However, the president elected not to appoint a chief academic officer until just a few weeks before the university opened its doors, and instead of a unique new faculty, a relatively traditional group of academics was assembled which, without leadership, was never willing to give the media a chance. That reluctance appears to have been intensified by the appointment of a zealot for the new technology who managed to irritate most of the faculty through his personal characteristics and extreme claims. Nor was an aggressive student recruitment effort made to convince prospective students that the daily trip was necessary. And as the institution opened, little attention was paid to faculty morale seriously damaged by the wide gulf between expectations and reality.

The institution continued but at enrollment levels below

those planned. There was, during the late 1960s, a general feeling in the state that good public policy would be served if the institution were closed. This has not yet happened. The lessons, however, are clear: Validate planning assumptions carefully and develop administrative practices consistent with institutional uniqueness.

Principles of Planning

The conception of collegiate planning is not new. Since the 1950s, techniques have been developed—through several definite stages—to aid rational long-range planning for institutions of higher education. In the mid 1950s, Sidney Tickton, then with the Ford Foundation, in anticipation of the enrollment bulge to come a decade later, urged each college and university to prepare a ten-year long-range plan. The Ford Foundation tried in a variety of ways to stimulate institutions to prepare master plans, and that stimulation did seem to produce some quite successful plans. Stanford University, for example, prepared a plan for expansion that was partially achieved through a $100 million development campaign. But for practical planning, the parameters within which planning takes place must be defined. Even with uncertainty about the future rate of inflation, the kind of federal programs for higher education that will be adopted, the forecasted birth rates during this century, as well as what people will want from collegiate education, planning models must be created that take into account such factors. Institutional decision makers must be trained to use planning data in prudent ways without being overawed by them.

Over time, there has grown up a consensus regarding planning that one can hear expressed all over the country in seminars and conferences and that comprises the substance of the growing literature of planning. A set of beliefs as to how this planning should be done has grown. Millett has codified this consensus in his booklet *Planning in Higher Education* (1977). Millett wisely points out that planning offers no immediate answers to problems but rather a rationalized approach to the future. It is in essence an anticipation and a seeking to prepare for both expected and unexpected eventualities. It assumes that human beings can modify the environment and reactions to it in rational ways and that human in-

stitutions can be improved. That improvement will be consistent
with the major tenets of American society of social pluralism, economic capitalism, individual responsibility, equality of opportunity,
and political, liberal democracy. Within that context, comprehensive planning involves several distinct phases:

* Anticipating the future
* Formulating strategic objectives
* Defining individual and social values
* Determining work objectives
* Inventorying current resources
* Calculating needed additional resources
* Developing work programs
* Making organizational arrangements
* Performing the work plan
* Evaluating accomplishments

Such a series of steps is equally applicable to the Department of Defense, General Motors, or the Catholic church. It can
be converted into academic needs and nomenclature and then become an agenda for institutional planning. As a general rule, institutional planning should consist of seven major elements. It should
consider and make explicit: (1) the statement of mission, (2) the
external environment, (3) internal assumptions, (4) program objectives, (5) foundation plans, (6) budgets, and (7) evaluation
plans.

Statement of Mission

Explicit in virtually all utterances about planning is the primacy accorded the development of a clear statement of institutional
mission and purpose. Although creating such a statement can be
regarded as but a meaningless chore, it can produce a document that
really governs the conduct of all programs and the making of all
decisions. The worth and validity of the statement of mission will
depend in large measure on how honestly and candidly the institution
understands the realities of the external environment and the nature
of determining the internal assumptions. Not facing those, or glossing

over them, can and likely will produce a plan leading to disaster. The statement of mission realistically reflects at least eight issues—both external and internal—and the real, rather than the idealized, alternative institutional responses to them. Responses to the external environment include:

1. *Response to the social environment*—for example, to what the supporting public expects. The early plans of the State University of New York at Old Westbury, Michigan State University at Oakland, and Nova University led to serious difficulties because the expectations of the supporting public were misunderstood.
2. *Response to economic trends.* It now seems true that institutional plans of the mid 1960s proved to be seriously wrong because of the assumptions of continued economic affluence and continued increases in financial support for research, faculty salary raises, and more elaborate physical facilities.
3. *Response to demographic trends.* It also now appears that the oversupply of doctorates during the 1970s was produced in part by failure to realize the significance in the shift in birth rates that began in the late 1950s. Many institutions expanded faculty and physical plant without realizing that the states in which they were located had begun to experience a real decline in population.
4. *Response to governmental planning.* Similarly, many doctoral programs were allowed to expand during the 1960s in the mistaken belief that federal support for research could and would increase exponentially, even though continued exponential increases of anything are contrary to laws of nature.

Responses to internal assumptions include:

1. *Choice of educational purpose.* Many choices are in theory available but, for any given institution, only a relatively few are realistic. The genius of a successful plan will rest on the correct choice made at the right time. Thus, Stanford's seeking to change from a strong regional university to a leading national university was the right choice at the right time. Had that decision been delayed from 1955 to 1965, it probably would have proved to be an impossible choice.

2. *Choice of quality standards.* This is a particularly difficult matter because the prevailing beliefs about the meaning of institutional excellence (except in the minds of some educational reformers) stress recruiting students with high academic aptitude, whereas in reality the number of potential students with high aptitude is limited. A decision on the part of an institution in 1977 to increase the SAT scores of its entering freshman class by a hundred points might very well produce an intolerable decline in enrollments.

3. *Choice of enrollment size.* This choice is also a delicate one. Knox College in Illinois, for example, which doubled its enrollments between 1955 and 1965, planned to double its size again over the next ten years on the mistaken assumption that the potential students were available. They were not and a new plan had to be created.

4. *Assessment of available resources.* Stimulated by an aggressive president who makes long-range future plans based upon past levels of success, the tuition-dependent institution which each year must balance its budget through annual giving may indeed be planning dangerously.

There are a variety of ways of arriving at statements of institutional mission, purpose, and goals. Possibly the most frequently used method in the past was adoption by the board of trustees of a presidentially drafted statement which was then published in the college catalogue. In stable conditions when there were generally shared values, this was not a bad device. The actual statement was more symbolic than directive, for most everyone knew what the institution was all about. More recently, more sophisticated techniques to determine purpose have been used, such as the Delphi technique. This in essence asks a number of people to rank-order many statements of purpose several different times, with more information provided each time until clear and general agreement is reached. This technique has the value of efficiency, but there is considerable doubt that it produces the broad and deep discussions from which emerge the powerful agreements of purpose that can be used to direct institutional behavior.

Generally, the chief executive officer has thought deeply about the mission of the institution and arrived at some conviction as to what it should be. Then, through many formal and informal discussions and statements, the central ideas can be clarified. In these discussions, the many imponderables must be made explicit, such as the eight issues just mentioned. Gradually, there will come agreement unless, of course, an institution is so torn and demoralized that different groups of people actually refuse to speak to one another.

Program Objectives

Second in importance only to the doctrine of the need for clear statement of mission is the postulate of the need for detailed planning in specific programs as the essential building blocks of a total institutional plan. Millett (1977, pp. 123-124) outlines the typical programs in a college or university and argues that each one should develop its own statements of objectives and plans for achieving them:

1. Output (productive) programs
    Instruction
    Research
    Public service
    Hospital operation
    Independent operations
    Student financial assistance
2. Support (overhead) programs
    Academic support
    Student services
    Institutional support
    Plant operation and maintenance
    Transfers
3. Auxiliary Enterprises
    Auxiliary programs

Millett (1977, p. 159) further argues that good planning requires that the leadership of each program be asked to develop clear statements of program objectives and candid commentary on at least six component parts: outcomes, action (work), actors (personnel), resources, time (completion), and evaluation of accomplishments.

It is this conception of program planning within subordinate units that is most revolutionary in collegiate institutions, possibly the most difficult to put into effect and the most distinctive from earlier versions of planning. The historic nature of what little planning took place in collegiate institutions was that it was presidentially centered and originated. As late as 1958, the generally successful Stanford Plan for the Future was carried on by the president and a few administrative associates. President Sterling of Stanford remarked that to ask schools and departments to plan would be to invite exaggerated hopes and likely frustration and disappointment. And even today, in the majority of institutions, although lip service is given to involvement of all constituencies in planning, actual responsible planning in the various programs (schools, departments, institutes, offices) is still superficial or incomplete.

A major question as to the validity of this new approach to planning is whether or not third-, fourth-, and fifth-level administrators—departmental chairmen, division directors, and the like—can be trained to do serious planning and whether faculties can accept the results. If they can, then something approximating management by objectives might be possible. And the results might resemble one of Millett's (1977, pp. 164–165) examples:

Program Objectives

Type
1. Quantity
    * Twelve hundred students will be enrolled.
    * Three thousand new student applications will be processed.
    * Attendance will average 300 people per game.
    * Class size in composition will be limited to 25.
2. Quality
    * A greater percentage of students will rate their education excellent in 1979 than in 1978.
    * Ten percent more students will succeed at four-year colleges than in our last study.
    * The budget request will be 100 percent free of mathematical errors.
    * Ninety-five percent of expenditure requests will have the correct budget account number.

- No expenditure requests will be forwarded to the business office if they exceed budget allocations.

3. Time
  - All budget requests will be in by February 1.
  - All equipment purchases will be processed in five working days.
  - All new faculty appointments will be made by the president by June 1.
  - The committee report will be made by November 1.

4. Cost
  - The cost per student will be reduced to $1,375 per FTE student.
  - The student personnel area will expend $138 per FTE student.
  - The teacher/student ratio will be 22:1.
  - Administrative costs will not exceed 7 percent of the operating budget.

Programs

Type

1. Instructional programs

   General
   - By September 1979, 75 percent of all college courses will be taught using behavioral objectives.
   - By July 1979, a foreign study program will be planned and readied for offering during the 1979–80 academic year.

   Specific

   English and Reading:
   - Each graduate in June 1979 will be able to read at the fiftieth percentile for grade 14 on a standardized reading test.
   - Each graduate in July 1979 will be able to pass a college test on the use of the library.

   Physical education:
   - Each student graduating in June 1979 will have the knowledge and skills to participate in two sports with carryover value to age sixty-five.
   - Each student graduating in June 1979 will have the knowledge and understanding necessary to be an intelligent spectator in two professional sports.

Automotive technology:
- Each two-year graduate in June 1979 will be able to tear down, reassemble, and repair a standard carburetor.
- Each two-year graduate in June 1979 will be able to install new rings in any standard-sized American-made automobile.

2. Student services
- By July 1, 1979, all counselors will be trained to offer human potential seminars.
- By July 1, 1979, a new academic advisement system will be developed and proposed to the academic senate.

Planning Data

Those who urge planning insist that a comprehensive plan should result, with mechanisms for periodically upgrading the several parts and the entire plan. While plans may be organized in various ways, a typical outline would indicate specific plans for: (1) instruction, (2) enrollment, (3) organizational structure, (4) personnel, (5) facilities, (6) management information, (7) income, (8) expenditures, and (9) evaluation (Millett, 1977). In the rationale for decentralized planning, each program or subordinate unit would be expected to plan for each of those elements in such a way that when the plans are reviewed and consolidated at higher levels, they constitute the total institution's master plan. Program plans can and do vary enormously with respect to complexity and sophistication. However, especially for institutions seeking survival, a parsimonious plan would seem to be desirable. Parsimoniousness here calls for the fewest specific elements than can indicate those courses of action most likely to contribute to survival. For example, each program or unit might develop the following information:

1. Instruction
- Broad rationale for the program and an indication of how the various elements in theory should interact
- Statements of degree requirements, actual courses to be offered, and any specific learning techniques
- Behavioral objectives for the program
- Proposed organization and management of the program

2. Enrollment
    - Statements of past enrollment patterns and tendencies
    - Statements of desired enrollments
        In majors
        In service courses
    - Statements of realistic enrollment goals and the factors that impinge on them
        In majors
        In service courses
    - Statements of problems associated with enrollments and ways they might be solved
        Attracting new or transfer students
        Decreasing attrition
3. Organizational structure
    - Duties and responsibilities of the various administrative officers
    - Duties and responsibilities of the various standing committees
    - Statements of how major administrative tasks are handled and by whom, for example, registration, course approvals, class schedules, advising, and examinations
    - Statements of the relationship between the program and higher, lower, or lateral programs and activities
    - Statements of any proposed changes in organizational structure or policy
4. Personnel
    - Lists of faculty and staff year by year for a period of five to ten years, and enrollments and advising loads associated with those
    - Statements of predicted changes in staffing through retirement, ending term appointments, and the like
    - Statements of needed faculty and staff for at least five years in the future in three formats:
        Drastic reduction in enrollment
        Steady enrollment
        Stable increased enrollment
    - Statements of actual and desired personnel policies, as on tenure and promotion
    - Where relevant, statements of plans for affirmative action

5. Facilities
   - Lists and descriptions of facilities used
     Those assigned to or used chiefly by the program
     Those used on a more occasional basis
   - Statements of needed renovation and explanation of the needs
   - Statements of needed facilities or capital equipment
   - Statements, in uniform style, of past, present, and future rates of space utilization
6. Management information
   - Statements and evaluation of information that is routinely collected
   - Statements and evaluations of information provided by higher authority
   - Statements of information not currently available but needed to accomplish the work of the program or unit
   - Statements as to how additional information might be obtained and at what additional cost
7. Income
   - Past and present income
     From tuition of majors
     From tuition of service courses
     From overhead and savings
     From grants and contracts
     From services
   - Projected needs for income
   - Projected plans for acquiring income
8. Expenditures
   - Past and present expenditures by category, for example, salaries, operating capital
   - Broad changes in expenditures over a five-year period and an explanation
   - Detailed budget changes for two years with increases arranged according to priority
   - Alternative ways of using increased expenditures, for example, a new faculty member, more teaching assistants, or increased capital expenditures, such as language laboratories

9. Evaluation
   - Statement of evaluation techniques in use, for example, student evaluation forms, faculty report forms, outside evaluations
   - Desired changes in evaluation and the approximate cost together with the uses to be made of evaluations
   - Techniques used for full program review

When every unit on campus is forced to ponder such matters and state what it wishes to do and how to do it, the results in aggregate may outline the institution's plan. However, that planning will be worse than fruitless if it is carried on in the absence of detailed knowledge of the external environment. It will also be destructive if there is infirm presidential leadership, which shifts from position to position as the political forces on campus shift.

The Planning Process

During the course of planning, at each administrative level, a series of questions should be asked—and answered candidly and realistically:

- What has been the historic clientele of the institution or unit and how has it changed with respect to financial ability, size, and educational desires?
- What are the real traits, attributes, and talents of the faculty and how may they best be used?
- What are the varying ways in which the institution is perceived by the alumni, students, faculty, administration, and board members and how can those differences be reconciled?
- What programs offered in the past have had strong or weak appeal—for what reasons and are those reasons still valid?
- What actual financial levels are needed for the institution to maintain itself or to change and are there realistic sources for that finding?
- Why have applications and enrollments changed over time and are there means within the power of the institution to modify any unfavorable trends?

- What can the institution do for students that realistically is of sufficient value to warrant its selection over all others and, in many cases, the payment of tuition more than three times that of public institutions?

Such questions should not be posed rhetorically but within an established administrative and organizational structure that can follow answers with definite implied alternative courses of action. Such a structure is suggested in Chapter Two. Here the use of outside consultation may be appropriate. Outsiders can frequently see reality more clearly than those whose economic, personal, or professional needs are intimately linked to the institution. Seattle Pacific University, for example, made effective use of three consultants, each with a different background but each concerned with private liberal arts education. Each consultant spent a week exploring the institution and then presented his conception of the institution and how it might proceed in the future. Those three alternatives then became the basis for serious board administration and faculty deliberation as to what the future should be.

As discussed in Chapter Four, such detailed planning may not be possible for institutions in crisis conditions. Colleges and universities in such a situation have resources for only the most urgent matters—enrollment, cash flow, and reduction of expenditures. If an institution can gain a few years of reasonable stability, however, it can then consider using more sophisticated approaches to plan for the future and to maintain a satisfactory degree of consistent stability. In a reasonably healthy situation, a first step for planning is the creation of a stable, responsible administrative structure, with people holding administrative positions who are prepared for those roles and are assigned definite and sufficient responsibility to fill the positions and be held accountable. In virtually every situation in which a reasonably established institution has run into a severe crisis, there had been a rapid turnover of second- and third-level administrative officers, an excessive concentration of details and decision-making power in the hands of the president only, a weak or nonexistent communication system, and a lack of generally shared critical information.

If an appropriate structure can be created, and if there is a reasonable level of faculty morale, then the institution can turn to planning for the future. This planning should not be vague, amorphous speculation and pie-in-the-sky dreaming but should be focused and well organized. It should take no longer than eighteen months —preferably only twelve months. There are a number of planning models that could be used. One developed by David G. Horner (in a 1978 oral seminar report) called "Strategic Planning in Higher Education" commends itself for several reasons, an important one being its modest cost. Horner argues that the bulk of the work can be done by existing administrative staff and faculty through asking faculty specialists to do many of the needed background studies. This model consists first of reexamining the historic mission of the institution, then making detailed analyses of the external and internal environment, then finding and examining many different opportunities and threats, then positing alternative strategies, and finally selecting the strategic mission for the future.

As a first step, the president would announce to the full faculty, preferably in a major speech, that the effort would be made and ask the full cooperation of the entire campus community. The president would further suggest an organization for the process. As a general rule, for the duration of the planning, normal standing-committee work—curriculum and the like—should be kept to a minimum. Then a new, temporary structure should be created, having as its major element a steering committee chaired by the president and widely representative of campus constituencies. This group should undertake a serious review of institutional missions and, at the same time, create two task forces to make detailed studies of the internal and external environments. As outlined earlier in this chapter, the external environment would include economic, demographic, regulatory, and sociocultural factors. The internal environment would include analysis of resources, desires of constituencies, problems of the past, the general higher education indicators and market, and the sorts and intensity of competition to be faced. This phase might require two months and should result in a series of reports that could be circulated to a number of newly created ad hoc committees for study and could serve as a basis for identifying and examining potential threats and opportunities. What these specific committees would be will depend, obviously, on the

size and traditions of the institution, but a sample list might include:
academic program; clientele, including recruitment, admissions,
and retention of students; finances; faculty needs and configura-
tions, including the full- or part-time issue; campus environment,
including student out-of-class life; and governance, including consideration of real or potential unionism.

Each of these committees, chaired by an appropriate administrative officer, would be asked to ponder as full a variety of issues
as possible and, finally, to prepare a report that might be organized
as follows:

1. The present situation, including evaluation of strengths and
   weaknesses
2. Possible significant changes, including possible favorable outcomes, unfavorable outcomes, and dangers—for example, turning
   coeducational might produce increased short-run enrollments,
   but, at the same time, change the character of the institution in
   such a way as to affect adversely the long-term enrollment practice
3. Estimates of the costs and possibilities of making the various
   changes suggested

When these reports have been completed, in about four months,
they should be widely circulated for criticism and reactions, all of
which should be given to the steering committee. That group, possibly working throughout the summer, would then identify a number of broad strategies based upon the information available. Each
strategy should be listed with as complete as possible evaluations of
strengths, limitations, dangers, and potentialities. A Western
women's college might list: coeducation; concentration on older,
part-time students; merger with a state system; major entry into external degree programs; reaffiliation with a religious denomination;
remaining a residential women's college but seeking a new clientele,
for example, followers rather than leaders; and creating unique
two- and four-year degree programs.

The ultimate decision about the strategic goals should be
made by the board of trustees upon the recommendation of the

institution's academic leadership. That decision is an act of judgment not of science. However, in arriving at the decision, maximum information should be used and the following criteria applied:

1. *Will the plan alienate any important constituency?* Dartmouth had to make sure of this before it became coeducational. A number of years ago, several efforts were made to merge two neighboring Catholic institutions. In one, there was a joint board vote of 19 to 1 in favor of merger. However, the one vote against was that of the president of one of the two institutions, who commanded a large faculty following. As long as he opposed merger, it could not work, even if legally mandated by the two boards and supported by the two religious orders.

2. *Is there persuasive evidence that there is a potential clientele—one with resources to pay tuition and that will continue well into the future?* To assume, without strong evidence, that there are students who would attend a liberal arts college if it became the only secular liberal arts college in the state, is to live dangerously. It is equally dangerous to assume that there is a long-term market of middle-aged women who would return to college part time, pay regular tuition, and meet traditional graduation requirements. Such assumptions should be carefully checked.

3. *Does the institution have the needed faculty to implement the plan and is that faculty supported by a reasonably secure financial base? Or does the institution have in hand the hard money to appoint and support needed faculty?* A plan that calls for the appointment of tenured professors to carry out parts of a strategic plan, on the assumption that its support will come as the plan unfolds, is questionable. The only reasonable departure might be if a foundation provided funds for, say, a five-year experiment with a major new program, the cost of continuation of which the institution would absorb if the program proved to be effective. However, such grants should be accepted and used only in such a way that if the plan failed, the institution would not be burdened by even one additional professor with tenure or one additional regular administrative appointment. This criterion calls seriously into question widespread use of seed money grants for major new programs. Many such grants have either placed additional drain on institu-

tions' resources in the long run or have resulted in the termination of the program once the grant funds ended. As a general rule, large seed money grants for major program changes should be sought only if the institution can almost support the program without external help.

4. *Does the strategic plan have the sequence for the implementation of the plan clearly stated?* For example, is there clear indication of how and when coeducation is to be put into effect, as well as the cost and expected results of each step? Does the plan indicate the conditions that would force retreat from the plan? For example, if new programs for nontraditional students are to be a major part of a strategic plan, are certain conditions specified which if not met would warrant an immediate retreat? This is a difficult criterion to put into effect, because retreat from a widely publicized new program may have serious adverse consequences for an institution's image. However, that risk must be run. If a two-year women's college decides to become a four-year institution, the plan to do so should carry with it a date by which a certain percentage of entering freshmen will finish the fourth year and receive the bachelor's degree. If that goal is not realized, the institution should be prepared to reassert its concern for two-year students while accommodating a marginal bachelor's degree program.

5. *Have the various things that could prevent the success of the plan been made explicit and countered with persuasive evidence?* In general, academic planners have been optimists and, in the 1960s, with some reason. However, it is urged that a more pessimistic posture be adopted, a sort of academic Murphy's Law—that every conceivable difficulty will in fact present itself. This need not create an impasse. Decisions must be made. But the search for weaknesses should lead to thoughts about overcoming them.

6. *Is the plan clearly an extension of the institution's tradition? Or if it represents a break, do the potential gains clearly surpass the potential losses?* Although a church-related institution may experience short-run gains by ending denominational ties, it may lose in the long run because it has become uncomfortable for its traditional clientele.

7. *If the plan does call for sacrifice of some programs and individuals, have the full consequences been weighed?* That is, if a

music department is no longer needed and faculty members are to be terminated, have all moral, legal, and economic consequences been examined and is the institution prepared to accept them?

8. *Is the plan in essence a simple, uncomplicated one?* An axiom of the military is that in war everything should be simple but the simple is always difficult. A strategic plan that calls for a major shift in institutional emphasis, creation of many new and complicated programs, adoption of new modes for the delivery of services, recruitment of new kinds of students, and implementation of new sorts of institutional relationships, all at the same time, is likely to fail because of its sheer complexity. To illustrate this point, a suggested plan of change for a two-year women's college to become a four-year institution is presented:

- Goal: a four-year institution with 50 percent of freshmen staying four years—to be achieved within ten years
    Year 1. Announce the change, recruit students, and begin curricular planning.
    Year 2. Intensify recruitment, continue curricular planning, and modify rules of student conduct.
    Year 3. Agree on faculty needs for the future, put limited number of upper-level courses into effect.
    Year 4. Begin scheduling faculty to accommodate bachelor's candidates and begin self-study to gain accreditation of the bachelor's program.
    Year 5. Continue faculty rebuilding, finish self-study, and announce final evaluation of the plan.
    Years 6, 7, 8. Plan a more carefully articulated curriculum, examine and rectify weaknesses, and intensify recruitment.
    Years 9, 10. Evaluate fully and decide whether or not to continue.

Effects of Planning

As implied, planning will almost always originate with administration. It must, however, quickly involve faculty in setting institutional goals and priorities, examining various alternative

courses of action, making definite recommendations regarding decisions, and having knowledge of all decisions once they are made.

Planning itself cannot produce wonders nor, indeed, can it
be expected to save institutions from problems, crises, or even ex-
tinction. However, planning does have value. It can help and it
does warrant reasonable financial support, even if a truly workable
plan is not produced.

First of all, planning is an admirable device for socializing
individuals and helping to create a sense of community. The vast
majority of institutional expenditures are fixed and do not vary
much from year to year. Salaries, physical plant maintenance, and,
when appropriate, debt payment absorb the bulk of available resources. Thus, there can be no sudden substantive changes. Yet the
discussions that take place between October and April regarding
the budget represent an ideal means by which people are encouraged to talk with each other about the purposes of the institution, individual problems, and institutional well-being. It is that
sort of sustained discussion that contributes to academic effective
citizenship.

Second, thoughtful planning and wide dissemination of results can be a means by which institutions, or systems of institutions,
maintain some degree of autonomy and restrain somewhat the
direct operation of political forces on the academic establishment.
Thus, the institution that accumulates impressive and good data
and displays these candidly is likely to be less vulnerable to political,
legislative, or agency intrusion than the institution that appears
secretive or whose officials appear to lack requisite information.
Impressive evidence skillfully displayed can be a powerful indicator
that the institution knows what it is doing and is trying to be accountable to the public. As a generalization, it appears likely that
every major new encroachment on institutional autonomy has
stemmed directly from administration action that was perceived as
seriously in error or administration ignorance of essential kinds of
information.

Third, planning has a therapeutic effect. Much of what
happens to higher education is accidental and irrational. Men and
women trained to believe that organizations are highly rational enterprises are likely to become anxious in the face of the unexpected

and the irrational. Among other things, a planning and managing system that has been maintained over time produces a collective memory. Awareness of vicissitudes of the past can make changes currently being experienced less frightening. For example, during the early 1970s, people talked of the steady state in higher education as though it were a unique and cataclysmic event. What many forgot was that between 1952 and 1958 and between 1930 and 1939, higher education experienced steady or declining states. In both earlier periods, enrollments declined, financial resources dwindled, professionals were out of work, and public regard seemed to deteriorate. While those episodes of the past do not present solutions, they do provide perspective—an essential ingredient in facing change with equanimity.

Fourth, planning and managerial processes cultivate institutional soil out of which can spring the unexpected new idea that makes life more interesting and, conceivably, more effective.

Intensive planning activities should produce a modification of shared values which can then be made into an ideological statement by the chief executive of the institution. This urges that an institutional plan should not be entirely a collective effort. Collective effort produces the raw material out of which the chief executive officer fashions a statement as close to consensus as possible.

Further Readings

Contemporary interest in planning is equal to that shown with respect to management, and the literature concerning it is also bimodal. Much of the material is cliché ridden but some writings are remarkably effective. Among the latter, Grinold and his associates document how a sophisticated planning model can actually be used in a complex university, and Millett provides a reasonable outline of the planning process that can actually be put into effect by most institutions.

DRESCH, S. P. "A Critique of Planning Models for Postsecondary Education: Current Feasibility, Potential Relevance and Prospectus for Future Research." *Journal of Higher Education,* 1974, *46* (3), 245–286.

DRESSEL, P. L., AND ASSOCIATES. *Institutional Research in the University: A Handbook.* San Francisco: Jossey-Bass, 1971.

GRINOLD, R. C., HOPKINS, D. S. P., AND MASSY, W. F. "A Model for Long-Range University Budget Planning Under Uncertainty." *Bell Journal of Economics,* 1978, 9 (2).

HUDSPETH, D. R. *A Long-Range Planning Tool for Education: The Focused Delphi.* Albany: New York State Education Department, 1970.

MILLETT, J. D. *Planning in Higher Education.* Washington, D.C.: Academy for Educational Development, 1977.

Organization for Economic Cooperation and Development. *Methods and Statistical Needs for Educational Planning.* Washington, D.C.: Organization for Economic Cooperation and Development, 1967a.

Organization for Economic Cooperation and Development. *Social Objectives in Educational Planning.* Washington, D.C.: Organization for Economic Cooperation and Development, 1967b.

ORWIG, M. D., JONES, P. K., AND LENNING, O. T. *Enrollment Projection Models for Institutional Planning.* ACT Research Report No. 48. Iowa City, Iowa: American College Testing Program, 1972.

PALOLA, E. G., LEHMANN, T., AND BLESCIIKE, W. R. *Higher Education By Design: The Sociology of Planning.* Berkeley: Center for Research and Development in Higher Education, University of California, 1970.

PALOLA, E. G., AND PADGETT, W. *Planning for Self Renewal: A New Approach to Planned Organizational Change.* Berkeley: Center for Research and Development in Higher Education, University of California, 1971.

SANDIN, R. T. *Power and Purpose in Collegiate Government: Role of the Faculty in Academic Planning.* Toledo, Ohio: Center for the Study of Higher Education, University of Toledo, 1969.

SMART, J. C., AND MONTGOMERY, J. R. (Eds.). *New Directions for Institutional Research: Examining Departmental Management,* no. 10. San Francisco: Jossey-Bass, 1976.

WEATHERSBY, G. B., AND WEINSTEIN, M. C. "A Structural Comparison of Analytic Models for University Planning." Berkeley: Ford Foundation Program for Research in University Administration, University of California, 1970.

Chapter 6

ᚼᚼᚼᚼᚼᚼᚼ

Emphasizing a Distinctive Educational Mission

In order to attract the kinds of students they wish to serve, institutions are frequently urged to develop a unique mission and statements of purpose consistent with that mission. Such urgings are reinforced by examples of institutions that have succeeded because they were able to find a clear-cut and unique purpose. Berea College in Kentucky has long devoted its attention to the youth of Appalachia and has achieved an enviable record of success in doing so. St. John's College in Maryland has also, in recent times, served a small but distinctive clientele with its prescribed program based on great works of Western Civilization. Virginia Military Institute leaves little doubt as to its purpose and the kind of student who would most profit from attending. Other old and established institutions whose missions evolved gradually, reinforced by traditions and the expectations of alumni, have faced enrollment and financial difficulties successfully—among them, even lesser-known colleges standing in the conservative, evangelical Protestant tradition. By the same token, institutions whose difficulties have continued are typically either new institutions that have not had time to develop an image or those older institutions that have tried to serve whichever students wished to attend.

The question is whether institutions, through reasonably rational means, can decide on a unique mission and create workable mechanisms to achieve it in a relatively short period of time. The task of doing so is difficult, and there are many more examples of efforts that failed than of those that succeeded. However, examining a few efforts may suggest tactics and conditions that might be considered by institutions seeking distinctiveness as a means of ensuring survival.

Examples of Distinctiveness

One institution that is attempting to create a new image with which to face the future is the University of Southern California (U.S.C.). It is an example particularly rich in lessons and principles from each of three major periods in its development. U.S.C. opened its doors in 1880 and, after flirting with the idea of expanding rapidly into centers throughout the state, hit upon a mission that would cater to the needs of southern California. It early placed emphasis on the professional schools and soon began to produce the majority of the doctors, lawyers, dentists, engineers, businessmen, and, eventually, teachers and school administrators practicing in southern California. The professional education offered was down-to-earth applied education with little or no concern for research, scholarship, or theoretical issues in the professions. The university also maintained a number of departments in arts and sciences whose members had little inclination to engage in research or graduate work. As the professional schools succeeded in producing applied professionals, a self-renewing process began, with graduates contributing to the alma mater that had launched them on their careers. Such contributions, plus tuition from newly rich southern California parents, provided the cash flow that enabled the president and a conservative board of trustees to create a policy still adhered to of never operating with a deficit and, when possible, of laying by reserves.

In 1958, a new president was appointed who undertook many things. He created the Master Plan and raised the money to build over forty new buildings. He evolved a highly successful development program which, year after year, generated needed operating funds and surpluses as well. He also made key decanal appointments which would eventually become the means for a major institutional shift in direction. And there were important things not done. During the 1960s, perhaps sensing that the time was not yet ripe, U.S.C. refrained from the intense competition for high-priced faculty. Appointments were relatively young; hence, by the end of the 1960s, U.S.C. was not constrained by a high proportion of older, tenured faculty whose salaries could drain an institution's budget. Nor did the president and the board of trustees relinquish administrative power to the faculty and the deans. U.S.C. was, during the 1960s, still a highly centralized institution, a fact that is clearly involved in the strong financial condition of the university: It is almost axiomatic that a strong faculty role in decision making is typically inflationary with respect to an institution's expenditures. An additional element was that, during the 1960s, students were also controlled by comparatively strict regulations, which may have prevented the outbursts of student dissent found at other California universities. This, in turn, may have been the factor in the steady increases in contributions from southern California wealth. Endowment jumped from under $10 million to close to $100 million.

The 1970s saw U.S.C. begin still a third period of development. As a regional university, it had grown in size, wealth, and regional influence. But it decided that its real future lay with the national arena, academic instruction, and graduate education and research. Thus, with ample reserves, it began to recruit star faculty members, seek research contracts, and undergrid its professional fields with research and theory. But it did so prudently. It continued to expand its traditional concern for vocational preparation and entered into continuing education in a major way. While it strengthened on-campus doctoral work, it also developed off-campus applied doctoral programs. It recognized the relationship between undergraduate tuition and economic solvency, and so allowed its undergraduate enrollment to increase and sought larger numbers of undergraduates having state scholarships or Basic Education Opportunity Grants. Although expanding undergraduate enrollments may have diluted the academic quality of the student body, it has made possible the expansion in graduate education and research. In this same connection, U.S.C. has actively recruited foreign students from South America, Asia, and more recently, the Middle East—students who typically do not need financial aid.

The University of Southern California may not achieve its avowed new goal of entering the first ranks of American universities. The times may be wrong. But it does stand as an amazingly well conducted institution. U.S.C. has changed over time but at no time has it changed in a radical way or sought impossible dreams:

1. It began its history by meeting definite community needs and it has never departed from that role.
2. It began operation with the conservative budget policy of no deficits and it has maintained that posture.
3. It began with strong central administrative control and still functions with a much stronger presidency than do other comparable institutions.
4. When it started to change direction, it first changed key administrator leadership and only gradually extended those changes downward to the faculty.
5. It appears to have been highly pragmatic about such matters as selective admissions, preferring increased enrollments and tuition to a more able but largely subsidized student body.
6. Many of its leaders would like U.S.C. to be regarded as an equal of Stanford or Berkeley but not badly enough to jeopardize the traditional strengths of the institution—service to the various professional fields, cultivation of the benefits of big-time football, and fiscal conservatism.

A second example of an institution with a distinct mission is a private liberal arts college located in a small town in the Middle West. During the 1950s, this college had enjoyed a modest success by stressing intercollegiate athletics and by appealing for support to the big business community in its region through a policy of questioning the use of public funds by private institutions. That particular pattern, which succeeded well for the two decades of growth of American higher education, proved inadequate to sustain the college during the seventies as private higher education everywhere began to experience difficulties. Intercollegiate athletics had come to be counterproductive as the school spent almost a fourth of its budget to enable it to compete with much larger institutions throughout the country. Winning football games in California may have made the athletic department feel good but it did not attract the loyalty of local alumni or the attention of the prospective regional students whose enrollment was essential for institutional survival. Enrollments began to drop, and a rather ineffective admissions office seemed powerless to reverse the tide. A local corporation had donated funds for the creation of a conference center which was intended to attract business conferences of all sorts and, indirectly, more undergraduate enrollments as parents of prospective students came to know the institution. The conference center had not become self-supporting, however, and was really a drain on the operating budget of the institution. The president had been in office twenty years and, in the pursuit of those activities that had succeeded in the past, had split the faculty and administration into two warring factions: the athletically minded on one side and the academic minded on the other. To the credit of the president, he sensed that his leadership might have become obsolete and so asked to be relieved of presidential duties. He was granted the title of chancellor and was given space on campus with secretarial help and a rather substantial salary to continue until a college-purchase annuity began to function. The arrangement proved to be a financial drain as well as an opportunity for the former president to continue to influence decisions, especially those that pertained to the conference center.

The newly appointed president, a highly talented and articulate young man holding distinctive political and economic views, sensed that a distinct mission for the institution was essential if enrollments, outside support, and public regard were to be generated sufficiently to sustain the college. He also sensed the conditions that would be necessary to achieve true distinctiveness: First, the mission would have to be consistent with the president's own philosophy as well as being reasonably consistent with at least some of the institution's traditions. Second, it would have to appeal to the likely clientele of the college—that is, to the children of the middle- and upper-middle-class business and financial community in the state, particularly in a large metropolitan area. Third, it would have to appeal to possible benefactors, whose help was essential for the survival of a college unwilling to secure public funds. And, fourth, it would require support from the faculty and administration.

In line with these conditions, the college was to become a center for a distinct ideology stressing the virtues of capitalism and the free enterprise system and preparing the young to enter into and to support that system. The steps the president took to achieve that mission were important. He first commissioned an outside management study that would recommend on the many malfunctions of the institution. These were obvious to him, as they would be to any competent consultant, but recommendations made by a consultant with no ax to grind would be better received by the board of trustees. The study was made, and the obvious recommendations were made and put into effect. The role of the chancellors was to become strictly honorific. Athletics were to be deemphasized and those administrative officers not in favor of deemphasis encouraged to leave. The conference center was to be kept on a self-supporting basis or, if that failed, was to be converted into additional space for the residential academic program. The admissions office was to be strengthened with a new director and an enlarged staff, the members of which would concentrate on relatively wealthy communities.

Central to the distinctiveness of the college was to be a center, which would be lodged in the conference center, that would do several things. It would bring speakers and scholars to the campus to conduct seminars, participate in conferences, and interact with students. These well-publicized events would attract the attention of the community and would assure parents of prospective students about the nature of the education offered. The president himself undertook a personal program of speaking and writing for a national audience, addressing himself to a number of issues and linking the name of the college with the particular point of view he espoused. He made it clear that support for the college and its center was a definite contribution to the fight against big government, deficit spending, relativist systems of values, and ever-increasing publicly supported social programs.

As this is written, the long-term future of this college may still be uncertain. The president reports that the college remains virtually full, with a satisfying admissions program drawing from a national clientele. The modest endowment has tripled, and the academic standards have shown steady improvement. For the short term, the results are impressive. The enrollment decline has been stopped, and the financial affairs of the college put in order. The college has achieved the image it desired and for which it planned.

Several principles seem to be involved here. First, the distinctive mission was based in the institution's own tradition. Although a radical departure from the past will usually fail, the mission of this college had appeal to segments of the population clearly relevant to the needs of the college—parents who could afford tuition and donors who could contribute to a college in whose ideas they believed.

Second, the president had a clear notion of what he wanted, the ability to communicate his ideas to others, and the determination to eliminate those who might subvert the achievement of those ideas. This may sound a bit strong. It is frequently argued that institutional strength and ability to survive is a product of diversity of opinion and freedom to dissent. But there may be times when unanimous support of a point of view is essential, and people who cannot embrace that point of view should leave rather than jeopardize efforts to change. When one examines institutions that have made major successful changes to ensure vitality and viability, it is found that, almost invariably, those who strongly opposed the changes have been replaced.

Third, and finally, appropriate symbols were also important. The center may not have had much real impact on the academic lives of undergraduate students but it did symbolize ideas of im-

portance to relevant constituencies. In a similar way, the $115 mil-
lion, two-mile-long linear accelerator at Stanford symbolized the
entry of that institution into big science.

Examples of Loss of Identity

Remaining faithful to a viable tradition appears the safest
cause to follow, based on the experience of some institutions that
have been tempted to depart from historic missions in an effort to
survive—typically with less than happy results. By and large, radical shift in style, purpose, or clientele has not proven easy to accomplish or particularly satisfactory. These difficulties are well revealed by the example of Lone Mountain College in San Francisco.
Until the mid 1960s, this college had been conducted by the Sisters
of the Sacred Heart to prepare young Catholic women from the
middle and upper-middle classes of San Francisco. The curriculum
was relatively pure liberal arts, stressing languages, music, the fine
arts, and those other subjects needed by cultured young women.
Then came the spirit of change in Catholic life and education generated by Vatican II, the moral dilemmas generated by the Civil
Rights Movement and the war in Vietnam, and a decline in the
student enrollment not unrelated to the expansion of the California
State College system and the University of California. These forces
and factors led the leadership of the school to seek to be of service
to people never before served, to make the curriculum more relevant
to changing conditions in urban America, and to increase enrollments by bringing new kinds of students to the campus. During a
few years of almost frenzied change, academic requirements were
freed and faculty encouraged to develop whatever kinds of new
courses or activities they wished, the institution became coeducational, and various sorts of outreach programs were developed. An
image of high innovativeness was projected that did attract some
external support but did not attract sustained enrollment of tuition-
paying undergraduate students to be educated by the resident
faculty trained in the liberal arts and sciences.

By the fall of 1977, Lone Mountain College had changed
so much that little save the actual physical plant remained of the
original institution. The religious order, although maintaining an

interest in the school and helping with its financing, had divested itself of all control in favor of a lay board of trustees. A completely new secular administration had been appointed, consisting of a president and vice-presidents for academic affairs, student affairs, finance, and development. The faculty had become unionized, and the union was trying to negotiate a contract, a task made more difficult by a deteriorating financial situation. There were a variety of on- and off-campus programs for many specialized groups, none of which appeared sufficiently strong to help maintain the total institution. The enrollment in the residential bachelor's program was small, and the need for such traditional liberal arts programs as mathematics had disappeared. On- and off-campus enrollments combined produced some 900 FTE students having available 42 different graduate and undergraduate programs.

With all of this activity, the institution projected an operating deficit for the academic year. The new president and his associates were determined to try to reverse the deteriorating situation. They failed, however, and Lone Mountain College closed in June 1978. This ultimate failure resulted from a number of questionable assumptions and some equally questionable practices. The first assumption is one that a number of troubled institutions are making. It is that, in some way or other, new kinds of students, especially minority group members, will be able to pay enough tuition to sustain the programs created for them. The reasoning is that the various state and federal programs of student support will provide enough revenue to maintain the institution. This is related to the assumption that innovative new programs will attract new students to replace those no longer interested in the traditional undergraduate program in the liberal arts and sciences. These two assumptions have produced many new and, for the most part, discrete programs taught by part-time or adjunct faculty. Although the successful ones have generated enough revenue to pay salaries (there were over 400 different individuals paid instructional salaries in the academic year 1976–77), the income has been insufficient to provide the needed administrative support, maintain the physical plant, or retire the debt. Thus, the more program activity, the worse the financial condition of the institution.

In retrospect, several observations can be made about the

case of Lone Mountain College. The institution shifted from its traditional role partly for ideological reasons but partly because of decline in traditional student enrollment. It might have been better for the faculty and administration to have focused on improving that traditional enrollment, rather than questing after new students. They might have failed, but observers believe that there were enough traditional potential students in the greater San Francisco area who might have enrolled had their needs, interests, and dissatisfaction been given explicit attention through such acts as modifying regulation of personal conduct. In addition, although the movement toward lay boards of trustees has been urged for Catholic institutions of higher education, that may not always be sound policy. Had, for example, the religious order maintained control of the college, both at the policy and administrative levels, a mechanism would have been available to strengthen the traditional role of the college. Certainly, it is difficult to conceive of the institution as having been in a condition worse than it actually achieved after secularization.

Another women's college in the West is a classic case of confused identity produced by several changes in mission. This is an institution whose leadership has been dedicated and well meaning and which has served some constituencies well. It presents an appearance of collegiate tranquillity, but its optimism regarding the rewards from major institutional change has been warranted typically only in the short run.

Since its opening at the turn of the century, the college has struggled to achieve a viable identity that would attract enough students to keep the place open. It opened as a four-year college but with a preparatory department. When it became clear that the college lacked the resources to be an acceptable bachelor's degree-granting institution, it became a two-year junior college. In the late 1950s, when the private two-year college began to experience competition from the lower-cost public two-year colleges and from the expanding state universities, and when foundations made grants to four-year but not two-year institutions, it once again became a four-year institution. When its ever-present financial problems appeared soluble through a substantial gift obtained at the price of a name change, it assumed a new name, in much the same way as

Trinity College became Duke University. When the anticipated funds proved not to be forthcoming and the name itself proved to be a detriment, it changed its name back to its original designation.

Although the college was able over time to produce an attractive campus, its very existence has always been insecure as enrollments fluctuated in response to even minor changes in the economy or other world and social conditions. Its many efforts to establish an endowment base for the institution failed, as did its efforts to maintain a stable program of annual giving. As it was typically successful in raising only part of the funds needed to construct new buildings, the institution seemed always to have to carry a heavy debt-service load and to pay for its buildings out of operating funds, usually in short supply.

As the college entered the decade of expansion of higher education in the United States (1957–1968), it did so from a temporarily stable financial condition. Its physical plant was reasonably complete for its enrollment. Its debt was down to $100,000, and its retiring president had at least pointed out the need for improvement of faculty salaries. In 1957, the college appointed, as so many other colleges were doing, an expansionist-minded president who, sensing the profound changes in store for American higher education, decided that the institution would be an active participant in them. To prepare for that future, he caused an intensive self-study to be made by the college that would become the base for a decade of development. He urged that the institution reestablish its four-year character. He retained the services of one of the nation's most respected educational consultants. He sought to upgrade the quality of students by requiring SAT scores for admission and by raising the grade point average required for graduation. He sought, but without great success, to increase endowment and annual giving and, at the same time, to improve faculty strength and salaries. And he also, in anticipation of larger enrollments, embarked on a building program made possible partly through gifts and partly through loans.

In short, the president, with the best of motives and intentions, led this college through exactly the same scenario as was being played in hundreds of private liberal arts colleges throughout the country: increased student selectivity made possible by a gen-

eral undercapacity for college students, anticipated steady enrollment increases based on assumptions of continued high birth rates,
added physical plant made possible by federal loan policies, and
increased faculty salaries mandated by increased demand for faculty
services. This combination of factors contributed significantly to the
financial plight of many private institutions in the 1970s. Increased
capacity and gradually declining demand made rationing of college
attendance based on aptitude more and more difficult. Increased
expenses for such things as faculty salaries forced tuition up, while
tuition remained low in improved public institutions. Eventually
then, enrollments were affected and began to decline, thus restrict-
ing the funds available to pay off mortgages on residence halls, new
libraries, and learning centers.

To these burdens, this college added still another. A business-
man offered a gift of many millions of dollars in return for which
the college would rename itself after him. The offer was accepted
and plans made to enjoy the sudden new prosperity. Overnight, the
college had become one of the best-endowed small institutions in the
country. However, reality proved to be different. Most of the funds
would not be available until after the death of the donor and his
wife, both of whom were in vibrant good health. Other potential
benefactors for the college withdrew, either out of conviction that
the college no longer needed their support or because they did not
like the donor.

From the date of the name change on, the fortunes of the
college declined to such an extent that when the president resigned
there was a $2.5 million accumulated deficit and an equally serious
decline in enrollment. With enrollment declines came faculty retrenchment, leaving a residue of the more lackluster faculty members
with low morale and no ability or resources with which to build
attractive new programs. For a short time, the college actually
closed its doors, after a reversion to its original name had failed to
stop the erosion. It was, however, reopened after board members and
the surrounding community generated the needed saving resources.
For the next eighteen months it survived and sought to chart a workable course out of its difficulties.

Since that time, a number of events can be recounted, although no plan or pattern is discernible. A new president was ap-

pointed who concentrated on broad external affairs. The board also appointed an executive vice-president, experienced in financial management but not in collegiate administration. This structure did not work, so, after a year in office, the president resigned and was replaced by the executive vice-president. The new president, the fourth in twelve years, attempted many things. To improve faculty morale, 10 percent salary raises were budgeted for academic year 1978–79. An admissions officer was recruited from a career in public relations; this person promised 300 new students for the fall of 1978. A director of development was obtained on loan from a local corporation and charged with organizing a development program. An acting academic dean was made academic dean but without being given a clear mandate to bring internal campus affairs to order. The president herself has used her considerable charm and ability to solidify relationships with the board of trustees, cultivate potential sources of funds, and put out public relations brush fires. She has also involved herself in many details of the academic program. This last is difficult to do in any rational or systematic way because the governance structure of the institution appears to be in shambles. The total faculty is the basic unit, and there are committees on the curriculum, professional status of the faculty, and resources allocation. There are also academic departments. However, as is true of so many similar institutions, decisions are actually made by the president, with the sometime advice of chief administrative subordinates. The president has also tried to formalize a statement of purpose that will stress the education of women and will position the institution to attract women who would not be inclined to apply to Catholic women's colleges, the Seven Sisters, or the few still operating two-year finishing-school sort of institutions.

It is difficult to predict the future of this college. Faculty morale has improved. There is a program for mature women that generates almost half the total enrollment. The president is skeptically optimistic. The board of trustees is involved. And early application rates are up a bit.

Whether the college succeeds or fails, it presents a number of lessons. The first of these is the danger of expansionism without an adequate base upon which to build. Nothing in the history of the college indicated capacity to grow in size, quality, and mission in ways that were attempted during the 1960s. But the prevailing bull market of that decade made the gamble irresistible. Similar temptations of the 1980s to enter many new markets for new kinds of students, but without an adequate base, could well lead to even deeper trouble rather than to salvation.

Then too, the institution possibly hurt its chances for long-term survival and growth by its frequent changes of image and mission. Starting as a four-year church-related college, changing to a two-year church-related college, loosening ties with the church, changing to a four-year secular college, changing its name and then changing its name again may have contributed to the temporary closing of its doors in 1976. The institution simply could not stand the shock.

Strong collegiate institutions, for the most part, manifest a remarkably stable image, and even not so strong but quite viable institutions retain a long-term consistency of purpose. This clearly suggests that a change of mission in quest of new students should be attempted only with extreme caution and with sufficient resources. As in the two cases just discussed, the examples of Antioch and Stephens reinforce the view that the weaker institutions had better make their stands on what they have been.

Antioch College developed a distinctive saga during the 1920s, 1930s, and 1940s, the elements of which were community governance, cooperative work study, academic rigor, general education, and political and social liberalism (Clark, 1970). Then, during the late 1960s, motivated by exactly the same pressures that powered the changes in Lone Mountain College, Antioch created a network of centers and campuses designed to serve new kinds of students. The economic condition of the entire institution has been deteriorating since, and as this is written, the institution must seriously consider its possible demise. Stephens College similarly changed from its historic mission of being a two-year college for women that stressed counseling and advising, occupational preparation, elements of high culture, and preparation of young women for a liberated but still traditional female role. In the mid 1960s, the institution became a four-year liberal arts college and sought to compete with the strong liberal arts colleges of the Midwest. Having abandoned most of the practices of the past, it began to experience enrollment problems, even at a time when other institutions were growing and developing financial reserves. One can only speculate on what the situation might have been had Stephens remained loyal to its earlier, successful style.

Both Stephens and Antioch argued that the changes were consistent with their past images: for Antioch its liberal traditions, and for Stephens its concern for the education of women. But for each that was only one element of tradition, and in retrospect not the most important. What seems to be necessary is for an institution to identify the major elements of its traditional mission as a basis for making decisions for the future. Thus, Dartmouth correctly decided that its essential character embraced a residential situation, academic rigor rooted in the liberal arts and sciences, and a high degree of interaction between an able faculty and an equally able student body. As long as these remained strong and vital, the college could and did become coeducational with no serious problems.

Identifying a Valid Mission

The problem is how to identify the true mission of an institution. Certainly, looking to formal statements of purpose and mission contained in the college catalogue is not of much help. As a general rule, such statements vary little from one institution to another. They seem to be so broad that any kind of prospective student can read them and conclude that the institution is tailored for his or her unique needs. A better way to determine the true character of an institution is to examine it candidly. Questions such as the following should be asked and answered: Over time, what sorts of students have actually enrolled and remained to graduate? What sorts of faculty accepted appointment and remained on contract as compared with those who refused appointment or who left after only a few years? What do alumni seem to value from their college experience, and what kinds of people contribute to the institution and for what reasons? Such information should be interpreted prudently, of course, because slavish adherence to the past could prove to be foolish. However, not to consider the past could be even more unwise.

To be quite practical, how might an institution seeking to

decide its posture for the future proceed to determine what it really is? First, the best evidence regarding students, faculty, friends, and alumni should be accumulated. Then outsiders should be invited to observe and report. For example, an anthropologist, an ecologist, a cartoonist, and several educational consultants might each be invited to spend a week on campus. They would be asked to look, listen, read, participate, and then report on what they perceived, as experienced observers can frequently see reality more clearly than can those who experience it daily and over time. Next this accumulated information should be discussed by the entire faculty, first in small groups at the department level and then in larger meetings. The faculty should attempt to answer the question "What is the essence of our institution?" The answers should probably not be made in the form of an elaborate report, although some documentation is necessary. Rather the discussions should provide the context in which actual policy decisions are made regarding such matters as budget projections, new buildings, admissions standards, and whether or not to enter new markets.

Chapter Five presented some specific outlines for long-range planning. To the extent possible, that information might also be made available in the discussions of institutional essence or mission. But again, following those suggested steps and accumulating good planning information will not lead to broad policy decisions that will determine institutional destiny. Policy decisions are made regarding specific issues but are conditioned by shared beliefs as to what an institution is. In this connection, several principles should be followed:

1. The president and administrative associates have definite responsibilities for institutional mission. However, they should not trust, nor be allowed to trust, their own intuitions. The ideal situation is for a strong president who well understands an institution to be checked and balanced by a strong faculty, board, and alumni. In so many of the institutions that made radical changes which then led to difficulties, the president or the board of trustees or both exercised far too much solitary discretion. A touchstone might be that in a critical board-of-trustee decision concerning a major departure from tradition (assuming that there had been

broad and deep discussion), the president would not be able to guess in advance what the outcome might be. This is different from board actions on normal operating decisions. In those situations, the president should know with considerable certainty what the board actions will be.

2. Alumni relations pose a delicate problem. As a general rule, alumni should have a voice, but not a determining voice in institutional policy. The presence of alumni representatives on boards of trustees is an effective technique. However, alumni feelings as to the essence of institutional mission are important and should be sought. No major shift in institutional direction should be attempted without alumni judgment.

3. With respect to any major shift in institutional direction and mission, a conservative posture should prevail. That is, discussions should be premised on the notion that in the absence of overwhelming and persuasive evidence to the contrary, the status quo will be maintained. This is not easy to accomplish in true situations of crisis or near crisis proportions, when there is the temptation to try anything. Yet it is in those moments of crisis that perspective is most needed.

4. Relatedly, institutions should resist embracing new trends even if there are successful examples to emulate. The trends, all too likely, will turn out to be fads. Or if they are valid developments, the conditions of the institution in which the change was made are certain to be different. Thus, change to coeducation, or merger, or enrolling new types of students may work well in specific institutions but not in most others. The successful history of American higher education in the large and influential institutions has been one of gradual evolution. That seems likely to be true in the future.

Further Readings

One of the major generalizations from this study is the value to an institution of a long, well-established image which, over time, attracts loyalty, students, and resources. The dynamics of such image building are well elaborated by both Meyer and Clark. The big question is whether institutions not having a well-established charter or saga can, under vexing circumstances, actually create one. The literature is silent on this subject.

CLARK, B. R. *The Distinctive College: Antioch, Reed, and Swarthmore.* Chicago: Aldine, 1970.

KEETON, M. T. *Models and Mavericks: A Profile of Private Liberal Arts Colleges.* New York: McGraw-Hill, 1971.

MEYER, J. W. "The Charter: Conditions of Diffuse Socialization in Schools." In W. R. Scott (Ed.), *Social Processes and Social Structures.* New York: Holt, Rinehart and Winston, 1970.

MEYER, J. W. "The Effects of the Institutionalization of Colleges in Society." In K. A. Feldman (Ed.), *College and Student: A Sourcebook in the Social Psychology of Education.* New York: Pergamon Press, 1972.

MEYER, J. W., AND ROWAN, B. "Notes on the Structure of Educational Organizations." Unpublished paper, Stanford University, 1975.

SELZNICK, D. *Leadership in Administration.* New York: Harper & Row, 1957.

WEICK, K. E. "Enactment Processes in Organizations." In B. M. Stow and G. R. Salanik (Eds.), *New Directions in Organizational Behavior.* Chicago: St. Clair Press, 1977.

Chapter 7

꙰꙰꙰꙰꙰꙰꙰

Upgrading Recruitment and Admissions Procedures

Collegiate institutional health and, ultimately, survival depend on enrollment and the tuition income or enrollment-based appropriations it generates. In spite of platitudes to the contrary which say that college students do not pay the full cost of their education, in most small, private liberal arts colleges, they do. In 1969–70, for example, tuition and fees in forty-eight small colleges totaled $135,651,000 and the cost of instruction was $97,752,000 (Jenny and Wynn, 1972, p. 9). If the state or district can be considered as a student surrogate, the full cost of education is paid, based on enrollment. The critical problem that must be solved is how to maintain or increase enrollment and, if upward limits are reached, how to keep income and expenditure in balance. The increase in

153

faculty salaries, expansion of physical plant and library holdings, and accumulation of reserves, which took place during the 1960s, were produced chiefly through doubling of enrollment and tuition, a phenomenon made possible because of earlier increased birth rates and rising expectations.

As institutions face the 1980s, during which there will be an absolute drop in enrollments of the normal college group of somewhere between one-half million and possibly two million students, they must in some way or other maintain or increase institutional enrollment or radically increase endowment and external income. Failing this, they must decrease programs consistent with decreased enrollment. This chapter addresses the problem of how enrollment can be maintained or increased.

Enrollment is clearly related to the broad mission that institutions set for themselves, although very likely not to the details of institutional statements of purpose or goals. Historically, for example, black, single-sex, graduate school preparatory, evangelical Protestant, or vocationally focused institutions cater to and attract quite specific clientele. To the extent that an institution does have a distinctive purpose and there is a large enough pool of college-age youth having the ability to pay tuitions and fees, survival and even health of the institution is reasonably secure. Thus, in a national, regional, state, or community complex, institutions properly struggle to find a distinctive position that will appeal to a certain segment of that total population. This struggle is clearly evidenced in Boston as institutions such as Northeastern, Boston University, Tufts, and, to some extent, Boston College seek an identity that allows them to compete with the pace-setting Harvard or M.I.T.

That search for identity must involve keeping in mind some or all of the major reasons why people attend college.

Reasons for Attending College

In the United States, young people have historically enrolled in collegiate institutions and continue to enroll for any or all of several reasons. Institutions that wish to enroll students must be able to respond to these reasons, even though responses to some must be camouflaged to protect both individual and institutional self-esteem.

Neither individuals nor institutions like to recognize the fact that college attendance for some during the 1960s served as a sanctuary from the draft.

The first and most important reason for attending college is the belief that it improves one's economic chances. Colonial colleges served as a route to the clergy, the study of law, and positions of political and financial leadership. Early nineteenth-century colleges lost enrollments when it appeared that the expanding frontier offered better financial returns than did attending college. The surging collegiate enrollments of the 1960s can best be accounted for by the fact that two and one half decades of relative national affluence allowed an exceptionally large generation to aspire to even greater affluence and to see that the road to this led through college. College is still seen as providing either preparation for a job, a credential needed for a job, or an accepted reputation of capability to hold a job. No college can survive if this demand is not met.

Another reason is the social and family pressure to attend college because college is good—good in itself or for economic, social, or political reasons. This point is illustrated by the Colgate student who claimed he was at Colgate because it was the only place he could get into which his parents would not be ashamed to mention when asked where he was attending school. It is also illustrated by the young woman who, although quite successful in her career, felt unfulfilled without a bachelor's degree because her father, mother, brothers, aunts, and uncles all had at least that degree and three of those held the doctorate.

Closely entwined with such pressures is the belief that college provides those traits of language, knowledge, and style that indicate membership in the upper classes. First, the act of attending college itself is symbolic of the leisure to pursue the nonutilitarian. But more importantly, the essential literary quality of the majority of undergraduate courses develops the idiom of the upper classes. An outstanding example of the power of this motivation can be seen in the spectacular evolution of a small female seminary in an out-of-the-way town in Missouri into Stephens College—the largest two-year women's college in the nation during the 1930s. The transformation took place when a new president created a collegiate program that simultaneously accommodated several major reasons for college attendance. In two years, at half the cost of a four-year program, the college provided students with a degree (AA), preparation for a vocation, at least a superficial awareness of high culture and language, and, at the same time, facility in the class-related recreations of horsemanship, golf, swimming, and tennis. The young women who attended Stephens during its ascendancy as a two-year institution came from reasonably affluent families without a college-attending tradition. Fathers of Stephens students were typically salesmen, manufacturer's agents, and small business-men—not lawyers, doctors, or college professors.

Students also enroll in an undergraduate institution to find an environment in which several important traits or characteristics of adulthood can be cultivated. College attending has been, and continues to be, important for mate selection. Whether the institution is coeducational or single sex, it plays an important role in this regard. The female institution located in a remote place maintains ties with male institutions and, in effect, signals that its students are ready for marriage and, by subtle techniques, who are and are not suitable mates for its students. College attending is also seen as an important means for meeting new friends and for learning how to get along with them. In a sense, going to college (whether off to a residential college or to a nearby commuter institution) is an act of separating oneself from one's family and creating a new and adult identity. Study after study indicates that the most potent forces for change in students are their relationships and interactions with their peers.

The reasons cited thus far are economic, psychological, and sociological. But there are intellectual ones as well. Going to college is a way of learning some interesting things or of deepening knowledge of something in which an interest has already been developed. Before students actually enroll as freshmen, they typically rank this interest in things academic as one of the major determiners of their decision to go to college. And after they graduate and reflect on what they wish college had stressed more, they also rank acquisition of knowledge quite high.

Another important reason why people enroll in an under-graduate program is to obtain support for some other part of their lives or to find help in solving vexing personal problems. This may be a reason felt by students themselves, their parents, or other important adults. Thus, a church-related college may be seen as strengthening religious beliefs, and a small college as a sanctuary for a timid and introverted individual.

Then there are a cluster of reasons that might be classified as ulterior motives. These might include attending college to avoid the draft, or to obtain basic educational opportunity grants or veteran's benefits as primary income, or to postpone entry into the work force and the assumption of adult responsibilities.

Conditions Affecting College Choice

No one has been able to establish with any degree of certainty why students select a particular institution. It seems likely that the decision to attend a specific college is made with little precise information about it or about other alternative institutions. Whether the fault lies with students, their parents, their high school teachers and counselors, or the collegiate institutions themselves, the fact is that students know very little about what they are getting into. In spite of such ambiguity, there are some generally recognized factors that contribute either alone or in combination to the selection of a particular school. It should be pointed out that student academic aptitude and socioeconomic level are probably the most relevant of student characteristics. Students with high aptitude and economic status do behave differently from other groups with respect to selection of a college. They tend more frequently to select the prestigious private, selective, and high-cost institutions. However, that does not describe the vast majority of institutions or the students that they must attract in order to survive.

The first institutional characteristic that serves as a determinant is geographic location—that is, the closer the institution, the more likely that a student will select it. Some students, particularly among the able and affluent, can and do select institutions far distant from their home, but as a general rule, institutions located close to a heavy concentration of college-attending youth will suffer fewer enrollment problems than those located in more remote areas. This assumes, of course, that the geographic location itself does not have an unfavorable image.

Additionally, there is the matter of tuition and fees. Students are inclined to opt for the less expensive institutions unless they can see clear advantages from paying more, such as better job prospects or more amenities. This accounts for the phenomenon of those few high prestige places whose high tuition parents and students will pay because of the anticipated rewards. In general, it seems to be the annual cost, rather than the cost of a full degree, that is the determining factor. For example, the Raymond campus of the University of the Pacific allowed students to complete a bachelor's degree in three years at a saving of almost one quarter over comparable private institutions. Its annual tuition and fees were somewhat higher, however, because the academic year was somewhat longer, and it was the higher annual cost that the students eyed and resisted.

Related to cost and location is the matter of convenience. If the institution can create programs that are convenient to the needs of various groups of students, it is in a considerably better competitive position than if it forces students to conform to quite rigid requirements. The Cooperative Work-Study Program at Northeastern was designed for the convenience of students from the greater Boston area who wanted to attend college but who could not afford full tuition and full-time attendance. Recently, a few institutions have been created that offer absolutely prescribed curricula. They give no credit for work done elsewhere, even though a transfer student might have had junior standing. One cannot be sanguine that those institutions will become truly competitive.

Another factor in selection is whether the student believes he or she can likely be admitted. Students apparently give this matter some thought. For example, they apply to three selective institutions of the type they most desire and to one less selective institution as an insurance policy so they can be certain of at least one acceptance. There is, as many have observed, a great deal of self-selection in American higher education, and this self-selection takes well into consideration the chances for admission.

Another important element, probably of greater significance to four-year and private institutions, is the matter of traditional relationships with the institutions. A family tradition of attending, neighborhood or church customs, or the fact that graduates from one high school typically select one or two particular institutions, do have influence. Members of the Baptist church in Morgan Park, Illinois, at one time considered Denison University as a likely place for their children, and those who elected not to go there were expected to provide a good reason for going against that tradition.

Then there is the matter of the image and reputation of the institution, which may be athletic, academic, social, or religious. People do perceive institutions as being different, and although those perceptions may be wrong or imprecise, they help determine college choice. Included in the institutional reputation is student perception of their chances of getting a good job on graduation or of being admitted to a desired graduate or professional school. Folkways, for example, say go to Wooster if you want to get into medical school, and choose Virginia Military Institute if you want the regular Army and cannot get into West Point.

Obviously, students look to whether an institution offers the program they desire. But even here, the ignorance of some students concerning what an institution actually offers can sometimes be deep, as indicated by the inquiries to Princeton regarding its law school.

It is difficult to gauge how effective persuasion is, but it seems to be involved to a degree. It may be the urging of a teacher, parent, counselor, coach, or admissions officer that convinces a student that a particular institution is the one to attend.

Lastly, the matter of whim or accident should not be discounted. A student waits until late August, then sees his or her friends getting ready to attend a college and suddenly decides to join them. Another student, quite by accident, hears of a new program and decides at once that it is for him or her.

Meeting Student Requirements

The enrollment equation with which institutions will have to work must include balancing the reasons and conditions just discussed, namely:

1. *Reasons for attending college*
   * Job preparation and to increase income
   * Social pressure that college is good

- College symbolizes and facilitates upward social mobility
- To develop adult roles, styles, and relationships
- Intellectual curiosity
- To help solve deep personal problems
- Ulterior motives

2. *Conditions affecting choice of college*
   - Geographic location
   - Cost
   - Convenience
   - Tradition of relationships
   - Institutional reputation and image
   - Presence of desired program
   - Chances of gaining admission
   - Persuasion
   - Whim or accident

The Carnegie Foundation for the Advancement of Teaching (1975, p. 81) has suggested that the institution capable of maintaining or increasing enrollment shows the following favorable pattern of attributes:

- Attracts all ages rather than only those eighteen to twenty-one.
- Provides for part-time rather than only full-time students.
- Is less, rather than more, dependent on teacher education.
- Has public state support rather than not.
- Is of an effective size rather than reasonably large.
- Is located in an urban rather than a rural location.
- Has comparatively low tuition and few local competitors rather than high tuition and many local competitors.
- Has a national reputation or a devoted specialized constituency rather than neither.
- Is older rather than younger as an institution.
- Made wise expansion commitments in the 1960s rather than becoming overcommitted.
- Has a stabilized undergraduate enrollment rather than a volatile graduate enrollment.
- Is related to the health professions rather than not.
- Is in a sound financial condition rather than not.

- Is closely related to reality rather than not.
- Is located in the South or California or New York rather than in other parts of the country, and particularly not in the North Plains and Mountain states.

Obviously, many institutions cannot conform exactly to this pattern. However, a first and major step in an institution's analysis of its enrollment situation should be to consider each of the reasons and conditions that influence college choice in the light of these attributes, and then—within financial, faculty, and logistical constraints —decide how best to meet some or all of them.

There are examples of institutions that have concentrated on only one or a few of these reasons and conditions. Parsons College in Iowa, with a wide-open admissions policy, met the ulterior need of young, underachieving males to avoid the draft. An Eastern two-year women's college stressed, in program and publicity, the social life leading to upward mobility mate selection. During the 1950s, the General College at Boston University stressed its heavy counseling program to help solve deep psychological problems. Nova University in Florida and some of the other nontraditional programs stress the convenience of a program conducted exclusively after working hours. Colleges located in remote areas have created branches and centers close to large concentrations of potential students.

The guiding rule for each institution should be that it examine, in realistic terms, what it can do with respect to each of the reasons and conditions, and then move rather quickly to produce the needed changes, whether those be creating specific vocational programs, adopting an open admissions policy, cultivating churches or alumni groups, or seeking legislative approval for state scholarship programs. This should be done with full realization of the various pools of potential students and the limits of these pools. The ideal college student in the 1950s and 1960s, sought by large and small and public and private institutions, was young (eighteen to twenty-two), able (combined SAT of 1100 and above), high achieving (high school average of B+ or better), and economically comfortable (family income of $16,000 or higher). Many institutions did each year attract more and more students meeting those criteria, because even though such students represented only a small percentage of high school graduates, the number of high school graduates was increasing rapidly.

The 1980s and 1990s will present different conditions. The number of eighteen-year-olds will decline by more than a fourth between 1979 and 1992—from 4.3 million to 3.2 million (Breneman and Finn, 1978, p. 4)—whereas the number of available institutions has increased by over a third since the early 1960s. In the future struggle for enrollment, the competition for that ideal student will increase. Additionally, criteria for determining other appropriate students will be developed and accepted and new kinds of students identified.

Attracting Traditional Students

Although attracting new students is one way institutions can maintain essential enrollments and the accompanying tuition or appropriations, the sounder approach would be to stabilize or increase undergraduate enrollments in the on-campus, traditional, core programs. Not only are those the activities that colleges and universities do best and for which physical facilities have been created, but they are also the heart of the institution that alone can give it integrity. Some institutions have so concentrated on new programs for new students that they have allowed the core activities to disappear and have lost all sense of direction except that set by the prevailing, short-term market. None of them has significantly improved its long-run chances, and several have encountered serious problems. As noted earlier, Lone Mountain College finally closed its doors; the Antioch system, as of 1978, had begun to disintegrate and to close some of its branches; and LaVerne College in California has had to reduce the variety of new activities and to concentrate on its historic core mission in order to survive.

The core mission of most American colleges is to serve undergraduate students. In the American ideology or mythology, higher education is equated with the undergraduate quest for a bachelor's degree. Although most community college students do not achieve that goal, the large majority of freshmen entering community colleges say they wish to obtain a bachelor's degree. It is true that some undergraduate programs in universities became highly selective through first building a strong graduate and professional faculty and thereby creating a reputation for academic excellence that attracted undergraduate enrollments. But for the vast majority of institutions, it is the undergraduate mission that determines image and attracts students.

Additionally, the undergraduate enrollment, especially that of the lower division, provides the financial base for institutional existence. Lower-division students, taught in relatively large sections and paying full tuition, provide the subsidy for smaller, upper-division courses and other specialized activities. Undergraduate students generally help support—through tuition, or appropriation in lieu of tuition—graduate and professional programs. Even those colleges that have entered into a variety of new programs, including external degree programs, support their administration and core faculty from regular undergraduate enrollments. The income from new programs can help balance the budget but it cannot support the elements essential to maintain an institution. With few exceptions, a collegiate institution having stable traditional undergraduate programs can add at least a few activities to attract additional enrollment from nontraditional clientele. An institution seeking to serve only a variety of new kinds of students, with each group provided a discrete program, does not appear capable of generating the resources needed for adequate administration and institutional continuity.

Another way of viewing the problem is to examine the characteristics of the private institutions that appear able to compete with lower-cost public institutions. Distinctiveness of program, but not radical distinctiveness, seems a major element of strength. Private institutions can and do remain somewhat smaller, facilitate a somewhat different life-style, and encourage somewhat warmer faculty-student relationships than the public institutions. To the degree that this is judged by prospective students as characteristic of a given institution, the chances of their applying and enrolling are enhanced. These characteristics are related to the matter of reputation, whether that be a strongly religious one or one involving a "good" academic program. It is no accident that a disproportionate number of the Carnegie Commission Level II Liberal Arts Colleges, called "invisible colleges," began to experience enrollment problems as early as 1967–68. Having an indistinct image, they lack appeal.

High selectivity of students and appeal to high-income students are also strongly related to institutional attractiveness. The highly selective, private institutions are able to maintain needed enrollment—even in a time of decreasing numbers of high school graduates—simply by lowering admissions standards slightly, giving them a distinct advantage over institutions that typically accept any high school graduate. The institution capable of drawing students of high-income backgrounds is not tempted to use operating funds to discount tuition to attract students. It can be much freer to use only designated funds for financial aid and can, by altering the mix of financial aid, actually increase the yield from tuition. The example of Brown University in Rhode Island is a case in point. By increasing enrollment slightly and by making loans and work a bigger part of the financial aid package, it was able to add to reserve from tuition income.

Two additional factors are not so clear cut. The institution that has long attracted students from outside its region is not so vulnerable to regional population changes or to changes in state higher education policy. Thus, colleges such as Colgate or Dartmouth are not dependent upon what happens in their immediate geographic region, whereas Kansas Wesleyan or Knox College are. A less understood phenomenon is the effect of the urban or rural location of an institution. In theory, a college or university located in a densely populated metropolitan area should be better situated to attract large numbers of traditional or new sorts of students simply because the pool is so large and transportation costs are so low. This may not be true in practice, however. Most of the vulnerable private comprehensive colleges or universities are located in urban areas but, at the same time, they lack real distinctiveness when compared with the public comprehensive institutions. It also appears that the less vulnerable Level I Liberal Arts Colleges are disproportionately located in rural or suburban situations.

One additional factor affecting the ability of an institution to attract enrollment is the degree to which it is dependent on tuition. An institution that relies on tuition for 60 to 85 percent of its operating budget is clearly more vulnerable and more tempted to resort to extreme measures to attract students than is one that relies on tuition for only a third of its budget.

It appears, then, that the institutions, public and private, that are likely not to experience severe enrollment and financial problems during the 1980s and 1990s are those with distinctive reputations and programs that appeal to high-ability and high-income students who come from both in and out of the region and which have resources such that tuition provides less than 40 percent of operating expenses. (See Breneman and Finn, 1978, pp. 187–190.) It is the task of institutions not so characterized to develop an admissions policy that will compensate for those lacks and will enable steady enrollment and income flow.

It is well to examine the degree to which less favored institutions can generate needed enrollments. Although a few institutions will be unable to maintain adequate levels and will die, many in weak enrollment and financial conditions can likely obtain a reasonable enough share of a reduced pool of high school graduates to sustain themselves. The fact that some institutions experienced serious enrollment problems during the 1970s, when the size of the high school graduating classes was still growing, suggests that admissions programs during that period were somewhat less than effective. Thus, a first major step would be to review admissions activities to determine the degree to which institutions are making or have made some common errors which, if corrected, might reestablish an effective admissions program.

Errors in Recruitment

Perhaps the most general error made by tuition-dependent institutions experiencing enrollment difficulties is to expend effort and resources to recruit the wrong sort of student. Excluding the educationally and socially desirable goals of serving certain disadvantaged groups, the sort of student desired by most established undergraduate institutions is one having reasonably high academic aptitude and the ability to pay the tuition needed to support the institution. There has been in the past and there continues to be a tendency on the part of educational leadership, including supposedly informed admissions directors, to overestimate the number of bright and prosperous potential students. In 1965, for example, the directors of admissions at the eight Ivy League schools estimated that there were 100,000 high school graduates with combined SAT scores of 1100 or above and family incomes of $15,000 or above. That year, the actual candidate pool of graduates was closer to 18,000 and, certainly, not larger than 33,000 (Doermann, 1968, p. 3). As a rough rule of thumb, estimate that approximately 20 percent of a high school graduating class will have a combined SAT score of 1100 and 20 percent of that group will come from families with incomes of $20,000 or more. Thus, the pool of students combining those traits is approximately 40,000 per million high school graduates—not enough for all of the institutions seeking such people.

When plotting an admissions strategy, institutions should study such data—not only national data but state and regional as well—to decide which group or groups it would be most realistic to cultivate. Some institutions without previous reputation for academic distinctiveness might ignore ability and concentrate on the pool of high school graduates not in college whose family incomes were $14,100 or above. Although that pool is still small, it might be cultivated—if institutions can find the right rhetoric to indicate their intentions. That rhetoric could very well eliminate any reference to selectivity or demanding educational programs.

A second major error in admissions is to try to attract students through cosmetic changes in the curriculum. In Chapter Eight the significance of the curriculum to institutional survival is discussed, with the conclusion that the educational program, as a means to attract students, is much less important than is generally supposed. But in institution after institution, the sudden realization of enrollment problems is followed by an effort to change the curriculum, at least in name, and to add new programs (without adding expense) that are presumed to be attractive to today's students.

For institutions facing enrollment problems—unless there is a marked dysfunction of the curriculum, such as heavy emphasis on teacher preparation or a rigidly prescribed total curriculum—there are matters far more important than attempting either a real or cosmetic change in the curriculum. Not that curricular change is without value. Perhaps every ten years all institutions ought to reexamine themselves, just to produce some intellectual ferment and to reconsider what the institution really is—even though no major curricular changes are actually made. But the tranquillity for such introspection is generally not possible for institutions in crisis or heading for crisis.

In this connection, it is instructive to examine how some institutions in financial difficulty in 1970 responded. Cheit (1971) examined forty-one institutions and found that about a third were in financial difficulty, a third heading for financial difficulty, and a third in good shape. Two years later, he found that the troubled institutions were progressing toward health, through such things as cost cutting, establishment of better management, and location of new sources of income. Few of the institutions adopted program reforms as a means of regaining health. There are, of course, some exceptions. The director of admissions at Brown believes that the major curricular changes of the early 1970s are related to an improved applicant picture, and two new programs at Chatham College in Pennsylvania are seen as effective in increasing enrollments. However, these programs were created some time earlier and not as a direct effort to improve applications or enrollment.

The third common error is for institutions to keep their tuition at levels significantly lower than those charged by their normal competition. For example, if the average tuition of private liberal arts colleges in a state is $3,000, the institution of 500 students that maintains a $2,400 charge is guilty of this mistake. There are three categories of potential students: the whichers, the whethers, and the nevers. It is argued that the bulk of students who attend a private institution in a region are individuals whose basic decision is which of several similar kinds of institutions to attend. To them, the $600 difference in price is not determining, and they will decide on the basis of other factors. The $600 might be somewhat more influential for the group who will decide whether or not to go to college. Most of these will likely opt for the much less expensive public institution. A few may be attracted by the $600 differential, but the cost will still likely be much higher than at a public institution. In studying the effect on enrollments of the tuition gap between public and private institutions, it is generally estimated that for each $100 drop in public tuition, there will be a gain of 1 percent in enrollment in public institutions and a loss of one half of 1 percent in private institutions. Applying that to this situation, an institution increasing tuition from $2,400 to $3,000 would likely lose fifteen students, representing a financial loss of $45,000. At the same time, the increased tuition would yield approximately $281,000 additional revenue from those students only slightly affected by minor price differences. Obviously, this matter must be examined in the light of the situation of each institution. In the absence of persuasive evidence, however, each institution should charge tuition at least equal to the average charged by its normal competition.

A related error is the tendency of some institutions to discount tuition for some students in the belief that the income from the partial tuition paid by these students would be completely lost if the discounts were not provided. It is believed that if serving the students so attracted requires no additional courses, staffing, or even administrative overhead, the net effect will be beneficial to the budget regardless of the tuition yield. In a 500-student institution with a tuition of $3,000, charging everyone full tuition would produce a yield of $1,500,000. Discounting $1,000 for each of 170 students would cost $170,000 and produce a yield of $1,330,000. Not to discount would mean that some students could not attend. If 50 could not attend, there would be a loss of income of 50 ($3,000 − $1,000) or $100,000 and an increase in income of 120 ($1,000) or $120,000 as income was increased from the other 120 students. This would be a net savings of $20,000. If fewer than 50 quit, there would be even more savings. But if as many as 57 quit, the loss in income would be $114,000 and the gain in income from the remaining students would be only $113,000—a net loss of $1,000.

Obviously, each institution must examine this matter in the light of its own unique situation. Are the students who are attracted by discounts really served at no extra cost, so their reduced tuition is all gain to the budget? If not, what are the costs? Would the quality of the students suffer if there were no discounts? Would a desired or necessary diversity be lost? Or would enrollments remain at a satisfactory level in number and quality? If one institution did not discount, in a state with fourteen similar institutions that did, it might be dangerous for that school. However, it seems unlikely that such a situation would obtain. A more likely situation would be one in which a few institutions did not discount, a few discounted only symbolic amounts, and a few discounted as much as $1,000 or even more for a few disadvantaged students.

As a general principle, an institution should not use its own unrestricted funds to provide student financial aid. What student aid is provided should come from the various state and federal programs and from special institutional funds acquired for that purchase alone. Even the use of unrestricted reserves for discount purposes is to be questioned. It is argued here that what marginal gains can come from discounting can be more than achieved through closer attention to other more positive admissions activities.

An unexpected but fairly common error is the toleration of an inadequate, ineffective, and frequently sedentary admissions staff. Since the mid 1950s, the role of director of admissions has evolved into a definite professional subspecialty with its own body of conventional wisdom and with considerable technical knowledge. No specific university training programs have been created—although several programs in higher education considered the possibility—but through in-service experience, conference participation, and the like, people have been well prepared for the role. In spite of this, technical failures in admissions seem almost to be endemic, especially in the smaller liberal arts colleges. In one institution, the director rarely leaves the office and simply concentrates on the details of sending out catalogues and receiving applications. In another, inquiries from prospective students are answered infrequently and irregularly. In still another, the only field admissions officers are part-time recent graduates of the institution, and in one large urban university, no contact is maintained with alumni. In many institutions, record keeping is casual and research nonexistent.

This sort of error is relatively easy to correct, but it does require definite presidential action and supervision to create and maintain a strong admissions office. In a number of situations, that effort should involve discharge of the entire admissions staff, search for and appointment of an experienced director, and development of a clear admissions strategy, including a well-organized research effort.

In the absence of a professional staff, institutions experiencing enrollment problems frequently engage in a frenzy of ill-advised admissions activities or make serious misjudgments about enrollment possibilities. Among the foolish things that have been attempted were distributing promotional frisbees during spring break at Fort Lauderdale, Florida, accepting high school graduates recommended by alumni on the first contact, and offering bounties to students of $100 for each new student recruited. Among the misjudgments were basing budget planning on the assumption that applications could be doubled within a year or that community college graduates, if properly cultivated, could be attracted in such numbers as to fill the vacancies caused by the historic 50 percent attrition rate. Inexperienced admissions staffs frequently appear unaware of state and federal programs of financial aid, research information needed to evaluate the admissions effort, and the cost-benefit equations for various sorts of admissions techniques, for example, high school visits and college fairs.

Transcending the failures of admissions staffs is the pronounced failure of some institutions to develop and communicate a definite image that is consistent with their traditions but attractive to today's students. The interaction of these two factors is very important. Institutions get into trouble if they remain so true to their traditions as to lose appeal as times change, but they also suffer if they change so much that they alienate their traditional core clientele. The College of Notre Dame in Belmont, California, is an example of an institution that appears to have struck an appropriate balance. It has maintained its posture as a liberal arts college for middle- and upper-middle-class northern California Catholic women but, at the same time, has adopted a limited number of carefully selected vocational and external degree programs to attract just enough additional students to balance the budget. Lone Mountain College seems to have failed because it did not maintain a vital core but, instead, created a wide variety of new programs, each tailored to a small group of potential students.

Steps to Effective Recruitment

Serious recruitment errors can be corrected only with considerable effort and difficulty, but they can be corrected. There are nine steps that should be taken:

1. Develop a definite and broadly shared concept of the nature of the institution and its mission.
2. Create a well-organized, well-staffed, and adequately financed admissions office.
3. Involve the director of admissions in the central administration of the institution.
4. Create a definite plan to involve the faculty in the admissions effort and to ensure that the faculty understands the realities of admissions.
5. Articulate admissions counseling with the on-campus counseling and advising programs.
6. Select and use the more effective admissions techniques.
7. Create and exploit a favorable market position.
8. Create a definite and well-understood financial aid program that is cost-effective.
9. Create a definite and consistent program of research on admissions.

The first of these steps seems so obvious and natural that there should be no need even to mention image and mission. Surely, institutions that have been in existence for a hundred years or more know who they are and what they do. But do they? During the relatively stable times before World War II, widely known (at least locally or in a state) and continuous images may have existed. Thus, Stephens College in Missouri was known as a finishing school and attracted young women from all over the country who wished to understand fashion, personal grooming, and the techniques of courtship, marriage, and family. Catholic institutions, large and small, were run by clerics and were understood to confirm the faith of young Catholics, strengthen their moral character, and prepare women for marriage, a religious order, or teaching, and men for business, law, or the priesthood. Stanford was a wealthy institution (so people thought) that catered to the socially active children of the upper classes in California, and Boston University and New York University were the most available vocational training institutions for young men and women from those urban areas.

These images or stereotypes began to break down after World War II at an accelerating rate as the decade of the fifties gave way to the explosive sixties and the troubled seventies. Church-related colleges became secular, single-sex institutions became co-educational, Catholic institutions adopted lay boards of trustees, and streetcar private universities in metropolitan areas sought national distinction as they priced themselves out of the local urban market. Some institutions made the shift to a new identity with relative ease, particularly if they began to change early enough, say, in the mid 1950s. Others have been less successful, and that group includes level II liberal arts colleges, urban level II comprehensive colleges or doctoral universities, and private junior colleges that are especially vulnerable. These must find, understand, and project a definite image appealing to a sufficiently large number of potential students if they are to remain vital or to survive.

Second in importance for maintaining an adequate undergraduate enrollment is the organization of a strong, well-staffed admissions office, which is directly responsible to the chief executive officer and which can develop and carry out a comprehensive admissions program. The size of the admissions staff will, of course, vary with the size of the institution, with increases in staff linked to enrollment increases. Private institutions have typically understaffed their admissions offices. As a general rule for institutions up to 2,000 FTE enrollments, there should be one FTE professional admissions officer for each 100 to 150 FTE enrollments. This would cost—including salaries, travel administration, and materials—approximately 10 percent of gross FTE tuition. This may seem high, especially to faculty. The question may be asked, At whose expense will such a formula be adopted? The only answer is that to solve a critical enrollment problem upon which the survival of the institution depends, even instructional expenses should be limited. Subject, of course, to detailed study of the actual situation of each institution, it could be urged that perhaps 4 percent of the educational and general expenditures of operating budget funds used for direct student financial aid could be reduced to no more than 2 percent, with the savings devoted to admissions. (This estimate is based on 1976–77 average expenditures as presented in Minter and Bowen, 1978, p. 71.) Additional funds would come chiefly from the instructional budget.

Thus, a 500-student enrollment institution would have an admissions staff of 5, and a 2,000 enrollment school a staff of 20. This staff, including the director, would concentrate on recruitment of students, generating more complete data, and coordinating the admissions efforts with the ongoing programs of the college. The actual decision making, with respect to the admissions of students, can and would become, for most institutions, a routine clerical task ensuring that each applicant meet general institutional requirements of high school graduation and recommendations from high school principals or guidance counselors.

Staff organization would be dependent upon different institutional circumstances and service areas. In most institutions that serve a regional market, dividing that region among the staff as a primary assignment and assigning each another category, such as Americans living abroad or coordination of alumni recruiting, would seem to be a reasonable arrangement. More important are the characteristics of the director of admissions. That individual should clearly be abreast of developments in admissions, understand in a fundamental way the nature of higher education in the United States, be willing to travel a good deal, be able to supervise straightforward research, and be able to coordinate a staff and relate its efforts to the rest of the institution.

A related matter is the administrative role of the director of admissions. As a general rule, the director should be considered a major administrator in the institution and should participate actively in all major policy deliberations. The specialized knowledge of the realities of admissions problems should figure prominently in setting budgets, pondering institutional priorities, and reaching most decisions concerning an institution. Too frequently, the director of admissions is regarded as more of a technical staff member and senior administrators remain unaware of actual admissions conditions.

Two major steps that the admissions staff and director should take are (1) inform the faculty of the realities of admissions and be informed by the faculty regarding the educational program, and (2) coordinate admissions activities and counseling with the on-campus counseling and advising efforts. Recruiting of students is selling, with the product sold being, in part, what the faculty does or believes it does. Each admissions officer should, thus, spend considerable time talking with various faculty groups, such as departments and special programs, so as to be able to interpret to prospective students what the institution actually has to offer. In institutions in the size range of 500 to 5,000 students, each admissions officer might well spend at least a full week each year in this activity, which enables the officer to seek out and gain faculty understanding and support. Such a prescription may sound quite routine and mechanistic, but it requires a definite mechanism for many important things to take place.

Coordination of admissions with advising is a more sophisticated matter. It is urged in the conviction that counseling and advising are two of the most important elements of collegiate education, and that admissions work is, in essence, counseling and advising. In an ideal situation, the admissions officer would be, in effect, a counselor who would advise applicants until the students actually arrived on campus. Then the counseling or advising responsibilities would shift to a definite on-campus professional—faculty member, counselor, or academic administrator. However, the admissions officer would maintain contact with his or her students and would assume partial responsibility for ensuring that these students return for subsequent years. This somewhat demanding effort can produce important side effects. Students can inform the admissions staff even better than faculty about what actually transpires on campus. Admissions officers can learn from students what to stress and what to minimize in their recruiting efforts.

The well-staffed admissions office properly located in the administration is the key to solving the enrollment problem of a private institution facing difficulty. Actually, the admissions effort is central to the success or failure of any private institution. It is the admissions activities of the prestigious liberal arts colleges and universities that ensure serious consideration of the institution by enough applicants to enable the institution to maintain high selectivity. Directors of admissions in high-prestige institutions are jealous of their own application rates and those of their chief competitors and seem to take pride when their rates increase sharply.

From successful admissions programs and from the growing research on admissions has come a body of techniques and practices that can be urged for all institutions. The first of these has to do with the use of time and resources. In the past, personal recruiting in high schools has produced the primary expenditure of funds. This activity consumed, on an average, 54 percent of the admissions budget and was followed by: direct mail (20 percent), campus days (10 percent), magazine advertising (7 percent), newspaper advertising (5 percent), radio advertising (5 percent), and television advertising (1 percent) (Murphy and McGarrity, 1978, p. 253).

Even though the high schools selected for visits are carefully chosen, it is an expensive, time-consuming activity. Typically, high schools are selected according to the criteria of past recruiting success, geographic location, academic reputation, established personal ties, size, and religious affiliation (Murphy and McGarrity, 1978, p. 257). Some institutions have begun to reduce the number of high school visits and to concentrate on other techniques. Northwestern University in Illinois, for example, has reduced the schools visited from 700 to 100 and strengthened its first contact by mail. This requires obtaining a number of lists of potential applicants, especially those provided by the College Entrance Examination Board, Student Search Service, which releases lists of high school juniors after each administration of the Preliminary Scholastic Aptitude Test. The individuals from such lists are sent a well-designed, brief, factual mailer, which asks prospects to respond if interested in further information. The names of those who respond are then placed in the candidates file and the individuals are visited during the summer before their senior year by undergraduates, alumni, faculty, or someone from the admissions office. Prospects are invited to attend any of a variety of activities, either on campus or in their home region. Throughout the fall, those who have expressed interest in Northwestern are given a variety of personal attention—possibly a letter from a relevant faculty member, participation in a weekend on campus, or another visit from an alumnus of the institution (Ihlanfeldt, 1975, p. 30).

This shift from a personal first contact to a direct mail first contact is a major change in admissions doctrine. While the situation of individual institutions will differ, as a general rule the number of prospective students receiving a first direct mail contact should be at least fifteen times larger than the number of entering freshmen desired, with over half of those classified as falling within a primary market. The market can typically be divided into primary (those whose profiles suggest that, if admitted, they would likely enroll), secondary (those who seem more likely to enroll elsewhere), and a third market of people who have been encouraged to apply but who fit neither the primary nor secondary characteristics.

Student decision with respect to college is a complex, slightly understood phenomenon. It seems clear, however, that prospective students do want specific sorts of information and that the information does make a difference in their decisions. Thus, during the admissions process, from the first contact, subsequent mail contact, personal contacts on campus, or group contacts, prospects should be informed about: instructional programs, class size, and faculty qualifications; costs and financial aid; institutional impact on graduates; admissions and transfer criteria; housing and student services; out-of-class activities; student accounts of campus life; student participation in decision making; institutional expenditures; institutional financial condition; and institutional goals. It should be a major duty of the director of admissions to ensure that valid information about such matters is available (not an easy task) and communicated to students.

A recent development in admissions work is the increased use of marketing techniques, market research, and the key concept of positioning. These have long been used by business but had been judged inappropriate and out of character for collegiate institutions. Marketing is here defined as human activity undertaken to satisfy some set of needs through exchange processes; marketing management is the systematic effort to improve the likelihood of a favorable response. Market research is the systematic accumulation of information predictive of possible responses, and positioning is the assumption, in a large market, of a distinct position especially desirable to some segments of that market. It is not the purpose here to enter into a detailed technical discussion of marketing; there is a growing bibliography available for that. Rather, it is to stress several major concepts that seem especially relevant for institutions during the 1980s.

The most important of these concepts is positioning. This is the adoption of a specific and unique role for each institution that will set it apart from other institutions and will have an especial appeal for at least one segment of the college-attending population. Some colleges, of course, have a well-defined position of long standing in the marketplace—Harvard, Antioch, and Oberlin are examples. But many do not, either from a conscious decision to try to be all things to all people or from a failure to examine and know themselves. It is argued here that the search for a viable position is one of the most important activities for institutions to undertake during the rest of the twentieth century. Kotler (1976) describes the four steps involved in institutional positioning:

1. The college administration should know how the institution is perceived in the market by its various constituencies.
2. Various alternative positions should be examined, along with the requirements for adopting any one of them.
3. One position that promises the best long-run opportunity for the college should be selected.
4. A strategy to achieve the desired position should be developed.

Several cautions previously mentioned must be stressed here. As a general rule, if a new position is sought, it should be congruent with the institution's past and its real, rather than idealized, capabilities. An historically unselective, academically modest institution should really not aspire to a position of great academic strength. In the past, some institutions have been able to do so, but the 1980s and 1990s will likely be antithetical to such a major transformation. Secondly, the market sought should be a reasonably stable one and not the result of a fad. Institutions that seek a position of serving older women in their own localities may well find that market exhausted rather quickly. Thirdly, the position sought should be reasonably consistent with the historic purposes and processes of collegiate education. The institution that seeks a position involving a rejection of the traditional patterns of higher education, such as formal courses, books, and a well-prepared faculty, is likely to find sustaining that position impossible.

Essential to finding a position is the conducting of market research to determine the institution's public image and the needs and desires of different kinds of potential students. Using a variety of techniques—surveys, interviews, or secondary reports—information should be obtained from the following groups: prospective students who did not respond to the first formal contact; applicants who did and did not enroll; high school seniors in the institution's service area; recent and more distant graduates; parents of students and other traditional adult constituencies of the institution; principals and guidance counselors in potentially supplying high schools.

Once a position has been decided upon in the light of the institution's past, its capabilities, and its sense of valid market demands, then the detailed steps of an overall marketing strategy should be put into effect. These would include:

1. Perfecting the programs and their descriptions, which are to be stressed
2. Developing a large critical mass of names of prospective applicants
3. Establishing good first contact with all prospects
4. Cultivating applicants
5. Cultivating enrollments
6. Evaluating the recruitment effort
7. Reiterating the entire process modified by experience

Recruiting New Kinds of Students

For many institutions, the most promising way to maintain enrollments will be to identify and serve new kinds of students: minority group members, older students, working people, members of the military, or those intellectually different from the previously typical college student. Examples of institutional effort in this regard are legion. Chatham College in Pennsylvania offers older women a chance to complete bachelor's degree work by attending part time. The University of San Francisco offers an accelerated bachelor's program to employees of the Bank of America, and the University of Southern California offers school administrators in California a chance to earn a doctorate while actively employed. Most institutions, even the distinguished research universities, have begun to investigate potential new markets.

The potential value of new kinds of students has been generally recognized since the late 1960s. At that time, public junior colleges in California began to stress their evening programs and to develop off-campus programs to be offered to special groups, such as employees of banks and other corporations. Large universities began to create centers in many parts of the world which, for some institutions, generated profits of $4 or $5 million, which could be used to offset rising expenses on the home campus. A few institutions even began to consider themselves educational brokers, offering quite specific educational programs for almost any purpose if the demand were present. New kinds of profit-making organizations came into existence to devise new curricula that could be offered in cooperation with an accredited educational institution. The for-profit corporation would create the courses, hire the faculty, and conduct the program, and the college or university would receive 25 percent of the gross tuition payments for awarding credit and degrees. Diligently pursued, such programs could generate enough income for an educational institution to offset even quite serious deficits. In one institution, enrollments of 1,200 students in three programs—master's level in education, business administration, and public service—generated $2.4 million, of which the accredited institution received $600,000 as unrestricted income. This amount almost eliminated the institution's anticipated deficit of $800,000.

Although many different kinds of programs have been offered, or at least considered, the most frequently encountered ones are educational administration, law, communications, public service, and general programs leading to an associate or bachelor's degree. As institutions ponder whether or not to attempt such activities, the following eight criteria should be used to reach a decision.

First, programs must lead to a credential, degree, or certificate that has a definite and positive relationship to an individual's income, present and future. This is not to minimize the intrinsic value of courses and programs for other purposes (avocational, joy of learning, and the like), but it does not appear likely that students will enroll in those sorts of courses and programs in sufficiently large numbers or pay sufficiently large tuition and fees to help improve the economic situation of institutions. An obvious exception would be public institutions that are allowed to receive appropriations based upon enrollments in avocational sorts of courses—such as junior colleges, which receive funds to offer a variety of adult education courses. However, if a taxpayers' revolt should take place, public support of such offerings will likely disappear.

Second, the course or program should be such that students can obtain tuition and fees through various student aid programs (Veterans, Basic Educational Opportunity Grants, state scholarship, or tuition exchange) or from employers (corporations or municipal government)—or tuition and fees should be low enough in comparison with the cost of similar programs and in consideration of the anticipated financial rewards to make the investment of personal funds worthwhile. For example, at Nova University in Florida the external Doctor of Education program for junior college faculty costs students about $4,000 for two years. This compares with the tuition of $4,000 a year or more charged by private universities for comparable but residential programs. In addition to this, students in the Nova program do not need to forgo income by stopping work. The real cost comparison between a Doctor of Education program at Stanford, The University of California at Berkeley, and Nova is dramatic.

	Stanford	U.C. Berkeley	Nova
Tuition	$ 5,400	$ 900	$1,800
Forgone income	12,000	12,000	—
Living expenses	5,000	5,000	5,000
Books	300	300	—
Travel	500	200	500
	$23,200	$18,400	$7,300

The yield for people who enter positions comparable to those they held prior to entering the program, for example, teaching in a junior college, would be an increase in salary of $500 to $1,000 per year just for possessing the doctoral degree.

Third, the course or program should be effectively taught at times convenient to substantial numbers of students, by faculty paid at rates less than those paid regular full-time faculty at the institution, and using relatively inexpensive modes of instruction (no laboratory work, no extensive use of large library holdings, no intensive supervision of clinical work, and relatively few formal class-room contacts). This point may be illustrated in several ways. A regular faculty member in a private institution in which the standard teaching load is three four-hour courses per semester will be paid a salary of $15,000 plus 20 percent to cover staff benefits, or a total of $18,000. Now assume that (and this is a generous assumption) one third of that salary covers departmental research, counseling, and administration. This means that the annual cost of instruction is $12,000 per faculty member or $2,000 per course—or $25 per credit hour for a four-credit course enrolling twenty students. An adjunct professor who has other income can usually be employed at a rate of $500 to $1,500 per course. In a reasonably typical external degree mode in which a class meets once a week for four hours and for which three semester hours of credit are given for the academic year, the cost per student credit hour produced, in the same size class, would be $3.33 per semester hour, even if the high fee of $2,000 were paid. This substantial amount of credit is granted on the grounds that students will be working independently in place of attending class.

Fourth, the course or program should be in a field in which there is a real shortage of credentialed individuals, or should attract people already in satisfying positions who wish to upgrade themselves for economic or status reasons. The California School of Professional Psychology, which operates three campuses, uses part-time faculty, and serves full-time students paying reasonably high tuition and fees, succeeds because of an almost insatiable demand in California for credentialed counselors of various sorts and for licensed psychologists. The Nova University doctoral programs are designed for people who already have jobs and who are seeking to upgrade themselves in junior college education, school administration, and public administration.

Fifth, the course or program should not require specialized teaching space, such as laboratories or clinical facilities. It should be offered in general instructional space during off-hours on a home campus, or at low- or no-cost space off campus, such as school buildings, office buildings, and churches. Further, the course or program should ideally be highly verbal and only modestly technological. Thus, law, principles of economics or administration, and social service would be appropriate, whereas dental technology, mechanical engineering, and nursing would not. There are, of course, exceptions—for example, when a corporation or a military installation contracts for a technical program to be offered by an institution, using the technical facilities of the contracting agencies.

Sixth, the course or program should, ideally, lead directly to an acceptable credential or license, without validation by any other agency. Thus, programs leading to an educational administrative credential would be appropriate where the state grants the credential on the sole basis of institutional certification that required work has been completed. There are exceptions to this rule, but they should be approached with caution. Graduates of law schools must pass the bar examination in order to practice, and yet, for some institutions, adding a law school can be suggested for fiscal reasons. The nature of the bar examination is such that bright students can and do cram for it and do succeed in passing.

Seventh, the course or program should be in a reasonably stable field so that portable course outlines and materials can be prepared relatively quickly and inexpensively with the expectation that they will not become quickly dated. Thus, programs in computer design would not be desirable, whereas programs in marriage counseling would be. The ideal field would be one having a large body of relatively unchanging conventional wisdom generally possessed by many professionals in the field. These professionals could be commissioned to produce instructional materials without doing a great deal of new research, thus keeping down costs. One major reason for the high cost of instruction in established graduate and professional fields is that professors are expected to engage in, and are paid for, continuous research and scholarship aimed at keeping their courses current with new knowledge. Obviously, new programs for new students adopted by institutions as an economic measure should not be accompanied by the substantial costs of these activities.

Eighth, relatedly, courses and programs should be such that they can be taught by any of a number of individuals generally acquainted with a field. They should not be dependent on being taught by a specific expert or by one of a limited number of highly qualified experts. Thus, a program in business administration should be sufficiently general so that someone from economics, business administration, experience in business, or even a military background could teach it, given reasonably clear course outlines, texts, and other instructional materials. It is the payment of premium salaries and the provision of unique working conditions that makes traditional university education so expensive. Even courses in law schools should typically be such that lawyers in general practice could teach them. Thus, special courses, such as a course dealing with subtle changes in the Fourteenth Amendment, should very likely not be offered.

These eight principles governing the creation of new programs for new students can serve as a guide to the institution seeking to expand enrollment in this manner. However, the institution should also be aware of a number of dangers and pitfalls.

The first of these dangers is that if new students are served on the campus itself, their very presence could so alter the character of the institution that, in the long run, it might lose its appeal to its traditional clients. Chatham College has created programs in management and communications for adult women that are quite popular. The proportion of the total enrollment that is composed of these women has grown and could grow still larger. However, the women of traditional college age on campus have begun to resist the presence of larger numbers of older women on campus. Should that resistance intensify, it could produce an enrollment crisis in the group of women aged eighteen to twenty-two. For this reason, in all except the quite large institutions, programs for new kinds of students might better be conducted off campus, or at night, or in the summer, so that participants will not mingle with the traditional students. The charm of the idea of integrating new and traditional students and using underutilized classroom space and faculty time is offset by the dangers of changing, for the worse, the public image of the institution.

The second danger is that of misjudging the potential market for new programs. Times of economic jeopardy produce distortions of judgment, as hopes are converted into assumption of reality. It is so easy to sense a major social need and then, without much additional inquiry, to translate that need into a definite demand large enough to sustain a new program. There is some evidence that the size of the pool of new kinds of students wishing new kinds of programs may be more restricted than the proponents of nontraditional education have claimed. Adult collegiate enrollments have, typically, come from the age group twenty-five to thirty-four, and the large cohort that produced the expanded undergraduate enrollments of the 1960s is currently passing through this age range. It will be followed by a much smaller group, which should produce lessened demand for adult education in the 1980s. Further, adult enrollments in the 1970s were derived from Vietnam veterans under G.I. Bill support, a force already on the wane. And because adult enrollments are vocationally driven, as the economic value of a college degree declines, as seems likely, motivation to earn the degree will also decrease (Breneman and Finn, 1978, pp. 154–155).

Not only are forces to increase nontraditional adult enrollment likely to weaken, but also the actual pool of students involved in external degree programs is quite small—54,000 enrollments in the fall of 1975 compared to over 11 million regular college enrollments (Sosdian, 1978, p. 1). And the demand may have stabilized. Most new external degree programs were created between 1972 and 1974, and the creation rate has since tapered off. The phenomenon may well have been that institutions finding themselves in financial difficulty about 1970 entered the new domain of the nontraditional and quickly absorbed existing demand. A few institutions may have saved themselves through such an effort. But the odds are against others doing so in the future.

In some cases, there may even be a sensed need for courses or for a variety of social or religious services, but to assume that individuals or agencies will pay enough to support these programs is highly dangerous. For example, to launch a program for intellectual upgrading of public school teachers on the assumption that individuals or school districts will underwrite it may court disaster.

There are no easy safeguards to avoid this danger. There are, of course, various ways to conduct market research in sample areas to try to discover whether or not a genuine demand exists. A survey of high school teachers, for example, might yield some information as to whether they wanted and would enroll in degree-credit programs. Results of such a survey should be used with caution because a teacher can indicate interest in the abstract and yet be unwilling or unable to follow through. As another tactic, institutions can run pilot programs to see whether they catch hold. This, however, can be quite expensive. Just to advertise a planned program, even if it is never actually offered, can put a strain on an institution that is well into deficit spending. A variant is to obtain grant funds from the state or federal government or a foundation to underwrite a pilot program. If the program takes hold, it would be expected to become self-supporting. This is not bad, if the grant covers *all* expenses and if the institution does not obligate its resources. Frequently in such situations, however, the actual costs are not anticipated and the pilot program becomes one more fiscal drain on the institution.

Those programs that seem to have worked have been generated by individuals whose insights enabled them to sense a likely situation at the right time and who were well aware of such financial realities as the availability of sources of funding for student tuition. For example, LaVerne College in California created many new programs to help finance itself when its president guessed that school teachers would pay for locally available courses and that military people would flock to base-centered academic programs.

As for other sorts of new students, serious questions of finance and institutional capability exist. On idealistic, theoretical grounds, a number of deserving groups and needs can be identified:

- The aging poor preparing for retirement
- The verbally untalented who need retraining for emerging jobs
- The unemployed ghetto young adults, with few skills and little hope
- The released inmate from prison who needs new job skills and new views of himself and society
- The chronically ill and the mentally retarded who need to learn new skills to cope with themselves and to survive economically
- The growing number of Hispanic adults who need English language skills as well as job skills to advance from the most menial sorts of work

In the absence of substantial public support, such people cannot afford formal education. Further, it can be doubted that the typical college faculty—whether of a community college or a four-year college—can reasonably meet their needs, even if the financial problems were to be solved.

It would appear that financially troubled private institutions existing on tuition may serve limited numbers of certain kinds of new students for a limited period of time. However, as a major source of revenue through the 1980s and 1990s, such new students should not figure prominently in institutional plans.

A third danger is the temptation to set up an administrative structure for creating new programs before the potential market has been established. A classic example is Kansas Wesleyan University, whose president appointed two specialists in continuing education and began a renovation of one unused residence hall to serve as a center for continuing education before it was established that the Salina, Kansas, region could support such activities. Stephens College in Missouri, for a time, maintained a vice-presidential office to develop new programs in a town well supported with educational institutions, including the flagship state university campus. The new program effort began to be a paying operation only after the institution linked up with the well-established University Without Walls program and created a less pretentious administrative structure to coordinate the activities.

There are no good solutions to this problem. Program development requires time and resources which institutions facing financial difficulty lack. But there are some techniques that might be used. The first is to contract an established educational brokering corporation to develop new programs and to identify the market, without expense to the institution. There are over twenty such companies operating in the West that are prepared to assume the risks and costs of developing programs, with the contracting educational institution sponsoring the program developed and awarding academic credit. There are, however, some serious problems in connection with this option. Since the companies are for-profit organizations, there is danger of quality reduction in order to ensure profit. Regional and special accreditation may raise questions about the propriety of having an accredited institution award academic credit for programs over which it has no real control.

A second technique for creating programs is based on the

belief that even in relatively weak and financially troubled institutions there are people whose regular duties, although necessary, could be suspended for six months to a year to allow time for new program development. From time to time, institutions have declared moratoria on normal committee activity and some administrative efforts to accomplish such things as institutional self-studies. It would be possible, for example, to free a tenured professor from all teaching and committee work for a full academic year to engage in program development. His or her teaching load could be shifted to others, with little substantive loss. Of course, not every professor would be interested in or talented enough for program development. Nor could every professor be relieved of teaching duties. The professor of chemistry in a one-man chemistry department in a liberal arts college that stressed premedical education would be indispensable. But even in a faculty of thirty, there is always some slack. Two warnings must be heeded here: Program development should not be assigned to a committee, and program development with such serious purposes as institutional survival should not be assigned as a part-time task. If the potential program is to be important, it should be important enough to demand the full-time attention of someone.

A fourth danger in the quest for new and financially viable programs is that those decided upon, on the basis of market analysis, will transcend the intellectual resources of the institution. There may be great demand for bachelor's degree programs in public service through which police officers and firefighters can upgrade themselves and earn higher salaries. But the run-of-the-mill liberal arts college, or even the comprehensive college or university, is likely not to have faculty who can offer technically valid course work. Thus, the institution would be forced to appoint adjunct professors or to offer a program of questionable quality or utility. As a general rule, institutions should not appoint part-time or adjunct professors if there are no regular faculty members or administrators qualified to judge the competence of the part-time teachers and able to oversee their work.

An intellectually ideal solution is for institutions to refrain from offering any program that is not directly derivative of the institution's strengths and for which there is not a sufficiently large critical mass of relevant faculty talent. Thus, programs in law enforcement would not be offered if the institution lacked real strength in law, criminology, and public administration. But that ideal very likely could not hold in the face of serious financial problems. The institution would be forced to appoint and use part-time or adjunct faculty to offer the needed specialized courses. But, at least, the supervision of the program could be made the chief responsibility of some faculty member with relevant training and experience who would monitor the adjunct faculty and the courses taught.

A potentially lethal temptation, in connection with seeking new clients through new programs, is to attempt too much. The economic value to an institution of serving new sorts of students with nontraditional delivery systems lies in keeping the cost to the students and to the institution lower than that of regular on-campus programs. As has been mentioned, this is typically done through self-service, low-cost labor, and low or no capital expense. Now, one or two such programs can probably be administered and monitored with existing administrative apparatus. Thus, a southern California-based liberal arts college could reasonably administer one or two liberal arts and business programs on military bases, particularly if these were close by. However, as more programs are added, the institution would be faced with the choice of either adding to the administrative staff or allowing the programs to proceed with inadequate supervision, monitoring, and record keeping. In extreme cases in which institutions have created as many as thirty to forty small programs, each designed for a special clientele, which at the same time have had a substantial cash flow problem, the small administrative staff was so inadequate that no one in the institution really knew until the end of the fiscal year how many part-time faculty had been paid, what courses they had taught, or what programs they had directed. Had the needed staff been appointed to handle the details of all of the programs, the small margin of profit each program generated would have been eliminated and the institution would have been in a worse financial condition than had it created no new programs.

Seemingly in contradiction to these observations are the many large and varied programs offered by the leaders in the field of off-campus education, such as the University of California at Los

Angeles, the University of Southern California, Boston University, and the University of Maryland. These are each efforts of $5 million to $15 million and do contribute to the profit of the parent university. But these institutions have large administrative staffs, equipment, and space that can absorb the handling of the details of added programs. There is, in reality, considerable hidden institutional subsidy that would be impossible for smaller or weaker institutions to provide.

Solving economic problems through program expansion should be seen for exactly what it is by institutions in serious financial difficulty. It is a highly dangerous step that institutions take to avoid death or deterioration. For many institutions, it is probably the only step that can be taken. But taking it also increases the likelihood of sudden death. For many liberal arts colleges in the Midwest and South, the choices during the early 1980s are likely to be (1) continue operations as usual, with slow death likely, or (2) experiment with new programs that might save the institution but, more likely, will hasten its demise.

Further Readings

Although colleges and universities have historically had to compete for students and some institutions have long and well-established admissions programs, the need for sophisticated, well-staffed recruitment activities is a relatively recent phenomenon in the majority of institutions. There is little monographic literature on the subject, although considerable experiential literature can be found in *College and University* and the *College Board Review*. The additional items presented here are simply samples of that sort of information.

ANDERSON, C. A., BOWAN, M. J., AND TINTO, V. *Where Colleges Are and Who Attends: Effects of Accessibility on College Attendance.* New York: McGraw-Hill, 1972.

ASTIN, A. W. *Who Goes Where to College?* Chicago: Science Research Associates, 1965.

BAIRD, L. L., AND RICHARDS, J. M., JR. *The Effects of Selecting College Students by Various Kinds of High School Achievement.*

ACT Research Report No. 23. Iowa City, Iowa: American College Testing Program, 1968.

BLOOM, B. S., AND PETERS, F. R. *The Use of Academic Prediction Scales.* New York: Free Press, 1961.

COLEMAN, J. S. "The Principle of Symmetry in College Choice." *College Board Review,* 1969, *73,* 5–10.

DOERMANN, H. *Crosscurrents in College Admissions.* New York: Teachers College Press, 1968.

JACKSON, G. A. "Financial Aid to Students and the Demand for Postsecondary Education." Unpublished doctoral dissertation, Harvard University, 1977.

KLINGELHOFER, E., AND HOLLANDER, L. *Educational Characteristics and Needs of New Students: A Review of the Literature.* Berkeley: Center for Research and Development in Higher Education, University of California, 1973.

LESLIE, L. L., AND FIFE, J. D. "The College Student Grant Study: The Enrollment and Attendance Impacts of Student Grant and Scholarship Programs." *Journal of Higher Education,* 1974, *45* (9), 651–671.

MAC DONALD, D. S. *Alternative Tuition Systems.* Washington, D.C.: American Association for Higher Education, 1977.

MC KENNA, D. L. "Ethics for Earthquakes and Other Emergencies: Moral Responsibility of Admissions Counselors." *Journal of the National Association of College Admissions Counselors,* 1978, *21,* 27–28.

MURPHY, P. E., AND MC GARRITY, B. A. "Marketing Universities: A Survey of Student Recruitment Activities." *College and University,* 1978, *53* (3), 249–261.

SHULMAN, C. H. *University Admissions: Dilemmas on Potential.* Washington, D.C.: American Association for Higher Education, 1977.

THRESHER, B. A. *College Admissions and the Public Interest.* New York: College Entrance Examination Board, 1966.

WING, C. W., JR., AND WALLACH, M. A. *College Admissions and the Psychology of Talent.* New York: Holt, Rinehart and Winston, 1971.

YOUNG, D. P. "Registrar, the Admissions Officer, and Academic Consumerism." *College and University,* 1978, *53,* 153–163.

Chapter 8

☙☙☙☙☙☙☙☙

Maintaining Enrollment

In the critical matter of student enrollments, the overarching principle for institutional survival, as seen in the previous chapter, is that the essential core of an on-campus undergraduate program must be maintained and that the new programs for many new kinds of students must never be allowed to dominate an institution's mission and financing. Having acknowledged that principle, an institution must then address the question of how to increase or maintain those traditional enrollments. It should be stressed that this question pertains to all institutions—junior colleges, state colleges and universities, even distinguished research universities. Without a solid undergraduate enrollment, the institution lacks both a central educational purpose and an essential stable economic base of tuition or appropriations. However, the issue may be most clearly seen in the smaller private liberal arts colleges. These institutions, if they are to be economically viable and able to offer attractive programs, should seek to maintain an FTE enrollment of between 1,000 to 2,700 or a total enrollment of between 1,200 and 2,500 (Carnegie Commission on Higher Education, 1971b, pp. 82–83), with the large majority full-time undergraduate students.

Reducing Attrition

The first and perhaps the most difficult way to maintain the necessary enrollment would be to reduce, in some way, the dropout or attrition rates. A typical enrollment pattern for a liberal arts college of 1,000 students would be: Freshmen = 400, Sophomores = 250, Juniors = 200, Seniors = 150. If the dropout rate between the freshman and sophomore years were reduced by 50 students, approximately 70 full-time enrollments would be added, which, with a tuition of $3,000, would add over $200,000 of income. But this is no nine days' wonder. During most of the twentieth century, attrition rates in United States colleges and universities have remained at a stable 50 percent of an entering freshman class. There are, of course, exceptions to this norm. Stanford typically graduates 85 percent of a freshman class in four years. And some of the larger state universities present patterns of a graduation rate of 60 to 65 percent of a freshman class within a ten-year period. Some of those graduates drop out and return, whereas others drop out and then enroll and graduate somewhere else. But the majority of all institutions experience a 50 percent rate of attrition. If that rate could be modified, severe anticipated enrollment shortfalls could be eased or eliminated.

Lowering dropout rates is a highly complex undertaking because students drop out of college for different reasons. Some may accomplish desired goals in a year; others cannot afford to continue. Some find the work too difficult; still others are bored. Some lack the needed psychological support of parents or friends to continue; others discover more satisfying ways of maturing. From the standpoint of the student, dropping out may be healthy or hurtful or make scant difference in the individual's life. Similarly, from the standpoint of society, the consequences are mixed or different, individual to individual. The consequences for an institution are not uniformly favorable or unfavorable either. However, it is assumed that for at least a proportion of students who drop out of college, the consequences are unfavorable to the students, parents, society, and institution, and that these students would have been better off to remain in college and complete a program or a degree that would at least have given the feeling of closure.

Now, how can these students be kept in college? Perhaps the greatest single factor is to contrive ways for almost all students to become directly involved in some significant activity, whether it be a sorority, football, student government, student publication, musical or dramatic groups, or participation in the actual governance of the institution. This suggests that the institution should develop a full program with enough different parts so that there would be something for everyone. A clear implication is that institutional resources should provide for professional leadership to make the needed arrangements. This, however, is dangerous. Adult professional leadership requires money, which can be provided only at the expense of other activities. Also, adult professional leadership may not be sensitive to the kinds of activities that will attract widespread student interest. The leadership may believe that a program of speakers and seminars in residence halls would attract students, especially if the programs have high intellectual content. But students may think otherwise or resent having professional leadership dictate which programs should be offered.

Probably in smaller institutions, the dean of students should spend fully one half of his or her time sponsoring, organizing, or stimulating activities with which students might identify. These would include: a system of residence hall and student government that would allow many different students to chair or be in charge of something; a vibrant intramural athletic program, with competition based on stable groups such as residence halls, fraternities, or clubs; student membership on all college committees, commissions, or task forces, especially the permanent ones; and a student publication program utilizing a substantial number of student staff members.

In making such an assignment of time, choices must be made. The institution must choose between having the dean of students spend time counseling individual students or organizing activities, between hiring an associate dean for activities or another admissions counselor, or between secretarial service for the dean or an assistant to the president. If the institution has decided that its major effort to improve enrollments will be through reduction of dropouts, the choice should probably be to strengthen the support of the activities effort.

But that effort can be further strengthened through academic or curricular arrangements. Through house plans, cluster colleges, and team-teaching arrangements, other groups can be contrived to which students can give affection and from which they can receive support. Organizing the freshman curriculum into one half required courses and the other half elective courses, and assigning the same students to the same sections of each required course, is a simple device. Thus, the first year might consist of freshman English, natural sciences, and humanities. For a freshman enrollment of 400, there could be sixteen teams of teachers and students taking or offering the same sections of the three required courses. Having the same people see each other in three different classes each week typically produces a cohesive group whose members share the same problems, successes, and failures. This is, of course, a version of the older general education requirements. Actually, those requirements can be well defended on the grounds that they allow the creation of these quasi-primary groups of considerable educational value, as well as being of value in holding students. The scheduling problem, given the modern computer, is not great. Given sections of English, natural sciences, and humanities are linked together. Students elect which English section they wish, which automatically assigns them to a specific section in the other two courses.

This is a simple model. In larger, more complex institutions, there needs to be a variety of continuous groups, because different students will follow different patterns. But the point is to create opportunities for as many students as possible to be involved in continuous groups.

A second highly important factor in keeping students in college is student creative achievement. Overly simplified, it appears that successful academic achievement is strongly related to staying in college, and that ways to improve that achievement will help the attrition problem. This is a difficult task since, in most colleges, there is a considerable variety of student ability to cope successfully with academic work. It is further complicated by the fact that little is really known about the effectiveness of various techniques for improving academic performance, such as remedial services, tutoring, or scheduling into sections of courses based on ability. However, several devices might be attempted. The first of these would be a more realistic statement of the actual academic demands the institution makes. Most collegiate institutions, quite properly, stress academic and intellectual values, but many overstress their own requirements. The majority of liberal arts colleges are essentially open-admissions institutions, accepting all applicants having a high school diploma and the ability, acquired in any of a variety of ways, to pay tuition. However, the rhetoric in the catalogue implies that rigorous academic standards are imposed and that students will have to struggle to remain in academic good standing. That rhetoric might be changed to stress that anyone accepted should expect to succeed if he or she makes a reasonable effort. This might be accompanied by a three-letter grade system in which students would receive A, B, C, or no grade. Thus, every student would be free of the vulnerability to failure. The truly inept student or the one clearly lacking in academic motivation would likely leave after making no progress toward accumulating credits, and the rest would perceive that they were making reasonable academic progress through accumulation of credits with adequate grades.

Some may see such a suggestion as lowering academic standards, but it is the contention advanced here that it simply codifies and makes explicit reality. In the vast number of relatively unselective institutions, grading is highly subjective and unreliable. It has tended to avoid F grades (out of charity) and has given D's, which traumatize the student but do not distinguish between solid achievement and no achievement. The three-grade, no-pass system is no real change, except that it eliminates the hurt egos that come from the D and F. And the system might keep a few more students in school.

While the evidence regarding the effectiveness of remedial services is limited, there are some examples that suggest that some sorts may help reduce attrition. In one northern New York institution, dropout-prone students were identified and half were randomly selected and subjected to a freshman year course dealing with academic survival. The class focused each week on solving the survival problems that the members were having. In one year there was a dramatic reduction in attrition among the experimental group, and continued high attrition in the control group. A similar effort was made in a west Texas institution, using trained student counselors to provide a highly structured treatment for academically risky students. The results were the same. A variant was an effort at the University of Houston to cut down on the attrition among minority group engineering students. This consisted of providing freedom from failure (no F grades given), organizing the students into an identifiable group with considerable counseling support, ensuring a cooperative work-study experience (to help financially), and presenting specially structured courses to develop intellectual skills needed to survive in a demanding engineering program.

Many other suggestions have been made, but the essence of a program to approach the attrition problem through academic achievement seems to consist of eliminating the trauma of failure and providing some group effort to develop the intellectual skills needed for academic survival.

A third approach to the dropout problem is the financial aid effort. Here the needs of students and the needs of the institution can converge, although typically they do not. Astin (1975, p. 157) has pointed out that of the various forms of financial aid that can be provided, work *on campus* seems most strongly related to student persistence in college. Off-campus work operates in the opposite direction. The implication for a serious effort to reduce dropouts would be a major program of student work on campus. This might ultimately result in half or more of the nonprofessional jobs on campus being filled by students. This would reduce labor costs because students' wages would be lower, provide students with needed funds, and, above all, provide one more way for students to identify with the institution.

Another broad approach to the attrition problem is to improve the entire campus environment to make it a more pleasant place. College campuses, particularly those of small liberal arts colleges located in small towns, can be desolate, lonely, and disheartening places. Especially in the Midwest, where many of the liberal arts colleges are located, a bleak climate during five months of the year, coupled with an unappealing campus, conspire to stimulate students to drop out. Of course, there is nothing that can be done about the climate, and the impoverished college may not be able to do much about the physical plant (cutting back on plant maintenance is one of the first economies institutions make when faced with financial trouble). But perhaps a few things can be done to make the campus a more pleasant place with greater holding power for students.

In Chapter Nine, some notions about faculty development are presented that might contribute to the attractiveness of faculty members. So serious, for several categories of institutions, is the need to reduce attrition that some of those approaches should hold high priority among institutional efforts to survive.

A more general approach to the attrition problem suggests three sorts of efforts that institutions might undertake. One is for admissions officers to pay greater attention to selecting those kinds of students whose backgrounds and behavior patterns are most congruent with the ethos of a particular institution. Thus, a college that operates in an open and highly unstructured way might be uncomfortable for an authoritarian student who requires considerable external structure just to keep anxiety at tolerable levels. Another college having a relatively ordinary faculty without great intellectual power could be disappointing to able and academically concerned students. It has been argued that a correct gauging of the environmental press of a given institution and the interest and personality characteristics of students could produce a student body generally in tune and satisfied with the institution. There are serious problems with such an approach. First is the question of whether it is sound education to seek a homogeneous student body. Students do educate each other, and a case can be made that a varied student body will contribute to a richer education than will a homogeneous student body. Second, there are significant technical and ethical problems in identifying student characteristics in sufficient detail to make decisions that involve variations in personality. George Stern and C. Robert Pace tried for years to develop complementary measures of personality and environmental press without ever being able to create a workable system. The task was complicated by the growing concern over the use of personality measure for administrative decisions. Lastly, the kinds of institutions that face serious financial problems must accept almost every student who applies. They cannot be selective even with respect to the traditional factors of aptitude and prior academic achievement, much less with respect to personal congruence with institutional ethos.

Much more plausible are the approaches of modifying student behavior to make it more adaptable to a given college program or of changing the institution to make it more responsive to student needs. Modifying student behavior might take any of several forms —for example, remedial work in writing or mathematics, counseling to improve self-concept and confidence, or courses to develop skills of academic survival. An extreme example of such an effort is the plebe summer at West Point, which modifies the reaction pattern of cadets so that they can survive the four years of rigorous training the academy offers. Changing the environment to meet the needs of students is another distinct possibility. This would range from seriously modifying the curriculum to adopting an academic calendar to minimize dropouts. (These concepts are developed in Ford and Urban, 1966, pp. 83–106.)

While there is little in the way of research to demonstrate the utility of any particular pattern of modification of students or of the environment in reducing dropouts, some speculation about effective techniques is possible. The first and most important of these techniques is the creation of a strong and active advising system. College students need a great deal of rather intimate support from professional adults as they cope with leaving home, pondering academic and career directions, just learning the ropes in a strange environment, learning to cope with the freedom of college life (only fifteen hours of class each week compared to the twenty-five to thirty of high school), and the variety of other problems associated with maturing. Unfortunately, in few institutions do they receive this help. Professional counseling staffs are too small and reach too few people. All too frequently, advising degenerates into the details of registration, and advisors are unprepared to render other kinds of help that the student might need. It can be theorized that even though the ostensible reasons students drop out are academic, financial, or social, the real reason is the lack of support available at the time it is needed.

It is critical that there be enough informed advisors to ensure that every student can quickly obtain help and that every student can be expected to see an advisor several times each term or semester. One structure might be to appoint every professional in an institution—president, librarian, professor—as an advisor expected to advise a proportionate share of students (1,500 students, 150 professionals = 10 students each). Each advisor would be required to see his or her advisees at each registration period, at the end of the school year, and once in December and once in February (months when morale is low). Each advisor would have a handbook giving details of the academic program, techniques of advising, sources for more specialized help, and the like. In addition, each advisor would be expected to participate in four to six seminars each year dealing with advising, counseling, characteristics of college students, or other relevant subjects. Further, the direction of the advising program would be the responsibility of the director of counseling, who would be expected to devote one third of his or her time to ensuring that the advising program was operating effectively and was being responsive to student needs.

There are, of course, problems with such an arrangement. Professors may feel that they should advise only majors in their fields. Some quite competent people cannot relate to students in an advising capacity. But it is argued that in the chiefly undergraduate institution, advising of majors is not all that important as compared with the other problems that undergraduates face. And most professors can be trained in the basics of advising, unless they are so misanthropic that they should not be teachers.

Of the many activities that an institution can undertake to reduce attrition, a well-developed advising system should be assigned highest priority for the small- to medium-sized institution. It need not cause significant additional cash expense. Advising may be considered part of each person's regular workload, as is the supervision of advising part of the workload of the director of counseling. The preparation of the advising handbook and the periodic seminars represent the total of special funds that must be expended. The retention of only a few potential dropouts would produce the funds for those expenses.

Rethinking Academic Programs

It has been consistently implied in this book that, for the most part, the particular content and form of the undergraduate curriculum does not affect enrollments one way or the other. That is, the majority of freshmen select a college for many other, and frequently not educational, reasons than its course offerings; once enrolled, students often stay for other than curricular reasons. But enrollment and student retention is affected to a degree by students' satisfaction with instruction and program options. For example, the presence or absence of such occupational programs, as nursing or business determines whether students desiring that particular program will attend a specific institution. A few highly visible and unique colleges, such as St. John's in Maryland and New Mexico, Reed in Oregon, or Evergreen in Washington State, have attracted a small but unique clientele, presumably because of their curriculum. And, as the recent history of Brown University illustrates, programatic change in the conventional liberal arts college can have enrollment benefits.

Brown is one of the eight members of the Ivy League, but over time it has ranked toward the bottom of the eight with respect to a number of criteria such as total endowment, application rates, endowment per student, and ranking of departments. (It should be pointed out that an institution with low ranking among that group of institutions is still in a highly favorable situation as compared to the vast majority of private institutions in the United States.) In 1969, with the stimulation of a group of talented undergraduate students, Brown University reorganized its entire undergraduate curriculum and its approach to teaching and advising. Formal course requirements were abolished and students were expected, under faculty guidance, to develop their own courses of study. New sorts of interdisciplinary courses were created to make the curriculum more attractive, and more recently the dean of the college was provided new resources with which to stimulate innovation in the educational programs.

At about the same time as this new approach began to be publicized and the image of Brown began to change to that of a highly innovative and attractive undergraduate institution, the university began to experience serious financial problems. By 1972, it had begun to budget serious deficits, causing substantial withdrawal from reserves—or quasi-endowment, in Brown terms. The institution responded by reducing expenditures, allowing attrition to reduce faculty size somewhat, reducing plant maintenance, and deciding to allow undergraduate enrollments to continue to increase as they had since the 1960s. This last was possible because although much of the Brown physical plant is old and many buildings need refurbishing, it did have enough capacity to absorb new students without adding any new residence halls after 1972. Like the other Ivy League institutions, it also allowed tuition and fees to rise and, at the same time, slowed the increase in grant aid by placing greater emphasis upon loans and jobs in financial aid packaging.

It is in connection with enrollment and increased gross and net tuition and fees that the new image of Brown is significant. In 1969, 8,422 freshmen applied, of which 2,304 were accepted and 1,150 matriculated. In 1978, 10,636 applied, of which 2,846 were accepted and 1,372 matriculated. The quality of the 11,512 freshmen applicants in 1979, as measured by the SAT scores, remained high (mid 1200s). The increase in the number of applicants to Brown moved it from the bottom of the Ivy League to a position at the top close to Harvard and Radcliffe. As of the spring of 1979, that number was still increasing. In the opinion of the director of admissions, Brown is now viewed by potential applicants as the one truly innovative institution among the high-quality, high-priced private colleges and universities. The director believes that if the other Ivy League institutions move to increase curricular requirements, that will put Brown in an even more favorable competitive position. It will be seen as the only prestigious institution allowing students real educational freedom. This desirable image is enhanced by a sort of middle position among the Ivy League schools with respect to a number of features. It is a university with graduate studies and professional programs in medicine and engineering, but its main effort is undergraduate education (1,400 graduate students out of 6,700 total enrollment). It is located in a historic residential area in Rhode Island that is part of an urban center but has many small-town characteristics—not as dangerous as New York City nor as isolated as Hanover, New Hampshire. It has a strong scholarly faculty but one whose chief concerns are with undergraduate curriculum, teaching, and advising. Over all, the institution has located a desirable, competitive position from which to face the future.

By the spring of 1978, Brown's financial condition had not completely recovered, but most indexes were favorable. It had increased reserves from $11.4 million to $16 million. It had increased the volume of research contracts and the overhead charged. It had increased annual giving from $750,000 to $2 million. It had begun seriously to cultivate alumni. The net tuition (the difference between total gross tuition and gross financial aid) had grown enough to make the difference between a red and a black financial statement. Officials at Brown are reasonably sanguine about the future. There are, of course, serious problems. Energy costs in New England are a substantial drain. The physical plant does need attention and some additions. The change in federal law increasing retirement age for faculty could hurt. The cost of federal regulations is a concern and could become destructive. Faculty salaries should be improved. But during the 1980s and 1990s, smaller numbers of children per family may encourage parents to make heavy educational investments in them. There is room for at least 100 high-cost prestigious private institutions in the country. Students considering those schools will likely be assisted by new federal and state programs to such an extent that by the 1990s a substantial amount of financial aid provided Brown students may be either state or federally supplied.

The Brown situation presents several features worthy of consideration by other institutions. First, it maintains a small top administrative organization as compared to other institutions of its type. It has a very small financial organization and no elaborate planning office. Its strong admissions office relies on the efforts of almost 3,000 alumni for active recruiting. Second, it demonstrates that a major curricular change can positively affect applications and enrollments if it is truly carried out and is not just cosmetic to conceal practice-as-usual. Not that all institutions could be as successful. Brown obviously had many advantages to start with, but it has demonstrated that at times curriculum can be important. Third, given the increased attractiveness of the institution, Brown, like many private colleges, has shown that changing the mix of financial aid can increase net tuition available to be used to operate the institution. By shifting from scholarship grants averaging $2,000 for 50 percent of an 8,000-member student body, with annual tuition of $4,000, to grants to one third with loans to the rest, an increase in net tuition of $1,333,333 was possible. That can help close quite significant budget deficits.

In addition to the case of Brown University, there are other dramatic examples of program appeal with respect to applications, enrollments, and retention. Within two years of the 1865 opening of Cornell University at Ithaca, New York, it had the largest entering freshman enrollment in the history of higher education to that date. Cornell offered a variety of applied courses and programs substantially different from the prevailing prescribed curriculum of the nineteenth-century college, and students flocked to take advantage of them. During the 1920s, Antioch College and Stephens College reversed a seemingly inevitable slide into bankruptcy through creating radical new programs that attracted students. In the case of Antioch, the combination of cooperative work study, community government, and a new general education program worked. Stephens offered a two-year program leading to a degree that combined vocational preparation, general culture, and role preparation for women highly appropriate for the times. More recently, Northeastern University has remained attractive in the dense collegiate environment of Boston through making cooperative work-study the central integrating element in most of its programs.

Informed critics and observers of higher education such as Earl McGrath have stressed the centrality of the educational program with respect to institutional vitality and appeal. They have urged institutions to tailor an educational program to achieve their distinctive missions and goals. Enrollments are also affected by the presence or absence of desired vocational programs. When, in the early 1970s, an oversupply of teachers emerged, state colleges that had concentrated on teacher preparation lost enrollments to area vocational schools that prepared students for fields in which there was great demand for workers. The success of some of the new non-traditional programs rests in part on the fact that they offer vocational preparation leading directly to jobs. However, the degree to which the curriculum and instruction are a vital factor in attracting and retaining students is still open to question. For example, The Carnegie Foundation for the Advancement of Teaching (1977, pp. 7–8) observes that "the curriculum is important, but it is not the most important aspect of undergraduate education" and that "no studies show that one undergraduate curriculum is clearly better than another."

Since the mid 1950s, there have been hundreds of studies seeking to determine the impact of college on students. In general, with the exception of Jacob (1957), these studies have presented evidence that college graduates know more, are somewhat more catholic in their tastes, manifest greater ability to think, and are more liberal and tolerant in their values than are those who have not attended college (Trent and Medsker, 1968, p. x). Bowen (1977, p. 98) goes so far as to estimate the magnitude of change based on the results of most of the studies. However, those changes appear to be related more to the generic college experience than to a specific college experience (Withey, 1971, pp. 42–43). They also are related to the knowledge and ability of students as they enter college. Astin (1972b, p. 193) found that postgraduate performance on the area tests of the graduate record examination were related more to measured aptitude of students as freshmen than to institution attended or program pursued.

Apart from the impact of specific institutions or educational programs on students, there is also the question of whether there is differential appeal. Institutions definitely do have differential appeal. The high-prestige colleges and universities since the late 1950s have demonstrated such appeal by receiving five to ten applications for every one student accepted. That seems likely to continue. But the evidence of the drawing power of a specific sort of undergraduate curriculum or of a well-defined teaching style is more difficult to find. Indeed, moderately to highly selective institutions exhibit a wide range of curricular structure from completely free elective systems to tightly prescribed curricula, and those institutions suffering enrollment problems show the same variety.

Some insight regarding curricular appeal can be obtained by examining some of the more radical and highly publicized curricular reforms of the 1960s. That decade produced major experiments designed to make college education more relevant to student needs and desires. But for the most part, relatively few students found them to be attractive. A number of institutions created cluster colleges to provide a major alternative route for undergraduates. At Western Washington State College, the University of the Pacific, Stephens College, and the University of Michigan, cluster colleges were developed in the expectation that significant numbers of students would elect them. In most of them, enrollments remained small. The clusters appealed to only a small group of somewhat unique undergraduates. Some new institutions were created to express unique and well-defined educational programs. Florida Presbyterian College, Florida Atlantic University, the University of Wisconsin at Green Bay, Evergreen State University, Metro-State College in Minnesota, and the University of California at Santa Cruz, all over time failed to attract the number of students anticipated and for whom those special programs were created. Still other institutions tried special techniques to make the undergraduate curriculum more relevant and more rewarding, including allowing students to create their own programs, undertake independent study, experience team-taught interdisciplinary courses, or have written evaluations of performance rather than grades. By and large those efforts failed, partly because of faculty reluctance but more especially because of student lack of interest or even outright antagonism (Levine and Weingart, 1973, p. 7).

Indicative of the reality of reform is Sterling College in Kansas, which in 1972 undertook to make the curriculum competency based. Under the leadership of an outside consultant, the faculty produced a statement of nine competencies which students could demonstrate in any of a variety of ways. Then new instructional activities were created to help develop those competencies. The new curriculum was put into effect with nontraditional ways of developing competencies. However, Sterling students select the college more because of its Christian orientation than because of its innovative curriculum and hence typically elect courses and traditional activities rather than the innovative options (Levine, 1978, p. 413).

Another kind of relevant evidence on curricular appeal is the fact that high school seniors select the college they will attend with very little knowledge of the nature of their desired vocation. They appear to know even less about the educational program of the institution they choose. Katz and his associates (1968) established that even students in such highly selective institutions as Stanford or the University of California at Berkeley knew only vaguely what the special programs of those institutions were and what would be needed to prepare for their eventual occupations. High school seniors seem to view colleges and universities in a generic way. George Stern has theorized that there are several distinctive collegiate environmental presses. Thus, in one institution the press is for intellectual activity, in another play, and in still another vocationalism. To measure this press, George Stern developed a college characteristics index. Administering this index to students on different campuses, he found that the perceived presses were quite different from one campus to another. However, administering the same instrument to high school seniors intending to enter those institutions, he found that the seniors anticipated substantially the same press regardless of the institution. Students typically expected the press to be an academic, intellectual one that could be epitomized as expecting that the academic goals of liberal or general education stated in the catalogue would be stressed. In the early 1950s, I discovered the same phenomenon in high school seniors in Arkansas. When presented a long series of outcomes of college education and asked to show which they valued most and expected to be emphasized in college, the seniors selected general education and critical thinking.

Still a different factor is what students actually do when given a chance to select courses. During the late 1940s and the 1950s, undergraduates were required to take 30 to 50 percent general education courses, about a third of their work in a major, and the remainder as a minor or as electives. From 1957 to 1967 there was only a slight drop in general education requirements, but from 1967 to 1975 there was a rather sharp reduction. During this same period, there was considerable experimentation with new sorts of courses intended to make the curriculum more relevant. There were courses in black studies, women's studies, specific sorts of problem solving, and a variety of interdisciplinary courses all intended to broaden students' educational experiences. Given greater freedom of choice, students strengthened their majors slightly and took the increased number of electives available to them in subjects close to and supportive of their majors (Blackburn and others, 1976).

Thus far a few tentative assertions seem warranted. There is no evidence that specific curricular or instructional practices have a measurable impact on students' choice of college. Many of the larger curricular innovations of the 1950s did not attract the numbers of students expected. Students typically select a college knowing little about the programs offered or even the nature of the vocations they desire to enter. Indeed, their judgments about college seem to be more generic than specific. Once in college, and given some choice, students concentrate most of their time on their majors and those courses that tend to support their majors and deepen their competency in them. Over half (58 percent) of undergraduate enrollments are in professional schools or divisions (Carnegie Foundation for the Advancement of Teaching, 1977, p. 6).

If these factors alone were used to guide curriculum construction for the troubled institution, a rather simple structure would emerge. It would consist of a limited number of general education courses, with at least the possibility of no such requirements. There would be as many majors, cognate, and professional fields as the institution could staff and finance. The institution would avoid radical and pervasive curricular changes that departed significantly from tradition but would allow changes to take place gradually as changes in faculty, students, and the disciplines occurred.

As shall be indicated, some deliberate curriculum changes can be made, but they should follow evaluations of fields and demands of the market place. Shifts in the content of courses should be allowed to follow emerging research findings from scholarship in the field as well as the developing interests of faculty and the changing needs of students. Thus, the curriculum should be viewed as constantly in flux, although from time to time a pattern of requirements emerges that is adopted by most institutions for a few years. As an eaxmple, in the general education movement of the 1940s and 1950s, institutions required students to take a sequence of interdisciplinary courses such as natural sciences, social sciences, and the humanities.

Redesigning Components of the Curriculum

It now becomes necessary to examine elements of the undergraduate curriculum from the standpoint of their contribution to institutional health and survival. Curriculum is here defined as the organized body of information, processes, and artifacts intended to produce the primary educational purpose of an institution. It typically consists of majors or concentrations, minors or depth electives, general education, breadth electives, and applied professional courses. Of these, the components having the greatest significance for program attractiveness are majors and general education. The availability of several types of electives is not likely to affect student recruitment or retention positively or negatively. Majors consist of a series of interrelated courses offered by one or several departments intended to develop a deep understanding of the subject. Depth electives are courses freely chosen by students with the intent to deepen their comprehension of their majors—these have been called minors in the past. General education is the part of the formal curriculum presumed to be essential for all or most students to prepare them for their nonvocational lives as individuals, family members, and citizens. Breadth electives are courses freely chosen by students to broaden their knowledge, understanding, or experience.

How may these elements be arranged and emphasized to attract and retain undergraduate enrollments while remaining consistent with the academic and intellectual values the collegiate institution is supposed to represent?

The Major. Beyond doubt, the major is the most important element of the curriculum both to students and faculty. It provides a focus for student academic and vocational aspirations and serves as a kind of intellectual home or primary group. It allows the faculty to express best their own training and what they believe to be most important. Majors can be in a single subject, such as

English, in several subjects, such as physical sciences, or in a vocational field, such as education, business, or nursing. A few institutions that attract a unique sort of student, such as St. John's College in Maryland, may not offer majors, but for the vast majority the major is one of the main attractions for students.

The question for institutions facing enrollment problems is what majors should be provided. Several criteria can help determine the answer to that question. The first is the presence of at least three professors of the subject whose courses collectively provide students different points of view and a broad coverage of the field. There is a tendency, in small institutions, to claim to offer a major in a field in which there is only one faculty member. This claim is likely to be at best cosmetic and at worst a potential fraud. It is argued here that any subject worthy of constituting a major should be sufficiently complex as to require several different points of view present. Thus, a history major should at least consist of American and European history and some other geographic or temporal subdivision.

This principle means that a small faculty of thirty should attempt to offer no more than ten majors and possibly fewer. What these majors should be depends on several different factors. The first is the training, experience, and talents of the existing faculty. Since the faculty has been created over time as a result of many different sorts of decisions, this criterion by itself lends a sort of random quality to the curriculum. But as faculties change, there is opportunity for conscious decision as to what majors should be added. Changing student interests and the changing job market should be examined and considered. For example, in the 1980s, education as a major might be gradually eliminated and replaced by a business major. One of the main responsibilities of the chief academic officer is to be aware of changes in demand and to make critical decisions about new faculty appointments. Actual student enrollment in majors should be studied with a view to replacement of majors that do not attract students.

Limiting majors to subjects for which there are at least three reasonably competent faculty and for which there is solid student demand will, in small institutions, leave out many subjects. This bothers some who believe in the ideal that a liberal arts college must offer a full range of majors in order to be honest and valid. This notion of an ideal, comprehensive institution of whatever type should be rejected. Comprehensive research universities can be excellent without a medical school, law school, or classics major. And a liberal arts college can be excellent without sociology, foreign language, religion, or music and with business, communication arts, or even agriculture.

There may be a few subjects so typically in demand and so essential to the transcendent purposes of undergraduate education as to be needed in most curricula, but the number is limited. English, mathematics, science, and perhaps history would be examples. Thus, the majors offered by the following two institutions would be equally valid—if they attracted students:

College A	*College B*
English	English
Mathematics	Mathematics
Biology	Chemistry
Psychology	Sociology
French	History
History	Religion
Elementary Education	Drama
Business	Journalism
Music	Art
Radio and TV	Political Science

General Education. The second component of the formal curriculum is general education. General education is designed to provide a common body of intellectual experience, a common universe of discourse, and a common awareness of the major domain of knowledge. In the past, there has been general agreement as to what general education comprised. In the Colonial college, Latin, Greek, Hebrew, and moral and natural philosophy were the essentials. In the 1940s and 1950s, natural sciences, social sciences, humanities, and communications were generally agreed upon—at least in theory. As a result of many forces—new fields of study, new kinds of faculty members, student rejection of requirements, and changing social conditions—that general agreement is gone. It is now necessary to question whether or not there should be a general education component and, if so, what it should contain.

There are three basic patterns available for general education, each with some strength and each with considerable weakness. The first is the free elective system, in which the student can elect any courses desired, presumably with some advice from an advisor. This can result in a balanced or a highly unbalanced educational experience, but it allows students a feeling of freedom and may be highly attractive. The second pattern is the distribution system, which requires all students to select some courses from each of three domains: science, social sciences, and humanities. This system allows students to make use of whatever courses are available, but those courses created for the needs of majors may not suit nonmajors. In addition, there is the illogicality of equating, say, a course in urban sociology with a course in child growth and development—both social sciences but quite different. The third pattern is a system of required courses especially created for general education purposes. This system has the virtue of being a serious effort to meet general education needs of students. However, faculty members may feel incompetent to teach such courses and the result may be quite superficial.

On balance, with stress placed on advising as essential and with the greatest likelihood of student support, a relatively free elective system seems a prudent course of action. Since the essence of undergraduate education is verbal, and verbal skills seem basic to vocational and nonvocational adult life, a one-year English course could be required of all students. Such a course, well conceived, could stress both writing and literature and hence could contribute to power of expression as well as to a common body of allusion, illustration, and metaphor. Aside from that and whatever courses were required in the major, students would be free to elect—always in the hope that they would discuss the possibilities with their advisors—the courses that would make the most sense for them. A desirable side effect of such a free market is that it would expose those courses and professors not attractive to students and, over time, would allow them to be replaced by others with greater appeal. Another desirable side effect is that this system would allow faculty members the freedom to develop courses that interested them. There is some reason to believe that a course taught by someone who is truly interested in and excited by the subject would have a powerful intrinsic value.

Some will argue that the free elective system abdicates the faculty responsibility to create a curriculum most likely to produce educated men and women. But as suggested earlier, there is no evidence that any one curricular pattern is any more or less effective than any other. It is the generic college experience that seems to produce change, not a specific kind of course or pattern of courses. If this is true, then the criteria of attractiveness to students and to faculty should prevail. It increasingly appears that a three-part structure consisting of a major, electives, and common work in English will likely be the most attractive and, over time, the most economical system. All institutions, and especially those facing difficulties, should refrain from adopting any radical or complex curricular organization. Actually, some of the most successful significant curricular innovations, such as Brown's, are quite straightforward solutions to very real problems. Dartmouth can be called highly innovative because it ensures that all students have experience with the computer, that student retention of a foreign language is increased, and that there is opportunity for all students to take small upper-level courses taught by senior and experienced professors.

Improving Instruction

What should be done regarding instruction that will help interest, enroll, and retain students? The answer is—a great deal and not much. Not much in the sense of some educational magic that will overnight change an institution into a highly desirable place because of its unique style of instruction. But a great deal in the sense that many traditional practices and processes can be improved.

With respect to teaching, institutions should not expect most professors to attempt and become proficient in a large variety of techniques and styles. It seems desirable that professors have a reasonable command of whatever it is they profess—history, sociology, or art—and that they be reasonably interesting people who clearly manifest an interest and excitement regarding what they teach. It is also desirable that professors be encouraged to regard students as important individuals. With respect to the acts of teaching, it seems worthwhile to encourage professors to seek to improve the organization of their courses, the clarity of assignments, the comprehensibility of their lectures, the focus of their discussions, the fairness of their grading, and the fidelity with which they keep office hours. Since there are some technological devices that can help some students learn more or faster or with greater retention, appropriate equipment should be made available and professors shown how to use it if they so desire. There can be no objections to encouraging faculty members to read such works as W. J. McKeachie's *Teaching Tips* (1969). And very likely, faculty members can learn how to improve their teaching from student evaluation forms. However, a number of currently popular theories of instruction do not appear to have much relevance for most professors in most institutions. The first of these is the so-called competency-based system of teaching. At a gross level, there is no problem. It can be and should be determined whether students can read, write a sentence, solve a physics problem, or write a computer program. But the advocates of competency-based education envision something far grander. They visualize a complex net of competencies, a variety of ways of developing them, and a precise system for determining whether or not students have acquired them. From time to time, a professor having special interests and skills might develop a competency-based course or program and make it work. And this should not be discouraged. But generally, professors should not be expected to seek to develop more specific competency than some knowledge and understanding of a subject and, when relevant, some ability to apply that knowledge and understanding. A similar notion is called a systems approach to teaching. This calls for the instructor to posit a sequential series of behavioral objectives and to demand demonstration of each desired behavior before proceeding to the next learning step. Once again, some professors teaching some kinds of courses may organize the work in some such fashion; for example, a professor interested in computers might develop a sequenced course requiring mastery before proceeding. But again, as a general rule, expecting the faculty to have the psychological sophistication needed to arrange such sequences is expecting the impossible. A much less sophisticated activity is the preparation of valid and reliable tests of knowledge in a course. Usually, faculty members fail to do even that well. And so it goes with more of the other complex organizations for learning. In some institutions, for some courses developed by a professor having unique interests and skills, an organization that forces students to work independently and to follow at their own pace a sequence of definite assignments works and is appropriate. But for the most part, learning is too inexact and professors too unskilled for such elegance.

The conclusion is that institutions should refrain from seeking any radical transformation of teaching. The course is a permanent fixture whether it be called disciplinary, interdisciplinary, or problem centered. Organizing the course clearly and well is important and should be encouraged. Verbal communication as the primary technique of instruction seems also to be permanent. Professors can be reasonably expected to have or develop their verbal ability. Also, for economic, if for no other reasons, the instructional norm will remain a single teacher and a group of students (obviously of varying size). Thus, team teaching or complex systems of grouping and regrouping of students are likely not possible except in quite unique situations.

There are hundreds, and possibly thousands, of interesting activities having instructional possibilities. These include tape-recording evaluations of student themes, role playing, behavior modification, videotape recordings, open- and closed-circuit television, computer-based or -managed instruction, nondirective teaching, programmed texts, and a host of others. All, however, appear to have utility limited to quite unique situations and users, and all appear to be more expensive than the traditional instructional format of a formal class consisting of an instructor and students pursuing a course largely by verbal means. It is upon that traditional mode of teaching that the success of an instructional program will depend. Nonetheless, if an individual professor wishes to experiment with an innovation, there can be no objection—so long as there are resources available and so long as the professor has the requisite abilities to use whatever technique is attempted. But financially troubled institutions should not divert resources to support such activities. The potential gains are simply not that great.

With respect to the instructional part of the educational program, the essentials can be quickly related. First, seek faculty members who have reasonable competence in a subject, who are moderately interesting people able to communicate with some facility, and who have respect for students as human beings.

Second, let the course be the basic organizing unit, with enough flexibility allowed so that within the course some variation of technique is possible. The point here is to refrain from making independent study, tutorials, mediated programs, or modules of instruction the organizing elements.

Third, let the principal physical elements of instruction be the classroom, library, laboratory, textbook, chalkboard, studio, when appropriate, and the professor's office. The point here is to avoid expressing educational fads in physical terms, which might very well include multimedia classrooms, lecture rooms having electronic response systems, or a network of television monitors in classrooms complete with remote response systems so that students can interact with a televised instructor. An affluent institution with external funds might create such things, but they hold little promise of being central to the educational effort of even those privileged places.

And fourth, with respect to evaluation or assessment, in spite of some quite valid criticisms some variant of the traditional letter grade seems best. There has been experimentation with comprehensive examinations, evaluation letters, periodic measurements of competency, contract learning—with credit granted when the contract has been satisfied—waiver examinations, and highly sophisticated oral examinations. For the most part, the more complicated and time-consuming techniques appear to fall quickly into disuse. In addition, they require abilities generally not present in a faculty. While letter grades tend to conceal and may become an end of education in themselves, they can serve as reasonably reliable indicators of gross student performance if a range of only three grades is used—and given the lack of precision in the entire process of education, gross indicators are all that should be used. Contemporary psychometrics allows for quite precise measurement of such things as attitudes and specific cognitive skills, but the tests are expensive to create and use and require a great deal of student and faculty time. The letter-grade system based on examinations, papers, or laboratory work is relatively inexpensive and is well understood and accepted by faculty and students alike.

A word here about course organization would seem appropriate. In the 1950s, Ruml and Morrison and McGrath suggested that classes of different sizes should be provided: a few large courses, 40 to 100 or more; some middle-sized courses, 15 to 25; and some quite small, 5 to 10. More recently, Bowen and Douglass (1971) have identified six different arrangements, each with definite educational and financial implications. First is the so-called conventional plan, which involves formal classes taught by an individual to between eight and forty students. Second is the Ruml plan just mentioned. A third plan consists of considerable programmed independent study with few formal courses. Fourth is a plan based upon extensive use of tutorials but so organized as to make maximum use of educational technology. The fifth plan uses a great deal of educational technology. The sixth plan, called "eclectic," consists of elements drawn from the other five. Bowen and Douglass (1971) have estimated the costs per class and per student for the different plans and discovered that there are important cost differences depending on what sort of course organization is offered. They further show that by using a pattern of courses derived from each of the plans, strikingly lower costs can be obtained than by using the conventional plan (p. 78). Summing up, they remark: "We conclude that there is no one best way of education suitable for all institutions, all subjects, all professors, and all students. We reject any single plan in favor of an eclectic plan that draws on conventional lecture-discussion and lecture-laboratories, large lectures, independent study, tutorials and mechanized instructions. We find that the eclectic plan is economically feasible" (p. 102).

In theory, such a balance of instructional modes makes sense for all institutions—those in and those out of trouble. However, for different reasons for different sorts of institutions, such a contrived pattern seems difficult, if not impossible, to achieve. It is significant that the two most radical plans are given the names of professors (Fred Keller and S. N. Postlethwaite) who actually have used the systems in their own courses and who then extrapolated as to what might be possible if everyone used the same system. The point is that professors are reluctant, as a faculty, to embrace any uniform style of instruction, especially if it involves considerable technology and complex logistics. Many institutions, for example, experienced difficulty in persuading foreign language professors to use language laboratories in any consistent way. Some one or several professors might devise a creative use of language laboratories that would be ignored by their colleagues. There are, of course, a few institutions in which all faculty use a similar mode and style of instruction, such as the Socratic discussion of Great Books at St. John's College. And at Evergreen State College, faculty members are all expected to use three general styles of instruction: a large-group team-taught course, a smaller-group single-professor course, and tutorials, generally in sequence over three years. But for most institutions, distribution of modes of instruction, if achieved, will result from some rather gross guidelines: First, an institution-wide, desired student to faculty ratio can be established. Second, courses that attract only a few students in a consistent pattern can be eliminated. And third, several broad categories of types of courses and cost per credit hour produced can be established and used as criteria or guidelines within which departments, divisions, or separate schools and colleges can be expected to operate.

Although in any given institution there may be professors who become interested and proficient in creating new kinds of courses, it is the position taken here that:

1. Most professors will not develop carefully programmed courses for self-paced instruction.
2. Most professors will be disinclined to develop and use, in any consistent way, courses that utilize the computer, videotape, audiotape, or other technological devices as a primary means of delivering educational services.
3. Most professors will be disinclined to manage, in a sophisticated way, carefully planned independent study courses for students.
4. Most institutions facing serious economic conditions will not be able to acquire or maintain the substantial amounts of educational technology needed. They will be unable to maintain a well-staffed center for the improvement of instruction. They further will be unable to underwrite faculty preparation of such things as programmed courses or computer-managed courses.

5. As a general rule, based on considerable observation, faculties in economically strong institutions will not, except for quite personal reasons, use prescribed patterns of course or organization or presentation. The fact of economic strength implies no real reason to adopt new styles. And in weak institutions, the resources to develop new patterns are lacking.

These are rather strong and, some would say, negative statements. It should be noted that there is no way they can be proven with any certainty, but they are based on a great deal of observation. At the University of Wisconsin, for example, an efficient way of teaching Basic Principles of Economics was developed and its value established by one professor. The approach was rejected by his colleagues and was terminated when the inventor moved to another institution. At Florida State University, an efficient way of using a computer to instruct teacher trainees in how to teach reading was developed, publicized, and allowed to fall into disuse, although state legislation mandated that such a course was required in order to obtain or update a teaching credential. Many of the approaches to teaching described in *Change* magazine during 1977 and 1978 in theory have general applicability, but the impression persists that they typically are used by the inventor and few others. Thus, the generalization is stressed that new and innovative ways of organizing the delivery of a curriculum will not likely help the financial condition of an institution or improve its attractiveness to students.

Principles for Curricular and Instructional Change

Some general principles may have a bearing on these matters.

Although there is no evidence that any one pattern for undergraduate curriculum is any better or worse than any other, it may be of value that the curriculum have a distinctive image with which prospective students can identify. Thus, the Dartmouth Plan, the Colorado College Modular Curriculum, the Brown University New Program, the older program of Functional General Education at Stephens College, the Core Program in Education Administration and Policy Analysis at the Stanford School of Education, the College of Basic Studies at Boston University, and the General College at the University of Minnesota each conjures up certain expectations in the minds of prospective students. If that image is based to some degree in reality, this is healthy. There is always the danger, however, that the image created will be purely cosmetic, covering over a weak and uninteresting program.

Some protection against cosmetics may be provided if a second, and essential, criterion is observed. It is that the curriculum be within the capabilities of the faculty. Thus, a curriculum that requires extensive use of educational technology demands a faculty qualified to use technology. A curriculum that focuses on ecology requires a faculty with more than traditional preparation in academic disciplines. A curriculum that purports to deal with personal problems of students through a variety of means requires a psychologically sophisticated faculty.

In a related vein, the overall curriculum should assume no psychological knowledge or sophistication on the part of the general faculty. Joseph Katz, K. Patricia Cross, and other curriculum analysts expect faculties to understand developmental needs of students or how to deal with differential traits and aptitudes. Such scholars have become proficient in psychological intervention over a lifetime of professional work, but few professors will be similarly prepared. As a general rule, faculty members may be expected to have formed, from experience, some conclusions as to what undergraduate students are like and which teaching techniques seem to work. And they might be expected to read a little, but a very little, concerning the psychology of late adolescents, adults, minority groups, or whatever specific group they instruct. Beyond that, those responsible for the curriculum should make no assumptions.

In spite of the earlier suggestion that the undergraduate curriculum should have a distinctive image, care should be taken that the nomenclature used with respect to the curriculum be relatively simple and linked clearly to traditional terminology. There seems to be a tendency when trying to create a new and attractive curriculum to create, at the same time, new names for things. At the University of Wisconsin at Green Bay, departments are called "options" and interdisciplinary activities are called "concentrations." Nova University has developed an entire new lexicon in which "modules" replace "courses," "major applied research projects" replace "theses," and "practicums" replace "term papers." At a more general level, "experiential learning" is a new name for learning through doing or even fieldwork. "Competency-based" curriculum indicates an attempt to measure outcomes, and a "systems approach" to education signifies that a course or program is organized. The use of new nomenclature can create problems. First, the new names may fool even the inventors into believing that they have produced something different. A good example is the phrase "nontraditional education," which is intended to imply something quite new that has great potential for human betterment. Yet, when one examines nontraditional programs in action, for the most part one finds just variations of the traditional course outline, bibliography, assignments, lectures, discussions, grading, fieldwork, and homework. As far as can be determined, the distinctive essentials of nontraditional education have little to do with what students actually do. Whether it be a program in business administration at the University of San Francisco, a program for junior college teachers at Nova University, or a program for school administrators at the University of Northern Colorado, the big differences may be summed up as: where—off campus; what—few classes and more homework; and who—part-time in place of full-time help. It probably would be better if the older language were used and efforts expended to improve the quality of each of those older, but still valid practices. A second problem is that new language, when used extensively, tends to confuse students and prospective students. One can at least theorize that some of the enrollment problems experienced by the University of Wisconsin at Green Bay may be due to the fact that prospective students cannot tell that an option is the same as a subject matter major and that a concentration is really a combination of major, minor, and elective subjects. In the absence of persuasive evidence against tradition, it is strongly suggested that nomenclature be kept simple and traditional. Thus, these words would be used: entrance requirements, graduation requirements, majors, minors, electives, reading lists, academic credits, grades, term papers, fieldwork, laboratory work, library, audio-visual aids, courses, and the like. When in doubt, simplify.

Similarly, the logistics of the curriculum should be kept relatively simple. The traditional pattern of courses meeting at regular times on specific days in the week and in a set place need not be invidiously regarded as lockstep. It furnishes both faculty and students with a definite framework for their activities, provides what is in effect a contract with respect to what each will do, and allows the availability of free time to be predicted and used as the individual wishes. Further, it is a way of dividing things to be learned into manageable limits. In addition, it allows for a more flexible schedule of activities for students who need or can use one without jeopardizing the needs of students who should have greater structure. One arrangement can be visualized in which there would be no class structure, with individual activities being scheduled as needed. A computer, in theory, could accumulate evidence about each student's progress and could actively provide for ad hoc groups as that progress warranted. Or another arrangement might provide for the class, but with individual students able to attend or not as they saw fit. The latter pattern seems preferable both financially and educationally.

In addition to the formal curriculum and instruction, other elements of the educational program should be considered as they bear on institutional vitality and survival. Thus, student involvement in campus activities is urged, as is the creation of small groups, such as cluster colleges, with which students may identify. Providing mechanisms to help students achieve well in the academic program also seems desirable, including some kinds of remedial programs. Especially significant would be serious efforts to improve the intellectual and psychological tone of the institution, which not only might reduce attrition but might also help attract new students. Above all, a well-developed, organized, and supported advising system seems one of the most important parts of the educational program, even though it is the one part that typically has been the most poorly used.

Conclusions

Although no particular curricular structure or content has proven to be superior to another and new and innovative styles of teaching have not established themselves, research and theory do suggest ways of making an educational program reasonably effective and more attractive to students. First, whatever curriculum is adopted should be tailored to the students and faculty at a particular institution. Perhaps one reason why the Harvard style of general education failed throughout the country is that it was devised for Harvard College and not for other sorts of institutions. Second, periodic combination and recombination of curricular elements and experimentation with a variety of teaching techniques are urged because such activities can create an atmosphere of life and vitality. It is the process of program innovation and change that is important, rather than the substance of any given change. Third, whatever curricular and instructional elements are used, attention should be given to logistics and finance to ensure smooth functioning and a minimum of frustration, whether it be over registration, library procedures, or classroom space. Team teaching can work well if an institution can afford the time needed for course organization but it will fail if it is attempted without time and resources. Fourth and finally, whatever curricular pattern is adopted for undergraduates should seek to be truly responsive to their concerns. The argument that a curriculum is good for students may be strong enough to gain passive acceptance of requirements but not strong enough to make it a truly vital force in the life of an institution.

Further Readings

The problem of how to retain students once they matriculate is at least fifty years old. By now there should have been a rich literature on the subject—but, strangely, this is not true. Once one has read Iffert, Summerskill, Pervin, and Astin, one has viewed the conventional wisdom. The curriculum may be involved and could perhaps affect retention, so a few illustrative documents are listed that indicate potentiality; however, the actual effects are as yet unknown.

ASTIN, A. W. "College Dropouts: A National Profile." *American Council on Education Research Reports,* 1972, 7 (1).

ASTIN, A. W. *Preventing Students from Dropping Out.* San Francisco: Jossey-Bass, 1975.

BUCKLIN, R., AND BUCKLIN, M. C. *The Psychological Characteristics of the College Persistor and Leaver: A Review.* Washington, D.C.: U. S. Office of Education, 1970.

Carnegie Foundation for the Advancement of Teaching. *Missions of the College Curriculum: A Contemporary Review with Suggestions.* San Francisco: Jossey-Bass, 1977.

CENTRA, J. A. *Strategies for Improving College Teaching.* ERIC/ Higher Education Research Report No. 8. Washington, D.C.: American Association for Higher Education, 1972.

CROSS, K. P., VALLEY, J. R., AND ASSOCIATES. *Planning Non-Traditional Programs: An Analysis of the Issues for Postsecondary Education.* San Francisco: Jossey-Bass, 1974.

DRESSEL, P. L. *College and University Curriculum.* Berkeley, Calif.: McCutchan, 1971.

IFFERT, R. E. *Retention and Withdrawal of College Students.* DHEW Bulletin No. 1. U.S. Government Printing Office, 1957.

LEVINE, A. *Handbook on Undergraduate Curriculum: Prepared for the Carnegie Council on Policy Studies in Higher Education.* San Francisco: Jossey-Bass, 1978.

LEVINE, A., AND WEINGART, J. *Reform of Undergraduate Education.* San Francisco: Jossey-Bass, 1973.

PANTAGES, T. "Studies of College Attrition: 1950–1975." *Review of Educational Research,* 1978, *48,* 49–101.

PERVIN, L. A., REIK, L. E., AND DALRYMPLE, W. (Eds.). *The College Dropout and the Utilization of Talent.* Princeton, N. J.: Princeton University Press, 1966.

SUMMERSKILL, J. "Dropouts From College." In N. Sanford (Ed.), *The American College.* New York: Wiley, 1962.

TINTO, V. "Dropout from Higher Education: A Theoretical Synthesis of Recent Research." *Review of Educational Research,* 1975, *45* (1).

WOOD, L., AND DAVIS, B. G. *Designing and Evaluating Higher Education Curricula.* Washington, D.C.: American Association for Higher Education, 1978.

Chapter 9

かかかかやややや

Increasing
Faculty Performance

Faculties are an indisputable resource in ensuring institutional survival and viability. Whatever is done in the academic program will
be done by faculty, and they can do it superbly, well, or poorly. The
degree to which an institution's faculty in aggregate performs well is
related, if not to application rates, certainly to retention rates. Apart
from the prestige colleges and universities and the highly visible denominational or special-purpose institutions (like West Point), students apply to a specific institution because of location, cost, parental
contact with the institution, or decisions of high school friends and
classmates. But whether they stay, once enrolled, seems related to
the degree of satisfaction with the social environment and academic
program. Both of these are powerfully determined by the faculty.

Faculty Role in Survival

An intellectually inert faculty, or one that does not manifest care and concern for students, is a reasonable guarantee of high student dissatisfaction and attrition. It is this intrinsic ability of the faculty that is a concern of faculty development activities and of the rational staffing policies to be discussed subsequently as essential to institutional survival. In addition, the faculty can be a source of new ideas and new programs that may contribute to overall institutional attractiveness. Although it is true that in the past the most profound changes in American higher education have been initiated by administrators or those outside of institutions (the free elective system by a president, reform in medical education by an outsider), faculty members can produce quite fertile ideas for change and reform, as the contents of hundreds of self-studies attest. The processes of innovation in all organizations, including academic ones, require a degree of decentralization if invention is to take place and a degree of centralization if adoption is to take place. The faculty is the decentralized element that must be relied upon to generate the new ideas, a few of which may help the institution through the difficult years that lie ahead.

It is also axiomatic that institutional existence, continuation, change, and even survival are related to the institution's traditions, saga, and perception of itself. Although former students, board members, and various constituencies help establish and maintain the image of the institution, it is the faculty that is the most effective collective memory and exemplar of a tradition. It is probably the president, as Clark (1970) has demonstrated, who is the one most responsible for creating a unique institutional image or saga, but it is the faculty that perpetuates it. It can be theorized that, especially among the private institutions, those whose faculty have long identified with the institution and serve as its collective memory will be most able to survive extreme adversity. The very hardiness of the small liberal arts colleges throughout the twentieth century seems to exemplify this point.

Further, it is this possession of tradition that enables faculties to grant legitimacy to proposals made by administration. In the American system of higher education, the president or his chief

associates typically propose, whether it be new graduation requirements, budget readjustment, or provisions for faculty discipline.
While boards of trustees give ultimate legal force to adoption of
those proposals, it is faculty action that assigns legitimacy to them.
Without faculty approval—even if given grudgingly—presidents
will rarely seek the legal approval for a proposal from the board of
trustees. This seems to be true even in the domain of financing,
which is clearly the explicit responsibility of the chief executive
officer. And without question, it is the faculty that legitimizes curricular changes, faculty personnel policies, and even such highly
sensitive matters as faculty reduction due to financial difficulties. As
shall be seen, one technique that institutions will increasingly need
to consider is the discharge of tenured faculty. When this has been
attempted without careful faculty consultation it has, for the most
part, produced such serious consequences for administration as immediate faculty demand for a union. This was well illustrated at the
University of San Francisco when it sent termination notices to over
a hundred faculty, some on tenure. The aftermath produced a union
contract and the summary firing of the president. At Mankato State
College in Minnesota, faculty finally granted legitimacy to the
termination of tenured faculty and to the processes by which the
terminations were carried out. And they were carried out without
incident.

　　This matter of legitimacy is clearly illustrated in major,
prestige colleges and universities, in which the president and the
board of trustees are ultimately responsible for all decisions. Prudent
presidents will typically make those decisions only after determining
the judgment of the faculty. This appears to be true regardless of
whether the decision concerns the disciplining of a faculty member,
action on promotion, or even institutional investment policy. It is
really the faculty that grants administrators the mandate to govern,
and that mandate can be removed by both overt and covert means.
The mandate is especially significant with respect to the various decisions that must be made to ensure institutional survival. In this
power to grant a mandate wisely lies one of the most potent opportunities for the creative energies of the faculty to be used for high
institutional purposes.

　　During the eighties, a key element in the financial and intellectual situation of collegiate institutions, regardless of type, will be how their faculties overcome common problems by making the creative contributions of which they are so capable.

Faculty Problems

A major problem is the cost of faculty, which has continued throughout the Sixties and Seventies. The acceleration began in 1958, with the dramatic exception of a few institutions and a few states that imposed moratoria on raises in faculty salaries and attempted to increase teaching loads. The cost increases were produced by: increases in compensation at rates higher than the rise in costs of other consumer goods; decreases in actual teaching loads from twelve hours to three in research universities and from fifteen or twenty hours to twelve in public junior and state colleges; growing use of more expensive educational materials; and increased institutional support for research in research and doctorate-granting universities and in comprehensive colleges (those institutions with the large majority of the total enrollment in the country). This cost increase was exacerbated by the simultaneous increase in the cost and variety of fringe benefits and the proportion of professors on tenure.

The shift may be seen by comparing the situation in one institution in 1957 with the situation in 1977. In 1957, the faculty was distributed by rank: instructors 19 percent, assistant professors 35 percent, associate professors 25 percent, and full professors 21 percent. Average salaries by rank were: instructor $4,500, assistant professor $5,500, associate professor $7,000, and full professor $9,000. Thirty-five percent of that faculty was on tenure, and the normal teaching load was four three-hour courses or twelve hours of classroom contact per week. Fringe benefits represented 9 percent of salary and included 5 percent retirement, 2 percent social security contribution, and 2 percent used for term life insurance and a slight contribution to health insurance. By 1977, the proportion of the institutional budget for faculty salaries had increased substantially through the combined effects of the elimination of instructor rank, a heavy concentration of faculty at the senior ranks with all on tenure (70 to 80 percent), a reduction in teaching loads to two courses (six hours), and an increase in fringe benefits to slightly over

20 percent of direct salary costs. There were also the added costs of elaborate audio-visual materials, computer time, expensive and sophisticated laboratory equipment, and more comprehensive library holdings.

Some of this can be justified. Faculty salaries in the immediate post–World War II period had lagged behind other segments of the professional work force (remaining at about the 1939 level of real wages) and had to be increased because of equity and to attract the needed professors for the enrollment expansion of the 1960s and 1970s. Teaching loads of eighteen to twenty-one hours in some institutions were excessive and probably produced superficial teaching (although this cannot be known). Further, the general trend throughout the society for workers to seek greater economic security through larger retirement, health, and insurance benefits established a pattern that educational institutions were constrained to follow. And the new or more refined educational materials can be presumed to be related to some qualitative improvement in collegiate education.

Justified or not, the financial strain of those increased costs on institutions as they face stable or declining enrollments and resources during the 1980s are considerable and, in some way, must be accommodated or rectified. However, the nature of faculty members and the faculty itself militate against any easy solutions. Faculty members are typically (clearly not always) highly trained to teach a specialty. When student demand for specialties shifts, as it did during the 1970s, and when the specialized faculty members are on tenure, there is need for faculty members to develop new specialties to conform to demand. Yet even minor shifts in specialty are difficult for an aging faculty. Can, for example, the professor of American history be reasonably expected to retrain himself or herself to deal with some aspect of business education or one of the emerging health fields (both high-demand fields in the seventies)?

Even if professors could, with reasonable facility, be retrained or retrain themselves, many are reluctant to do so, in part because of a deep suspicion of administration and considerable ignorance regarding institutional finances. Even distinguished professors in sophisticated research institutions are persuaded that central administration has substantial reserve funds that could be expended to support faculty members, even when demand for their services has declined. The situation in research universities is especially vexing. The shift in student demand for courses and programs is frequently accompanied by shifts and declines in external funds available to support research in a specialty.

Expecting professors to shift their interests is difficult for many reasons, one of which is the ambiguousness of the professorial role. Professors teach, engage in research and scholarship, render various kinds of professional services, participate in administration, and generally reflect upon the nature of man, society, and the universe. Which of these is really the most significant activity, deserving of continual institutional support? For example, consider a faculty in teacher preparation that did all of those things. The recent decline in student enrollment in teacher education programs does not lessen the need for research and reflection on education. A strong theoretical case can be built that even faculty whose courses have been eliminated should be retrained because of the contributions they make to the intellectual fabric of the school or department. Such a case is especially difficult to refute when advanced by an academic department that expanded during the 1960s, added faculty coverage for new subspecialties, and gained a reputation as an outstanding department. Suggestions that some members of the department should turn their attention to another discipline are met with the complaint that even with no students some subspecialties are essential if a department is truly to reflect its discipline. The same phenomenon is also found in smaller institutions whose entire faculty can argue that even if there is a decline in student enrollment in French and German, it is impossible to conceive of a true liberal arts college in which the literature, language, and culture of those two nations are not represented. The nature of the academic, intellectual institution is so ambiguous that it is impossible to establish that elimination of a particular specialty or subspecialty would not jeopardize the educational and intellectual impact.

This problem of the essentiality of academic subspecialties was aggravated during the 1960s when the expansion through research and scholarship of virtually all academic fields was reflected in a proliferation of courses and positions. Obviously, expanded curricula result in an expanded conception as to what an academic institution is. Thus, just through extension of the frontiers of research and scholarship and the consequent course proliferation, a larger and more expensive institution was created, which in theory should be maintained even when enrollments and resources stabilize or decline. Additionally, the expanded version of the college or university was solidified through the granting of tenure to 70 to 80 percent of the faculty staffing those new programs.

Perhaps undergirding such factors is the essentially conservative posture taken by faculty members with respect to educational practice and policy and institutional organization and structure. Although faculty members are more liberal than the general population concerning political, social, or economic matters, they typically resist changes in the curriculum (except growth), in styles of teaching, and in their conception of the academic institution. Resistance to change deriving from such conservatism is reinforced in the face of financial threat, when the faculty resist cutting back on courses offered not only on ideological grounds but also on the economic grounds of preserving faculty positions.

Although difficult to prove, a distinct possibility is that faculty resistance to change during the late 1970s and the 1980s may be related to the aging of the faculty. The big enrollment jumps in higher education came about between 1958 and 1968. Faculty appointed to serve those students were relatively young products of post-World War II doctoral programs who were in their thirties or early forties. Because of the high demand during the 1960s, those faculty members were promoted rapidly and granted tenure early. Thus, by the end of the 1960s, a faculty was in place aged mid forties to mid fifties, whose members would tend to remain in their positions given the deterioration in job opportunities that began in the early 1970s. It can be theorized that throughout the 1980s such an aging professoriate will be increasingly unable or unwilling to respond to new demands and situations unless externally motivated.

Thus, as institutions move into the 1980s and can anticipate overall decline in enrollments and a likely decline in resources— possibly absolute but certainly relative to previous levels of support —their faculties present a composite of problems. Faculties wish to offer an expanded and proliferated curriculum but with a reduced number of courses taught by each faculty member as compared with the teaching loads of the 1940s and 1950s. Faculty members are older, hold higher ranks, receive higher salaries, and are generally on tenure. Many of the academic fields that were much in demand during the 1960s, such as teacher education or theoretical physics, no longer attract large enrollments, yet are staffed with tenure faculty in numbers appropriate for an expansionist period. Such faculty members are unable or unwilling to change to new fields more in demand and are reluctant to embrace changes that might jeopardize their conceptions of themselves as professionals, their departments or institutions as idealized entities, or their economic well-being.

Faculty members who fight to keep teaching their particular specialties even when enrollments have dropped precipitously are not evil. They often realize that they do not have the accomplishments and reputation to get another job given the generally bad economic situation in higher education. This makes them dependent on their current institution and anxious and suspicious when administrators make decisions affecting them. These professors have worked hard for many years to become very knowledgeable in a narrow specialty. To justify this hard work and specialization they have had to convince themselves of the great value and excitement of their specialty. Students' decisions not to take their courses undermine this assessment and set up cognitive dissonance that they must work to dispel by insisting that their liberal art or science is important even to those students interested in the new professional fields. For example, in an institution with serious enrollment problems, two soft-money programs (management and communications) had been created which attracted high enrollments. The time came, however, when those programs could be continued only by shifting to them two tenure track positions from elsewhere in the institution. Despite the life-or-death characteristic of the situation, the members of the faculty committee could not bring themselves to believe that students would prefer courses other than the ones the faculty members taught. The arguments used were the classic ones: It would not be a liberal arts college without advanced French. To reduce music would have a chilling effect on the cultural tone of the institution. Replacing a history position with one in management would send out managers who lacked the broad social perspective that only the study of history can develop.

These problems will be more intense in some kinds of institutions than in others. The private liberal arts colleges of only local or regional reputation had begun to experience serious enrollment declines by the mid 1970s and, unless unexpected changes take place, will face even more serious declines during the 1980s. State colleges and universities will face similar conditions a few years later. By the mid 1980s, even the flagship state universities (in at least some subordinate schools and colleges) and prestige private colleges and universities can expect lowered application and acceptance rates, although probably no absolute decline in enrollments. They very likely will not become open-admissions institutions. Even public junior colleges, which have expanded enrollments by emphasizing programs for adults, had begun to experience some enrollment and resource decline by the late 1970s and can expect further deterioration during the 1980s. The chronic faculty problems must be solved if such institutions are to survive.

Faculty Development

Although reducing the number of faculty and increasing the overall student–faculty ratio is the most direct faculty-related approach to institutional survival, improving the quality of faculty and increasing faculty involvement in institutionwide concerns may, in the long term, be even more significant. Certainly, during the 1960s, a few institutions changed their image and increased viability by concentrating on faculty improvement. Knox College and Stanford University, under strong presidential leadership, increased strength and attractiveness by first recruiting outstanding faculty members and increasing their remuneration, then by recruiting more and more able students, then by increasing the amount of external support, and finally—only after the first three steps had been taken —by creating new and improved physical plants. But that was during an expansionist time. Whether the same techniques could be used in a more stable situation is conjectural.

The argument is made that, during the late 1970s and 1980s, institutions with a high proportion of their faculty on tenure (70 to 80 percent) will be unable to recruit new faculty members and, with them presumably, new ideas. The only way such institutions can be self-renewing is through a conscious effort to help faculty members renew themselves. Advocates of this point of view range from the Carnegie Commission on Higher Education to the University of California system to the Lilly Foundation, all of which have urged that a substantial portion (2.5 to 5 percent) of budgets be devoted to faculty development or faculty renewal. So popular has the concept become that there has evolved something that might be called the "faculty development movement" and a new professional subspecialty has arisen of what might be called "faculty developers." These include directors of centers for the improvement of instruction, assistant deans for faculty affairs, and directors of learning resources centers.

The techniques used present considerable variety. There are the centers for improvement of instruction which provide advice and consultation regarding instruction, assistance with certain technical aids for instruction, and small grants to help faculty members improve their instruction. The University of Michigan, Michigan State University, and Cornell University are all examples of institutions that have created reasonably successful centers. There are foundation-supported activities such as the former Danforth Foundation Liberal Arts Workshop, which brought together faculty members from twenty-five to thirty colleges each summer to discuss educational matters. There are the consortia of institutions that stress faculty improvement and assist faculty members to travel abroad, participate in conferences, or jointly plan new programs. Some institutions, with external funding, have created university fellows programs, which allow younger scholars time to think about new professional interests and directions as well as devote some time to institutionwide concerns. There are also grant programs, such as that attempted by the University of California, which make funds available for various individual efforts to improve instruction. And then there are the many examples of fall faculty conferences, various leave-of-absence policies, professorial development consultation between faculty members and academic administration supervisors, and salary improvement programs to encourage individual faculty members to develop and change.

It is difficult to gauge the potential of faculty development as an approach to strengthening institutions. In part, this stems from a certain ambiguity of the phrase. Many of the more widely publicized efforts seem to have equated faculty development with improvement of instruction. When such a narrow conception is used, the number of actual faculty members directly affected in any institution is so small as to be insignificant in modifying institutional destinies. Faculty development is conceived of as related to any or all professorial activities, such as time to develop new courses, time to generate research proposals, general or specific work conditions, released time from teaching for junior faculty members, encouragement to teach experimental courses, or creating an environment that encourages greater faculty interaction. Such a broad conception does not allow for any real testing or generalizing, except to affirm that an institution in which a great deal of attention is given to faculty needs is likely to be a more attractive place for faculty, and hence for students.

For the purposes of this book, faculty development will be conceived of as those specific activities undertaken to help faculty members: (1) improve the attractiveness of their courses (to improve student retention), (2) create proposals that attract external financial support, (3) develop genuine interest in significant institutional problems and a desire and willingness to help solve them, or (4) improve talents and abilities needed to render professional service to the end that the externally perceived values of the institution are enhanced and enrollments and financial support increased. The focus here is on the relatively short range that can help institutions survive a difficult decade. Again, it should be stressed that what is attempted is related to type of institution. What may be possible in a junior or community college or liberal arts college may be quite inappropriate for a national or international research university.

Intellectual stimulation. Several categories of development activities can be suggested, with the first being improvement of the intellectual tone of the institution, the sense of community, and the sharing of values. The reasoning here is that the total institutional press on those who experience it is, in some way, related to institutional desirability and support. There is, of course, no way to establish that this is so, except to indicate the likelihood of its being so from anecdotes and episodes. One college became more desirable after faculty members were encouraged through grants to do intellectually stimulating things during the summer. Another institution seems to have improved as the result of a direct effort to encourage greater faculty use of the library. Still another small institution seemed to enjoy a changed and improved intellectual climate after a small group of faculty were financed to visit other comparable institutions to see what they were doing and to gain perspective. For the smaller institutions in general, the following activities seem to have reasonable potential for success:

1. Summer travel, study, or research grants for at least 10 percent of the faculty each summer for a period of three to five years so that an adequate critical mass of faculty is produced who have done something intellectually new and interesting within a reasonably short period of time.
2. Participation of four to six key faculty members in an intensive summer experience such as the former Danforth Workshop, which extended from two and a half to three weeks. The group typically returns to campus with a plan (in which the members are personally involved) to attempt a significant new development of some sort. The important ingredient is the cadre of important people dedicated to institutional improvement.
3. Creation of some major campus-unifying intellectual activity, such as a freshman-required, interdisciplinary course taught by a majority of the faculty—for example, Amherst's American Civilization or Stephens' Ideas and Living Today, both of which are now gone but were at one time potent campus unifiers—or a campuswide reading program, such as a book-of-the-semester scheme which expects faculty and students to be reading the same book at the same time. Here it is possible that a well-selected, well-publicized, and integrated series of outside lectures might help, especially if the theme could be shown to have definite implications for each of a substantial portion of the

entire faculty. Such a theme might be the theme of this book: institutional survival. It should be stressed that such an effort should not be attempted year after year, as faculty members do become saturated and on occasion even overstimulated.

4. Occasional use of the traditional techniques, including hiring a particularly well regarded consultant to spend a few days to a few weeks on campus, assisting at least with the financing of each faculty member to attend one professional conference each year, providing resources so that departments can meet for both social and intellectual reasons several times each year, or externally subsidizing a visiting-scholar program which each year would bring to the campus different kinds of talent to interact with students and faculty.

None of these techniques should be expected to produce radically changed environments. Yet each, in some institutions, might contribute to making the campus more intellectually alert and more desirable for students. The majority of the private liberal arts colleges are parochial and not at all intellectually stimulating. They may reflect a comfortable sense of community and a sense of civility. In the past, they have served their immediate communities well by preparing the needed school teachers, nurses, church workers, and local businessmen and by providing relatively inexpensive undergraduate preparation for those few students who would go on to medical, law, or graduate school. Enrollment and continued attendance was a matter of convenience and geography. The validity of those reasons no longer obtains, and students who are enticed into enrolling are likely to find the collegiate environment dull and dreary, to be escaped by dropping out. In such a situation, even a small improvement in the intellectual vitality of the campus may help to slow or even decrease the dropout rates.

For the larger, more complex, and frequently research-oriented institutions, total institutional effort to modify the intellectual tone of the campuses is likely to prove fruitless. Large campuses are like large urban areas, harboring a multitude of activities and ideas but without any single focus. However, the impact of faculty in smaller groups, such as departments or programs, must be presumed to have some influence with respect to institutional survival. It should be obvious that large, complex institutions represent a considerable range of attractiveness to students and to faculty, with the prestige private research universities and prestige state flagship institutions at one end and the quite large but regional universities or comprehensive colleges at the other. Yet all need to devote some attention to the attractiveness of their environments in an era of increased competition for students and funds. Several techniques can be suggested.

First, the large institution should establish, as a matter of broad policy, conditions that encourage faculty members to establish good relationships with relevant members of the surrounding community. The faculty in business should be encouraged to consult with and serve the regional business community. Educational faculty should be urged to view service to the schools as being at least as important as teaching their classes. These service activities serve especially well to provide real clinical material to be used in classes, thus giving students the distinct impression that the course work is preparing them for the "real world." They also establish contacts that lead to future enrollments and support from significant elements of the community. Of the private doctoral and comprehensive universities that seem to be most secure as they face the uncertain future, those such as Creighton University in Omaha and Northeastern University in Boston, which have made faculty relationships with the community an essential element, are in the best possible position.

This point is so significant that it requires elaboration. The period of expansion of higher education during the late 1950s and the 1960s allowed a few institutions to change character radically and to become national universities in which the faculty gained much of their intellectual stimulation from relationships with various national groups. Stanford is perhaps the prime example, having changed from a solid regional institution serving well-to-do West Coast youth into an institution of first rank. But a few others made similar changes, such as Notre Dame among the Catholic institutions, Duke University, and to a somewhat lesser extent, Washington University in Missouri. The chances of other institutions changing in a similar direction appear rather remote. But it seems to be still possible for private institutions to establish or reestablish ties with the local or regional community and from that to create an intellectual climate that will attract and hold students and will also attract needed supplemental resources.

Second, without eliminating institutionwide activities such as lectures, consultations, and events, greater emphasis should be placed on and resources provided for smaller, intellectually stimulating units. A large institution becomes an interesting place when there are many different, interesting things taking place, each attracting a small but involved group of people. Thus, for the greatest intellectual benefit for faculty improvement generally, $5,000 fees paid a Henry Kissinger or Gerald Ford would be better spent by giving ten departments $500 each to be used as these smaller units saw fit. This observation is made with the full realization that a Ford or Kissinger speech might make headlines, but headlines do not contribute to general faculty development.

In general, responsibility for the intellectual stimulation of faculty should, for the most part, devolve on the professional school or department. It is within those units that the spirit of collegiality can best prevail and significant intellectual development take place. This is consistent with the observation concerning all large organizations that fertile invention of innovations requires decentralization. Of course, centralization is also needed for some purposes—but for the purpose of faculty intellectual development in large institutions, decentralization should be the rule. Specifically, this means that budgets should reflect the fact that it is the smaller unit that will be the most active.

Curriculum and instruction. The second category of faculty development is the improvement of the curriculum and of instruction. As mentioned in Chapter Eight, evidence is lacking that improved technical educational processes and content are an essential ingredient, above minimal levels, in institutional survival. Nevertheless, a case can be made that improved instruction and better curricula are possible and that these might, in concert with other factors, help institutions to sustain and maintain themselves. There are a variety of techniques that purport to contribute to improved instruction. These include: use of student evaluation of teaching; videotape recording of teaching and subsequent critique; rewards for effective teaching; assistance in the creation of audio-visual aids;

class visitation by colleagues or administrative superiors; handbooks or kits showing how to improve lectures, discussions, examinations, or tutoring; seminars or symposia on instruction; and even full courses on college teaching. And there are many different curricular patterns from which to choose or which could be modified, ranging from a prescribed curriculum based on great books to no requirements whatsoever. The task here is to identify broad approaches that can be used in a cost-effective way to improve total institutional viability.

The first approach, and the one requiring the least expenditure of extra funds, is a comprehensive system of evaluation of faculty members. This is premised on the belief that individual faculty members like to know how they are doing and, within reason, want to improve. Evaluation of faculty should be multi-faceted and should consider the several different traits essential to a professor. One such list, applicable to large and small institutions, includes the areas of teaching, ability to communicate, scholarship, reputation, and academic good citizenship. Evidence should be accumulated with respect to each of these. Each faculty member should be expected to ask at least one class each semester or quarter to complete a teaching evaluation form, with results being sent both to the individual and to the academic administrative superior. Each faculty member should also be expected to complete an annual report indicating the full range and complexity of professional activities. Immediate administrative superiors (deans, division heads, or department heads) should be asked to rank all faculty they supervise on each of the five traits. Results of all such information or other material judged relevant by the professor or supervisor should be part of the professor's file. At least once a year the professor and supervisor might review the file in a conference to plan future professional development for the professor.

Secondly, the duties of academic administration (deans, division heads, department heads) should be specified and codified. They would typically include, as previously noted in Chapter Two: (1) titular head of the unit, (2) advocate for the unit, (3) budget preparation and management, (4) execution of unit policies, (5) educational planning, (6) adjudication of differences, (7) fund raising, and (8) faculty development. A clearly defined proportion of administrative time should be devoted to faculty development, and ability to engage in that sort of activity should be considered in making administrative appointments. If administrators take seriously faculty development responsibilities, the need for a special administrative role of faculty developer would be obviated or at least reduced considerably. It is the point of view here that faculty development is best handled by the head of an operating unit rather than by a staff office. It is in the school or department that faculty loyalties lie. Further, since administrative heads are already accounted for in the budget, no additional cash outlay is needed.

However, if an institution has some extra resources, or can obtain resources from external sources, such as federal or foundation provisions for faculty development, a special office for the improvement of instruction may be created and may contribute to overall curricular improvement in the institution. There are several models that might be followed, but all should possess several characteristics. The center should be administratively responsible to the institution's chief academic office. Its head should be a faculty member with an appointment in a regular teaching department. The center should be viewed as a service and its head have no administrative control over any faculty not on appointment to the center. The range of activities can vary but should include: (1) counseling and advice regarding problems of teaching and examining; (2) maintaining an inventory of audio-visual equipment and training people in its use; (3) maintaining a fund from which small improvement grants can be made to faculty; (4) subject to external funding, sponsorship of educational experiments; and (5) maintaining knowledge of curricular and instructional developments and experiments throughout higher education and dissemination of that knowledge to faculty and administrators.

Given substantial resources, there are hundreds of ideas that may be tried to improve collegiate instruction. *Change* magazine has published a résumé of what has been attempted in a report entitled *Faculty Development in a Time of Retrenchment* (Group for Human Development in Higher Education, 1974), and the Southern Regional Education Board (1976) has published *Faculty Development Centers in Southern Universities*. Both of these reports stress outside consultants, seminars in college teaching, changed reward systems, seminars on the psychology of college students, published work on college teaching, sponsored experiments, retraining programs for mid academic career changes, great use of audiovisual materials, and the like. The value of these activities to an institution seeking to maintain itself in an unfriendly environment is neither rejected nor accepted. Logic allows a presumption of value, as does the rhetoric with which such activities are urged. But the question intrudes as to what activities present a favorable cost-benefit equation for an institution struggling to survive. It should require persuasive evidence of likely effectiveness before an institution in financial difficulty is urged to expend 2.5 to 10 percent of its instructional budget for specific programs to improve instruction. The fact that institutions seeing themselves in financial difficulties do a great deal of experimentation with innovation is not proof of much except that institutions in trouble will try almost anything. Careful evaluation of faculty, administrative responsibility for faculty development, and some services such as those provided by centers for improvement of instruction represent a parsimonious program that can be urged.

Scholarship. The third category of faculty development relevant here is the improvement and enrichment of scholarship. Although there does not appear to be any relationship between published research and educational effectiveness, it can be argued at least that there is a positive relationship between intellectual interests and activities and educational effectiveness. Collegiate education is essentially an intellectual enterprise, and it seems reasonable to suppose that a person intellectually alert is likely to be more effective than a person without serious intellectual curiosity. It would seem prudent then to encourage and facilitate the intellectual growth of faculty through research and scholarship. As can be seen by visits to different campuses, there are considerable differences between faculties with respect to intellectual concerns. Some faculties appear overall to be dull and their members chiefly concerned with family, recreation, local community affairs, church affairs, or campus politics. On other campuses, faculty members, without rejecting such concerns, appear well read, urbane, cosmopolitan, and aware of the freshest developments in their special fields. Those differences are not unrelated to institutional attractiveness.

How then can an institution create, generate, or maintain a reasonable level of faculty scholarship? First, the myth of the purely teaching institution should be eliminated. It is argued that the public junior colleges and the invisible liberal arts colleges are solely teaching institutions and that faculty are not expected to engage in research. A more promising posture is for all institutions to insist that scholarship (of any of various sorts) is an essential part of faculty appointment and that demonstrated scholarship will be considered for purposes of promotion, salary increases, and the granting of tenure. That demonstration need not be publication of a book or of an article in an established journal, although this should be highly regarded. Evidence of scholarship might include revised course outlines, presentation of papers in informed colloquia, distribution of mimeograph copies of papers, display of new paintings, or the giving of a recital. Whatever the sort, evidence should be demanded and used.

Provision should be made for the conduct of scholarship on salaried time. In diary studies and other time-use studies, regardless of type of institution, faculty claim they spend about fifty-five hours per week in professional work. That is probably an inflated figure, with forty-five hours a more likely one. For a full-time faculty member in a junior college or liberal arts college, a reasonable time use might be:

Classroom contact hours	12
Class preparation	12
Advising students	7
Administration and committee work	3
Evaluation of student performance	3
Professional services and activities	2
Scholarship	6
	45

Time use in other types of institutions would, of course, be different, but whatever the arrangement, research and scholarship should be considered as an essential part of the professional role. Especially should the significance of scholarship be included in negotiated contracts with professors' unions.

Once overall policy with respect to scholarship is established and sanctions indicated, all sorts of encouraging activities can be undertaken. One institution sponsors a research club that meets each month to hear and discuss papers prepared by its members. Another institution earmarks between $5,000 and $10,000 a year to be used to make seed-money grants to encourage research efforts. Another institution maintains a director of research specifically charged with encouraging research activities and helping faculty members to obtain external grants and contracts. Still another institution publishes annual reports indicating the research interests and activities of all faculty members, whereas another subsidizes the publication of books written by faculty members. Inventive presidents and deans can create all sorts of incentives.

Mental Health. The last category of faculty development is one of the most difficult to engineer or, for that matter, to discuss— yet it may be the most potent for an improved and more attractive institutional climate. This is the fostering of better mental or emotional health of faculty members on the supposition that improved mental health is related to improved professional performance. People in different professions face different emotional problems and those who enter college teaching are no exception. Professors tend to be more liberal than the general public, thus producing some tension with various other constituencies of the college or university. They also tend to experience conflict between their required role as teacher and their desired role as scholar, and some give the appearance of marginal individuals who have used their not inconsiderable intellectual abilities to move from one reference group to another without ever really achieving that goal. In addition, they daily face a generation gap as they deal with their students in almost a parent-surrogate role. All of these factors can and do produce tensions and behaviors antithetical to an attractive institutional environment. Professors may demonstrate a preciousness regarding their disciplines which relegates students to a role of necessary nuisances. They may, as defense against their own anxieties, project their feared weaknesses onto their students. Thus, fear of imperfection may lead to unrealistic demands of perfection on the part of their students. At the same time, fear of not being loved can lead to courting student affection or deliberately alienating students. The catalogue of potential problems is long.

As to what institutions can do financially and with propriety to help improve mental and emotional health—there are no easy answers. Professional counselors could be encouraged to extend their concerns to faculty. Seminars, symposia, conferences, and colloquia dealing with personal problems of professors could be attempted. Special attention could be given to professors who are struggling against discrimination, such as women and minority group members. But the chief responsibility must rest with deans and department heads, who should be sensitized to the emotional needs of faculty and who can provide support when needed. An academic vice-president who makes a point of knowing every faculty member by first name and the research interests of each, can make one of the most important contributions to a good institutional climate regardless of cost. A dean who maintains an open-door policy and who encourages faculty members to drop in to talk about whatever is on their minds can also be highly influential.

Revising Personnel Policies

Faculty development programs may make an institution more interesting and attractive. However, reasonable efficient use of the faculty is also important. There are several ways of doing this; increasing teaching loads is the most direct method. It is strongly argued that the course loads of twelve to twenty-one contact hours per week of the late 1940s were too high but that the course loads of three to nine hours of the late 1960s are too low. Although there may be need for some variation because of individual circumstances, some course load guidelines can be suggested according to type of institution:

- Research universities: two courses per quarter or semester
- Doctoral universities: three courses per quarter or semester
- Comprehensive colleges: three to four courses per quarter or semester
- Liberal arts colleges: three to four courses per quarter or semester
- Junior community colleges: four courses per quarter or semester

The lower loads for research universities are intended to accommodate research and graduate education. The higher loads for junior colleges reflect the limited number of different courses taught, the general absence of any research expectations, and the fact that all courses are lower division, typically elementary, and not as likely to change quickly. Research faculties may contend that such a load cuts into the time needed for research, thinking, and the one-to-one kind of instruction that takes place in conferences with graduate students. That claim, with some obvious exceptions, is simply rejected as spurious. There exists too much testimony of graduate students that they work primarily on their own without much contact with professors (unless they are teaching or research assistants), and there is no evidence to suggest a qualitative difference between the graduate education at major universities during the 1930s, when heavy loads were the rule, and the 1960s, when light loads prevailed. Junior college faculties may also claim discrimination and demand load parity with other public institutions. However, teaching three sections of History of Civilization with one preparation and one section of American History with another preparation does not appear to be an excessive load in the absence of significant research or professional service expectations.

At the same time, class size and student-faculty ratio should be increased. Over time, research has not established significant and demonstrable values of small classes as compared to large classes. With few exceptions, undergraduate classes might reasonably range from 15 to 100. Classes that consistently enroll fewer than 10 students should become candidates for elimination. The prevailing mode of instruction, even in classes called seminars or discussion classes, is still the lecture, and the lecture given to fewer than 10 students is almost a travesty. Lectures delivered to over 100 students become impersonal and more difficult to follow and can be counterproductive.

Such a rigid policy ought, of course, to allow for exceptions. Thus, a faculty member who can demonstrate a real need for a small seminar and who can establish that it will be organized and conducted differently than orthodox courses might be allowed to offer it. However, the burden of proof should rest with the proponent and such courses should be allowed only with acceptable overall institutional ratios.

Along with these principal approaches to productivity, institutions might well consider limited use of less expensive labor, self-service, and substitution of the use of capital for labor. Some of the recently created nontraditional institutions have made almost exclusive use of such techniques. That is not suggested here. However, in the faculty-as-interchangeable-parts types of institutions (liberal arts colleges, junior colleges, comprehensive colleges), perhaps one third to one half of the FTE faculty might be part-time or adjunct faculty and, in the universities, the same percentage might be teaching assistants. These would be employed at lower compensation because of less experience and preparation and would receive fewer or no fringe benefits on the grounds that part-time faculty would typically be employed full time elsewhere.

Independent study (self-service) is costly if carried on in ideal form, but in actual practice, although it is fully supervised, it is an inexpensive way of enriching a curriculum and providing for individual differences. Each faculty member is assigned an independent study course number with which to register students for subjects not normally part of the curriculum, for example, Student Personnel Work in Higher Education. Since, theoretically, there are some educational values to be obtained from having students work by themselves, and the danger of serious harm to students is minimal, a case can be made to increase the amount of independent study through a requirement of at least one independent study course in each degree program. Faculty load policy could be established that would assume four or fewer independent study students as an essential part of a normal load.

Related to greater use of self-service is substitution of greater use of capital for labor. Here the library is one of the more obvious examples, but so are computer-based and managed instruction, tape and videotape collections, open- and closed-circuit television, and programmed texts of various sorts. Although the evidence thus far does not show that such uses of technology are more economical than orthodox lecture and discussion, eventually they may prove to be of financial advantage.

To ensure some stability in a reasonably efficient use of the faculty, several principles should be used. The first principle is that of centralized position control. This, simply stated, provides that all vacant positions revert to central administration for assignment or reassignment and do not remain the property of the department or school. During the expansionist period of the 1960s, departments and schools assumed that once a position had been assigned to them, the position was permanently lodged there. Gradually, central administration lost any real power to redeploy faculty to meet changed conditions. That sort of departmental or school luxury can no longer be afforded. For example, as education enrollments decline, education positions should become available to handle enrollment increases in business, and this can only be accomplished centrally.

The second principle is that of limitation of the number of tenured appointments possible. As a general rule, an entire institution should have no more than 50 percent of the faculty on tenure, a school no more than 60 percent, and a department, program, or division 70 percent. This policy should be tied to a rigorous up-or-out policy so that at the end of six years for assistant professors and five years for associate professors, the individual must be granted tenure or else be terminated. A similar hard-and-fast rule should govern retirements and leaves of absence. In general, institutions should establish that the normal age for retirement is sixty-five and that after that age tenure and retirement contributions cease. Although the law prevents forced retirement before age seventy, individuals should be counseled to retire or to accept part-time teaching responsibilities. No leaves of absence of more than two consecutive years should be allowed. If an individual became, for example, the U.S. Secretary of State, he or she could take two years' leave of absence and return to a tenured position—beyond that, the choice would be forced return or termination. The purpose of such policies is to ensure institutional flexibility. Unfortunately, some individuals will be hurt in the process. It is assumed, however, that by the end of the 1980s the supply of persons with doctorates will drop and that these policies will contribute to relatively stable market conditions.

A third principle is part of the doctrine of position control. It is that every request for a continued assignment of a vacant position or the granting of a new position must be accompanied by an exploration of various alternatives for meeting the claimed need. Thus, a request for an assistant professor position should examine meeting that need with four or five teaching assistants, a nontenured lecturer, or part-time appointments—or by using other comparable courses already staffed but possibly underenrolled. The analysis should be an honest one, going into immediate costs, long- and short-term program objectives, and advantages and disadvantages of each option examined.

A long-established, but relatively little used, technique to maintain a more economical academic program is to limit the proliferation of courses. In a stable enrollment situation, course proliferation results inexorably in smaller classes and higher per-unit costs. McGrath (1961) established that departments in liberal arts colleges offering few courses suffered no qualitative disadvantage when compared with departments offering large numbers of different courses. He also showed that, at the time of his analysis, colleges that reduced the number of courses could actually pay the remaining faculty considerably higher salaries. As institutions reduce their faculty size and increase the student–faculty ratio, they should, at the same time, limit the number of different courses a department can offer. There are several ways such a limitation might be set, the easiest being by means of a ratio between courses offered and requirements for a major. The policy might be established that a department would be allowed to offer no more than the total number of hours required for a major plus 20 percent. Thus, a department requiring a thirty-semester-hour major could offer those courses plus six hours additional. To ensure against creeping proliferation, it should also be established that departments could offer whatever new courses they desired, but that for every new course offered, an existing course would have to be eliminated.

A related technique is to eliminate courses that duplicate each other in various departments, as does statistics offered in mathematics, psychology, education, sociology, and economics. The argument can be made that the illustrations from each field are so important as to mandate special statistics courses in each, but such duplication in a stable or declining situation is a luxury that many institutions cannot afford. Obviously, there are limits to the elimination of duplicative courses. Statistics, social psychology, and intellectual history, however, are clear examples of courses that could serve several different departments.

Then there is the matter of required general education courses offered during the first two collegiate years. Although the educational arguments for such requirements may be questionable, there are strong economic arguments to support a required core of courses. Required courses make course enrollment prediction possible and, by their nature, can produce larger classes. Additionally, as the courses remain substantively stable over time and hence require less course revision and extensive teacher preparation each year, professors who teach them can carry a heavier course load than would otherwise be possible.

There is danger, however, that a limited and streamlined curriculum will not provide for quite important individual differences among students. To ensure that variety and yet keep costs and long-term financial commitments down, each department might be allowed to offer, perhaps every other year, specialized courses taught by a part-time faculty member. Thus, in a small school of education, courses on collective bargaining and on education and the law might be offered one year and courses on institutional research and state budgeting the next. Students would obtain the needed exposure to those subjects, but the institution would not use up a tenured position to provide such topical coverage. In cosmopolitan areas in particular, it should be possible to find well-prepared people who could and would willingly teach courses dealing with a specific author, advanced language training, new developments in income tax law, or the team approach to nursing. Of course, care should be exercised that too much part-time instruction does not become the rule. There is need for a solid base of full-time faculty and well-established courses. But as many as one third of all specialized courses could well be offered by part-time or adjunct faculty.

In complex, research-oriented universities, the "every tub on its own bottom" doctrine has much to commend it as a financial technique. The general principles are also applicable to other types of institutions. Overly simplified, this doctrine proposes that every major academic unit produce the funds necessary to sustain its program. This could be done by generating tuition from enrollments, grants, and contracts and by means of special programs such as summer workshops or conferences. First the school would develop its base budget, defined as the amount of money necessary to maintain the essential academic program for a specified number of students—for example, a base budget of $1.5 million to provide graduate professional education for 350 FTE students. Next the school would undertake to generate that budget first through a percentage of tuition collected (75 percent seems reasonable), which might produce $1.1 million, and then through funds from such additional activities as increased enrollments without increase in faculty or administration, grants, contracts, or special income-generating programs. If the school in any given year failed to maintain its financial situation, the university itself could help it by advancing funds through loans. However, if the school failed to maintain itself for three consecutive years, it would be required to bring its budget into balance at a new and lower figure. This would normally be done through administrative economies and then through actual termination of faculty appointments. The same sort of calculation of a base budget can be done for departments in smaller institutions. The fundamental principle is that the academic unit should be forced to attend to economic matters, live within its income, and face the consequences if it fails to do so. There are two problems or issues here: First, it is difficult for some service activities, such as counseling or health services, to generate enough income to maintain themselves. Second, institutions may feel some activities and programs, such as museums and classical language departments, are essential to the main purposes of the institution, even though they may never be self-supporting. With respect to the first issue, refined accounting could conceivably be developed that would show the proportion of tuition devoted to providing a particular service and would then allow calculation of the income generated by the service. Additionally, attempting to establish the actual cost of health service, for example, might raise the question of whether the service was really needed or whether it could be replaced by some other method, such as insurance in some form. With respect to the second issue, it is true that some essential programs must be supported without regard to their power to generate income. But the number of such activities is limited, and institutions should not attempt more than their resources will allow. One loss-leader department in a liberal arts college is about all it can afford.

Deciding on Tenure

As the reality of a deepening financial problem in higher education has been gradually perceived, the validity of tenure has come under question. Tenure is presumed to be a device to safeguard academic freedom. The college professors working at the frontiers of knowledge and dealing with youth at an impressionable age are seen to be particularly vulnerable to attack by all sorts of pressure groups. Their new knowledge may run counter to prevailing belief. In their courses, they likely will teach the young notions contrary to the beliefs of parents. In addition, the work of a scholar may take a lifetime to complete and, until extensive research is completed, the scholar is vulnerable to criticism of being nonproductive. A safeguard is the provision that a professor, after a probationary period (typically six years) and after having been judged worthy by his or her peers, is granted an appointment without limit, save for proved incompetence or demonstrated financial exigency.

In practice, through much of the twentieth century, the granting of tenure was a relatively informal act after which the faculty member and the institution just assumed that tenure was operating. Not until the 1960s did institutions generally provide a document indicating that tenure had been granted. As the proportion of faculty on tenure hovered at 50 percent or less, tenure was not seen as a particular burden to institutions. There were from time to time, to be sure, complaints that tenure protected the incompetent and some instances in which professors holding tenure were discharged for presumed political, personal, or moral reasons. But for the most part, tenure was generally accepted as a benign but important element of academic life—a possible fringe benefit to compensate for a remuneration lower than that of the other major professions. The period of faculty shortages during the late 1950s and most of the 1960s, however, produced dysfunction in the system. Faculty members in short supply could and did demand earlier granting of tenure, a posture reinforced by the American Association of University Professors (A.A.U.P.), which insisted that service at other colleges and universities should count as probationary time. For example, a professor who had spent two years as an instructor at each of two institutions could demand tenure at a third institution after three years' service as an assistant professor. In some states—California, for example—state law provided for junior college faculty to acquire tenure within three years.

At the same time that enrollments were increasing, so were faculty salaries. These factors combined to produce a situation in the 1970s, when enrollments and financing of institutions began to stabilize, in which many institutions had 70 percent or more of increasingly high-salaried professors on tenure, with no chance of reducing that figure until well into the 1980s. Financially troubled institutions, forced to reduce faculty and taking the option of discharging nontenured faculty first, quickly found themselves with virtually all faculty positions filled by tenured professors.

At this juncture, other ways of appointing faculty were advanced, including: seven- to ten-year renewable term contracts; creating tenured and nontenured positions, with the nontenured position paid at a higher rate than the tenured one; eliminating tenure and replacing its protection with length-of-service provisions; and increasing the length of time required to acquire tenure and making the requirements more rigorous. None of these, with the exception of applying more rigorous standards for a tenure appointment, has been widely adopted. A few places have instituted the term contract, but that system has really worked as a covert tenure system. Contracts are typically renewed, even in questionable situations, often with the rationalization that since renewal is actually not tenure, a professor who really is a nice person should be continued.

What should be a proper stance regarding tenure for the remainder of the twentieth century, especially for the financially troubled institution? Despite real or potential flaws, a well-administered and monitored system of tenure is still probably the best system. It is well regarded by faculty, and its elimination, even if only symbolic, would likely produce serious morale problems as well as the immediate unionization of faculty, with the contract providing job security based on length of service. The granting of tenure has a symbolic value indicating that merit and competence do count. The fact that faculty members have tenure also probably safeguards against panic-driven reduction in faculty size to intolerable levels and hence helps ensure some program quality. And over a relatively short time, the excessive proportion of faculties holding tenure can be reduced to manageable limits. To use an extreme case, an institution that replaced all regular positions that came open through normal means with part-time, nontenured faculty for four years could enter the fifth year in a reasonably satisfactory tenure situation.

For all institutions, except perhaps 100 research and graduate-training institutions, and in spite of the damage it may do to some younger scholars, the policy of terminating nontenured faculty before tenured faculty should be followed. It is argued that such a policy excludes new blood and fresh ideas, and this may be true. However, the length of time the aging faculty will predominate is limited; hence the intellectual damage is likely to be slight. By the end of the 1980s, by not filling vacancies or by replacing them with junior faculty or part-time faculty, the age and rank balance can be restored. A more difficult problem is the contention that a draconian policy toward the nontenured will seriously erode affirmative action programs to increase minority group and female faculty appointments. Some of this will, beyond doubt, happen. A modified-quota system, particularly in the larger institutions, may be necessary until the early 1990s, by which time the number of qualified minorities and women available for appointment may well increase. At the same time, the total number of doctorates produced each year may have decreased as young people respond to the unfavorable academic market for Ph.D.'s during the 1980s and seek other career goals. Stress is placed here on the larger institutions because they employ the largest number of faculty and hence can make a difference in the total number of minority members and women employed. They are also likely to have more flexible financial resources. Most of the approximately 600 invisible liberal arts colleges and the smaller state colleges and universities, even in aggregate, will appoint only a few faculty from previously disadvantaged groups and, more properly, should concentrate on surviving in the future rather than on helping to solve social problems of the present. Urging institutions to turn their backs on the problem of eliminating discrimination may sound like socially irresponsible doctrine, but the question can be raised as to which option makes better sense—concentrating on institutional survival even at the expense of some continuation of discriminatory policies or accepting likely institutional demise by attempting to solve social problems without the requisite resources.

Dealing with Unionism

No discussion concerning faculties and faculty policy for the 1980s and 1990s would be adequate without attending to the

matters of unions, collective bargaining, and contracts. Faculty
unions have quickly become an essential part of the academic scene
and could come to pervade all of American higher education. By
1978, there were over 500 institutions in which a union had become
the bargaining agent for faculty, and those institutions employed
almost one fourth of all faculty in the United States. That number
could well increase as a direct result of the financial uncertainties
over the next several decades.

The question of unionism is especially relevant for this book
because of the characteristics of the institutions now unionized and
the characteristics of those in which conditions encourage unions to
exist. Unionized institutions are typically public and are the least
prestigious representatives of that sector. They are, for the most
part, community junior colleges, state colleges, a few middle-level
state universities, and a few large systems of higher education.
Among the public institutions, the original state colleges are the
ones most likely to experience the financial constraints produced by
drops in enrollment. But even the public community junior colleges—the largest group in the ranks of the unionized—can experience enrollment problems, especially if public support for large
adult and off-campus programs should be curtailed.

Unions seem to develop in response to a limited number of
factors, including endangered faculty compensation, curtailment of
presumed essential support services, vulnerability of programs to
elimination because of enrollment shifts, and seemingly arbitrary
actions on the part of central administration. These factors are also
present in a large number of privately supported liberal arts colleges
and quite a few middle-level private universities—and it is quite
possible that those could become unionized in a relatively short time.

Perhaps the first consideration in discussing unions is to
decide what position the board of trustees and administration should
take concerning unions. Some union spokespersons have argued that
the decision of a faculty to elect a union is entirely a matter for the
faculty to decide and that the board and administration should
remain neutral or even indicate approval of the potential of collective bargaining to produce great institutional improvement. Such
apologists reason that collective bargaining is a way to develop institutionwide agreement as to purpose, produce an effective and

efficient system of management, dissipate tensions and emotions, and harmonize the efforts of all constituencies for the good of the institution. Another point of view is possible, however, which holds that although unions will clearly not destroy institutions or traditional academic values and that educational quality is possible in a union situation, on balance the best in American higher education can better be preserved and enhanced in the absence of a union. That position would argue that boards of trustees and administration should oppose moves to unionize and, in the event of an actual election, should actively participate in the debate against electing a union.

Perhaps the most important thing a president can do in opposition to a union is to try to eliminate or prevent the development of those conditions in which unionism flourishes. Thus, there would be wide participation of faculty in consultation in reaching decisions. Presidents, deans, and department heads would refrain from arbitrary actions and from allowing real or perceived inequities to develop. In the face of financial difficulties, administration would bear more than its full share of budget cutbacks and it would do whatever was reasonably possible to secure the financial well-being of the faculty. The long-range planning statement by the Stanford central administration of its intention to keep faculty salaries well within the top 10 percent of its kind of institution is probably the best insurance that no faculty union could be elected at that institution.

A partial checklist for administrators seeking to avoid even serious discussion of a union can be prepared based just on practices that have contributed to unionization:

1. Consult broadly with various faculty and student groups before every major decision affecting people, working conditions, or economic well-being.
2. Ensure consistent application, and the appearance of consistent application, of policies to all relevant groups and individuals.
3. Maintain a steady ratio between administrative and faculty costs and thoroughly document and explain any significant shifts in that ratio.
4. Cooperate fully with the senate and accept most recommenda-

tions unless they seem seriously to threaten institutional survival. Explain in detail to all constituencies why recommendations are not accepted.

5. Avoid making all major decisions affecting groups of people until after at least a half-year discussion of the various factors involved.

6. Use a variety of techniques to keep members of all major constituencies informed of all significant decisions and the unfolding of all important problems and issues.

Institutions can and will survive with or without unionization. However, institutions facing serious financial troubles and real problems of survival would be better served without a unionized faculty for several reasons. The first is the economic one that negotiations typically focus on economic improvement for the faculty, even when the institution may lack the resources to provide for that improvement. It is perfectly legitimate for faculty to wish increases in compensation that keep up with inflation. But from time to time, institutions may need to declare a moratorium on increases in compensation, if only to prevent the budget base from increasing at rates faster than income increases. Increasing salaries by 7 percent each year increases the base-salary budget by almost one fourth by the third year. Contracts are typically two to five years in duration and typically call for annual increments of some sort. Yet within a two- to five-year period, all sorts of financial problems can appear that can make conforming to a contract difficult or impossible. Consider the following example.

In 1974, an institution of 1,200 students charged tuition of $2,900 to contribute to a total operating budget of $4,000,000, of which $2,280,000 went for faculty and professional salaries. However, the actual expenditures were $4,200,000 or a deficit of $200,000, which would be sustained for the next three years. Institutional policy forbids tuition and room and board charges to be increased in the same year and allows these increases to be up to the rate of inflation, that is, 7 percent. Thus, in the three-year period, tuition income would go from $3,480,000 to $3,723,600. At the same time, a three-year union contract calls for 7 percent increases in faculty salaries for each of three years in order to bring faculty compensation into line with that paid by similar institutions. Thus, the base-salary budget would increase from $2,280,000 to $2,793,098 over the three-year period, or a jump from 57 percent of the total budget to 66 percent of the total budget. Now assume that in the third year there is a shortfall of 100 enrollments, producing a net loss of income of $304,500. The contract would thus have increased the percentage of income paid in salary to 72 percent and produced an annual deficit of $330,500. Just being able to restrict raises for the third year would cut $182,726 from the salary budget base, plus an increase of $12,761 if the 7 percent raises were put back into effect the following year. Of course, a contract can be written to allow for moratoria on salary increases as well as more severe actions, but flexibility in dealing with changing and frequently deteriorating conditions would appear to be greater in the absence of a contract.

A second problem with unions involves the use of merit performance and quality in judging faculty for retention, promotion, and salary increases. It is possible for contracts to provide that evaluation of performance and promotion and salary changes be management prerogatives, and some do. However, there is a tendency in union thinking to make longevity on the job the most important criterion so long as individuals perform adequately. This point of view is especially characteristic of American Federation of Teachers (AFT) unions. Judging faculty performance is at best a highly subjective art, although the reliability of the process can be improved. As it is subjective, the act of judgment is especially vulnerable to being considered a grievance and subject to the grievance procedures. Thus, the sheer fact of a contract will tend to increase the emphasis placed on seniority and to decrease other factors on the basis of which judgments can be made. This tendency is antithetical to the basic concept of intellectual quality upon which a college or university is based.

A third operational difficulty is that a union contract may limit the number of part-time or lower-priced people used to deliver educational services. The faculty union quite properly seeks to preserve the economic needs of its members, and this would include safeguarding the jobs of full-time faculty members. However, as indicated earlier, institutions may wish routinely to have as much as one third of normal faculty serve part time and at a lower compensation level. At times, as when an institution wishes to redirect the emphasis of a faculty through not filling positions with tenure-track appointments, the proportion of part-time faculty could go as high as 50 percent for a year or so. The existence of a contract could seriously eliminate that tactic for solving institutional problems. The union intent is exemplified by the fears of both the AFT and AAUP. The unions have denounced the growing use of part-time faculty although they recognize that the economic values to institutions are significant. Part-time teachers are paid at lower rates than full-time faculty, receive fewer fringe benefits, require little office space, and can be hired only as needed. The leadership of unions, however, points out that part-time faculty are likely to be less-qualified, to do less research, and to provide fewer services to students than full-time faculty. (See Magarrell, 1978, for a discussion of this issue.)

Another sort of problem, occurring especially in public institution systems in which bargaining is handled by an office of the executive branch of the state, is that bargaining may produce for union members financial gains for which no appropriations have been made. The situation in the Pennsylvania state colleges is illustrative, with the individual campuses being told that they must find, out of their own budgets, the funds to pay for provisions added to the union contract. An institution operating on a tight budget could be told to lower faculty teaching loads but, at the same time, not be provided with resources to employ additional professors to staff courses, many of which may have been mandated by other state laws. Funds to do so can thus come only from increasing tuition, cutting back support services whose workers are not covered by a union contract, or reducing operating budgets (such as those for supplies, equipment, and travel).

One further problem is that, in some situations, a contract can actually limit the consultation in which management may engage as it attempts to solve critical problems. When presidents are faced with a financial crisis, for example, it is good that they consult with other administrators, board members, schools, departments, faculty groups, student groups, and other relevant constituencies. In some situations, however, the contract calls for consultation only with the union on such matters as class size, salary, retrenchment, and conditions of work—all of which are deeply related to decisions leading to institutional survival. Of course, the contract may allow consultation, but the fact that it can be denied makes that possibility highly dangerous.

There are other objections to unionization clearly related but not central to the issues of survival. There is the danger that the adversary relationships implied by collective bargaining may jeopardize historical collegial relationships. There is the possibility that faculty concern over economic matters may jeopardize serious decisions on educational matters; for example, a needed change in general education requirements might be postponed because it could adversely affect the economic well-being of some of the faculty. In a similar vein, stating precise work loads could very well result in less actual service to students by encouraging all faculty members to put in only that time specifically stated in a contract. For example, in a faculty of 100, there might be 25 who put in 50 hours a week of clearly relevant professional service, 50 who work a steady 40 hours, and another 25 who routinely work only a bare minimum of 30 hours a week. This would yield 4,000 faculty hours per week. A contract calling for 35 hours per week for everyone could, in theory—and impression suggests would—reduce the faculty hours to 3,500 (a rather substantial loss of service).

If administration has been unable to create conditions that limit interest in unionization or if external events have been so serious as almost to force faculties to ponder relief through a union, and an election for or against a bargaining agent has been called for, the president should be prepared to work actively against a union. This may include writing letters to faculty and asking board members to prepare memoranda requesting that deans and department heads campaign against the union and document likely or possible unfavorable outcomes from a decision to unionize. There is nothing illegal in such presidential efforts, and the evidence suggests that when such opposition is well organized, there is substantial chance that the union can be defeated (Mortimer and McConnell, 1978, pp. 70–71).

But if the effort fails and a bargaining agent is elected, then the contract becomes the place for administration to ensure the rights to do those things needed for institutional survival. Generally, there are three categories of subjects that might be raised at the bargaining table. The first category comprises the permissible subjects, which management may or may not consider proper. These would include statements of mission and goals, budgeting procedures, program evaluation, and organizational and administrative structure. As a general rule, administration should resist trying to bargain for as many of the permissible subjects as possible and should include them only when there appear to be clear institutional reasons for doing so. Then there are the mandatory subjects of work loads, pensions and other benefits, grievance procedures, safety conditions, and a management-rights clause. And there are a few prohibited subjects, such as provision for a closed shop (in some states, an agency shop) and, in some states, any subject that conflicts with existing state or federal law.

Management should know these categories well and be able to detect when the union bargainers attempt to obtain inclusion of a subject that would limit managerial flexibility. The management bargaining team, usually headed by a vice-president, and others who can speak for the institution should prepare themselves well with facts about the institution and should know which matters must be covered and which should not be covered. A key criterion is that management should not bargain over anything it presumes to have a right to control.

The following matters must become part of the contract, particularly for institutions facing problems of survival:

1. The right of management to decide when an institution is in financial difficulty, and the criteria to be used in reaching that decision, should be sharply stated. Some variant of the criteria cited in Chapter Ten might be appropriate but with the proviso that management may increase the number of those criteria should conditions change.
2. The right of management to decide upon the size and composition of the faculty should be stated, including its right to use a variety of procedures to obtain and retain that size and composition. Included in this section should be a statement of the right

to retrench and of the specific procedures to be followed to terminate the appointments of part-time, tenured, and non-tenured faculty. Especially crucial is the statement that management has the right to decide when retrenchment is essential and is obligated only to demonstrate how the relevant criteria have been used to reach that decision. The broad general statement such as that of the AAUP should be avoided: "an imminent crisis which threatens the survival of the institution as a whole and cannot be alleviated by less drastic means" (Angell, Kelly, and Associates, 1977, p. 235).

3. If the contract deals, as it must, with faculty salary, benefits, and grievance procedures, there should also be a full statement of faculty obligations and the various sanctions that can be applied by management, ranging from a reprimand to immediate termination without further compensation. This section will be a rather lengthy one but management increasingly needs it to ensure that the institution can obtain the full services of the faculty.

4. Possibly deserving of explicit statement is the right of management to decide upon the qualifications of people allowed to teach courses. This seems especially desirable during a time of possible retrenchment when faculty members—say, in foreign language—see their enrollments dwindle and seek to start a new career—say, in African music and dance. Faced with a possible loss of jobs, faculty members can with ease make a case for their ability to exploit some marginal experience as a basis for offering new programs. Sometimes this is possible and legitimate, but more often it is not. Management should have the right to decide not only for the good of the institution but also to prevent jurisdictional disputes within the union. In one institution, for example, a dispute developed as to which department—speech and drama, anthropology, or English—should have the right to offer a program in African drama.

5. Management should also state the full range of professional activities that faculty should and may engage in, and reserve the right to evaluate those required and to consider that evaluation for purposes of reappointment, promotion, tenure, and salary

changes. Thus, it would be proper to expect research and scholarship and to evaluate it.

These are rather stringent suggestions, but they should be advanced in a firm but not an arrogant manner. While the essence of collective bargaining is a presumed adversary relationship, it is not an antagonistic one. Faculty and administration in colleges and universities were socialized by the same forces and share many of the same powerful values. However, there is one value that ostensibly is shared but concerning which there may be profound differences: the matter of institutional survival. Faculty union members may argue with reason that their own best interests are bound up with institutional survival but, at the same time, may be so close to their own personal, professional, and economic concerns that they make demands that will weaken the institution. It is part of the distinctive role of administrators in American institutions that they must put the survival of the institution first and decide as rationally and objectively as possible the steps most needed to ensure that end.

To recapitulate, presidents and their associates should try to create conditions and practices that will lessen the likelihood of faculty desires for a union. If a union is proposed, they should actively participate in an election and oppose the formation of a bargaining agent. If an agent is elected, they should limit the contract as far as possible but, at the same time, reserve to management those rights essential for a quick response to new and frequently dangerous conditions.

One last matter needs to be addressed—what to do when a faculty union decides to strike. This usually happens when faculty perceive that the bargaining agent has not resolved those faculty concerns that led to the formation of the union in the first place; or it comes from a feeling on the part of union leaders that there is faculty loss of control over the resources necessary to acquire or maintain professional status. When it appears that a strike is likely, management should formulate a strike plan which will indicate acceptable compromises to avoid a strike and a rationale for either closing an institution or keeping it open. Such a rationale should consider such matters as when in the term the strike takes place. Remaining closed if the college has not yet opened might be wise, whereas remaining open toward the latter part of the term might also make sense.

Further Readings

The area of faculty problems has chiefly an exhortative literature; that of faculty improvement has a growing literature composed of, for the most part, untested suggestions; that of faculty personnel policies is covered chiefly in fugitive literature from individual institutions; and there is a growing literature with respect to both tenure and unionism. The citations below illustrate the best of what is available.

AAUP/AAC Commission on Academic Tenure. *Faculty Tenure: A Report and Recommendations.* San Francisco: Jossey-Bass, 1973.

ANGELL, G. W., KELLY, E. P., JR., AND ASSOCIATES. *Handbook of Faculty Bargaining: Asserting Administrative Leadership for Institutional Progress by Preparing for Bargaining, Negotiating, and Administering Contracts, and Improving the Bargaining Process.* San Francisco: Jossey-Bass, 1977.

BERQUIST, W. H., AND PHILLIPS, S. R. "Components of an Effective Faculty Development Program." *Journal of Higher Education,* 1975, *46*, 177–211.

BOYD, J. E., AND SCHIETINGER, E. F. *Faculty Evaluation Procedures in Southern Colleges and Universities.* Atlanta, Ga.: Southern Regional Education Board, 1976.

CENTRA, J. A. *Faculty Development Practices in U.S. Colleges and Universities.* Princeton, N.J.: Education Testing Service, 1976.

COHEN, A. M. (Ed.). *New Directions for Community Colleges: Toward a Professional Faculty,* no. 1. San Francisco: Jossey-Bass, 1973.

DURYEA, E. D., FISK, R. S., AND ASSOCIATES. *Faculty Unions and Collective Bargaining.* San Francisco: Jossey-Bass, 1973.

DYKES, A. R. *Faculty Participation in Academic Decision Making.* Washington, D.C.: American Council on Education, 1968.

GAFF, J. G. *Toward Faculty Renewal: Advances in Faculty, In-*

structional, and Organizational Development. San Francisco: Jossey-Bass, 1975.

Group for Human Development in Higher Education. *Faculty Development in a Time of Retrenchment.* New Rochelle, N.Y.: Change Magazine Press, 1974.

HAMMONS, J. O., AND WALLACE, T. H. S. "Sixteen Ways to Kill a Faculty Development Program." *Educational Technology,* 1976, *16,* 16–20.

HOPKINS, D. S. P. *Analysis of Faculty Appointment, Promotion and Retirement Policies.* Academic Planning Office Report No. 73–2. Stanford, Calif.: Academic Planning Office, 1973.

KEMERER, F. R., AND BALDRIDGE, J. V. *Unions on Campus: A National Study of the Consequences of Faculty Bargaining.* San Francisco: Jossey-Bass, 1975.

LIPSETT, S. M., AND LADD, E. C., JR. *Professors, Unions and American Higher Education.* Berkeley, Calif.: Carnegie Commission on Higher Education, 1973.

MILLER, R. I. *Evaluating Faculty Performance.* San Francisco: Jossey-Bass, 1972.

MILLER, R. I. *Developing Programs for Faculty Evaluation: A Sourcebook for Higher Education.* San Francisco: Jossey-Bass, 1974.

MIX, M. M. *Tenure and Termination in Financial Exigency.* Washington, D.C.: American Association for Higher Education, 1978.

MORTIMER, K. P. (Ed.). *Faculty Bargaining, State Government and Campus Autonomy: The Experience in Eight States.* Denver, Colo.: Education Commission of the States, 1976.

MORTIMER, K. P., AND RICHARDSON, R. C., JR. *Governance in Institutions with Collective Bargaining: Six Case Studies.* University Park: Center for the Study of Higher Education, Pennsylvania State University, 1977.

ODIORNE, G. S. *Personnel Administration by Objective.* Homewood, Ill.: Irwin, 1971.

SHULMAN, C. H. *Employment of Nontenured Faculty: Some Implications of Roth Sinderman.* Washington, D.C.: American Association for Higher Education, 1973.

SMITH, A. B. *Faculty Development and Evaluation in Higher Education.* ERIC/Higher Education Research Report No. 8. Washington, D.C.: American Association of Higher Education, 1976.

SMITH, B. L., AND ASSOCIATES. *The Tenure Debate*. San Francisco: Jossey-Bass, 1973.

STECKLEIN, J. E. *How to Measure Faculty Work Load*. Washington, D.C.: American Council on Education, 1961.

TICE, T. N. (Ed.). *Faculty Bargaining in the Seventies*. Ann Arbor: Institute for Continuing Legal Education, University of Michigan, 1973.

YUKER, H. E. *Faculty Workload: Facts, Myths and Commentary*. ERIC/Higher Education Research Report No. 6. Washington, D.C.: American Association of Higher Education, 1974.

Chapter 10

☙☙☙☙☙☙☙☙

Controlling Program
and Faculty Costs

F or the institution attempting to survive, retrenchment will be of
vital concern. It will be necessary for administration to face a
double challenge: (1) to eliminate deficits and maintain deficit-
free operations, and (2) to effect reductions in both programs and
personnel.

Eliminating Deficits

Deficits represent the negative difference between current
revenues, including whatever proportion of gift income is used for
direct operating expenses, and total expenditures. (A positive difference would be a surplus.) In some cases, operating deficits can be

266

misleading; for example, an institution might show an operating deficit in the same year that it registered significant increases in endowment or value of physical plant. In general, however, especially in stable or declining circumstances, collegiate institutions should try to abstain from having operating deficits unless they have sufficiently large reserves accumulated from past surpluses to cover the deficits without having to invade endowment or use gift income for more than about 1 to 20 percent of annual revenue.

Table 1 presents a reasonably typical example of an operating deficit and the administrative approaches that can be used to solve the problem. In this chapter, only one side of the budget-balancing effort will be considered—reducing expenditures. Ways of increasing income have been considered in other chapters.

Table 1. Expenditure and Income Profile for a Hypothetical Institution

Expenditure	Ideal	Actual	Revenue	
Instruction	1,865,000	2,095,000	Tuition & Fees	3,200,000
Research	400,000	400,000	Grant contracts	550,000
Public service	300,000	300,000	Private gifts	850,000
Academic support	312,500	312,500	Endowment	150,000
Student services	560,000	600,000	Other	250,000
Institutional support	995,000	995,000		5,000,000
Plant operations	525,000	725,000		
Scholarship	540,000	540,000		
Principal and Interest	115,000	145,000		
Loan fund matching	100,000	100,000		
Total	5,712,500	6,212,500		

Note: Enrollment = 800, FTE Faculty = 62, Endowment = $1 million, Physical Plant = $25 million.

This hypothetical institution ran a deficit of $50,000 in 1972, $75,000 in 1973, $100,000 in 1974, $200,000 in 1975, and $500,000 in 1976. It has an accumulated deficit of $925,000, which it has accommodated through bank loans using the endowment and physical plant as security. However, the bank has indicated that it will make no further loans until the annual deficit has been ended and a 50 percent reduction in the accumulated deficit accomplished. In October, the president reviewed the budget situation and projected the situation for the next year. He anticipated a 10 percent increase in tuition and fees or $320,000, a possible $50,000 increase in gifts, and a possible increase of $50,000 in other income. However, there would be a $35,000 increase in debt services, a $72,500 increase in plant operation, and a $108,000 increase in scholarship funds—a total of $215,500 in increased spending. Since the total increase in revenue would be $420,000, there would be a net increase in revenue of $204,500. This would still leave another deficit of $295,500, with no funds available for improvement of staff or faculty.

Review of expenses revealed that instructional costs, costs of power, costs of debt service, and some costs of student services were the items showing substantial increases. The task then became clear: to develop a budget that would shift from −$295,500 to +$150,000 and to develop a plan that would eliminate the accumulated deficit within four years. (The appendix lists 319 ways in which colleges and universities have tried to cut costs, according to the Management Division of the Academy for Educational Development.)

Institutions facing such a situation have attempted various techniques that should be avoided at all costs. The most direct has been an across-the-board budget reduction large enough to attain the budget goal. Such a technique overlooks such intractabilities as the price of gas, oil, and electricity or the need for some academic programs absolutely essential for a viable college. A second technique has been to increase momentary cash flow by acquiring ongoing programs purchased through loans and using the income generated by them to operate the parent institution. Also concentrating on the income side, some institutions have contracted with noneducational organizations to generate new and popular programs that could be offered at a profit; a typical arrangement is for the institution to award academic credit in return for a percentage of the gross income each program generates.

Much more effective in the long run would be to set yearly goals for the entire institution aimed at producing budget equilibrium at the end of a given period—that is, keeping yearly increases in expenses equal to yearly increases in income. Then each major unit within the institution would be assigned a goal ranging from no reduction to considerably more than the institutional average. In the hypothetical institution used for illustration, these steps would be taken: Institutional goals for budget reduction would be thoroughly discussed first by the president's cabinet and then with the faculty budget review committee. This would ensure that faculty opinion is expressed early in the process. Once unit goals have been set, the responsibility for deciding how they will be met would be the concern of each academic division, the library, the registrar's office, the student affairs area, and the other major administrative units. It is typically difficult for chief executives to assign this responsibility to subordinate units, partly because they feel that they know better where cuts should be made because of their broader perspective and partly because faculty groups in the past have frequently been unable to agree on financial matters that impinge on the careers of individual faculty members. It is the point of view argued here, however, that subordinate units will act responsibly if they are expected to act responsibly and that their decisions or recommendations will be taken seriously by central administration and the board of trustees. Trouble comes when faculty members begin to deliberate only to see their efforts discounted when the president, perhaps in a moment of panic, takes unilateral action.

Each administrative unit should be asked to: (1) set a date by which recommendations will be made, (2) specify the parts of a program to be modified, reduced, or eliminated, (3) specify the individuals whose positions might be modified or eliminated, (4) present a written estimate of the short- and long-term implications of the proposed changes, and (5) draw up a detailed presentation of several alternative ways in which the goal might be reached. When the administrative unit recommendations have been completed, the reports in aggregate should then be examined and commented on by the senate and the president's cabinet, first alone and then in joint session. Then, before the proposals are finally sent to the president for decision, the aggregate plan (without names of specific individuals directly affected) should be aired in a full faculty–staff meeting.

This procedure is long and requires much meeting and consultation time, and time is short. However, if the full crisis significance of the problem can be communicated to all campus constituencies, it is possible to reach tentative decisions in a relatively short time. The actual duties of faculty on any collegiate campus are sufficiently flexible that in a crisis many matters and activities can be postponed to provide time for the needed deliberations. Students would really not be hurt if, for example, a full week in late October were suddenly declared an independent study week to allow faculty to debate the financial affairs of the institution. A possible timetable might be:

- October 15: Budget goals for the institution announced and divisions and other units charged to produce proposals
- November 1–7: Detailed planning carried on in the divisions and other administrative units and recommendations prepared
- November 8–14: Cabinet and senate review of proposals
- November 15: Campuswide discussion of the proposals
- November 16–29: Presidential review and decision
- December 1: Announcement of decision and dispatch of letters to individuals whose duties are to be modified or terminated

Cutting Programs

Since reduction of major expenditures will normally involve the elimination of some programs or parts of programs, it is well to examine how this can best be done. There are some general criteria for program elimination: Is the subject or discipline one that seems to be evolving and developing? Does it attract capable scholars and students? Does it also attract continuing financial support? Are there adequate outlets into which graduates can be placed? Is the program linked to other programs in the institution so that it interacts with them and lends combined strength to the entire institution? But these criteria are so general that, except in flagrant situations, those responsible for programs that are being considered for elimination or retrenching can make defenses that are difficult to answer.

If leaders in an institution believe program retrenchment is needed, the following specific criteria can be applied to determine which programs are likely candidates. These criteria will be applied differently in different institutions but, in general, they are applicable to all types of institutions.

First, it should be determined if the program exhibits an

excessively high cost per credit hour produced. There are many ways of arriving at cost indexes, each based on certain assumptions. A relatively simple method is to use total faculty salary, or a proportion of total salary for part-time teaching, recognizing that salary actually goes to support many different activities but that the teaching function is the most central. Thus, for each faculty member, one would compute enrollment in each course taught in an academic year, multiply by credit hours, then divide the salary by the resultant credit hours produced. The cost per credit hour produced would then be computed for a full department or program and comparisons made between departments, programs, and the full institution. Such a comparison might reveal that Sociology costs $12.50 per credit hour produced, Russian $41.66, and Music $50.00. Similar computations could be prepared for each identifiable instructional department or program in the institution, with means median and standard deviation computed as a method of displaying high-cost programs. Cost alone, of course, is not sufficient for program elimination. Some very high cost programs may be essential for the institution's mission, for example, music in a liberal arts college. But cost should not be ignored.

Second, implicit in the cost estimates but speaking to a somewhat different aspect is actual course enrollment. As a general rule, lower-division courses (except for clearly tutorial or individual practice courses) that consistently enroll fewer than ten students should be examined, as should upper-division and graduate courses that enroll fewer than five students. Within a department or teaching program, isolated but consistent examples of low enrollments might be evidence for faculty reduction, whereas a general pattern of low enrollments would be evidence for possible program elimination.

Third, the number of majors should also be considered. A liberal arts college of 1,150 students might legitimately offer majors in fifteen of the liberal arts and sciences and perhaps five professional or applied majors (nursing or elementary education, for example). There would normally be a graduating class of 200, or an average of ten majors per department or program. The actual number of majors can be computed over a period of time—say, for the last five years—the averages computed, and the extremes displayed for consideration. As a general rule, an average of four majors per year per full-time faculty member would seem to be a reasonable expectation. When the major productivity of a department or program falls significantly below that norm, the unit should be scrutinized rather carefully.

Fourth, placement records of graduates are another appropriate consideration but one that should be used prudently. Some departments in the liberal arts colleges are clearly not vocational in character—for example, English, except for teaching or graduate school. But for those that are, such as education, nursing, chemistry, and business, what students do subsequent to graduation is significant for program evaluation. If placement of education graduates has declined rather consistently for four or five years, that should be cause for concern.

Fifth, in those institutions in which research grants and contracts represent a major source of institutional funding, changes in level of funding should be noted. If there appears to be a consistent decline in external support over four or five years, and if previous external support had been central to the functioning of the unit (one third or more of total operating budget), this fact should certainly be considered, as should also the types of grants and contracts received. If, for example, a program is created to train research workers in higher education and to do basic research regarding the nature of higher education, a decline in research support and a shift to service-type contracts should be taken quite seriously.

Sixth, frequently, programs are justified more for their impact on external relations than for their contribution to on-campus educational productivity. Intercollegiate athletics—especially football—music departments, and religious programs in some denominational colleges are examples. In some situations, those claims are clearly warranted. The fact that Stanford won the Rose Bowl twice within three years contributed beyond doubt to the steady increase in contributions from alumni. But these claims should be carefully examined. In one institution, intercollegiate football was justified on the grounds that it attracted students and benefactors. Closer scrutiny revealed, however, that few tuition-paying students enrolled because of football and that actually the schedule of playing more out-of-state and out-of-region games tended to alienate rather than attract good will and benefaction.

Consideration of such factors will reveal prime candidates for reduction or elimination, but the process by which these candidates are chosen is critical. At the outset, all constituencies should know that departments and programs are being examined. When a unit has been selected for consideration, a series of steps should be taken. First, the prudent academic vice-president or dean should meet with the faculty of the unit and discuss the data and possible actions deriving from them. The faculty should be encouraged to consider the issue and to make alternative suggestions, which might include: (1) improving productivity indexes; (2) initiating new activities or offering new services; and (3) joining other departments or programs to increase productivity and/or to improve service. Next, the chief executive officer and the head of the questioned department should each nominate an outside consultant to visit the campus, study the situation, and make recommendations. If the recommendation is to eliminate the program, a tentative date should be indicated, probably twenty-four months in the future. During that time:

1. Letters of proposed termination to nontenured faculty should be delivered.
2. A search for other positions within the institution should be undertaken for tenured professors.
3. A search should be undertaken at other institutions for positions for both tenured and nontenured faculty.
4. Opportunity should be provided for the head of the unit to appeal to the board of trustees regarding the decision to terminate the unit.
5. All faculty, administration, staff, and student groups should be kept informed in writing as each significant step in the process is taken. Ill will typically comes from rumor and ignorance. All concerned have a right to know, and their knowing will ease a difficult action.

Extreme care should be taken to avoid adding programs or significant expense while the process of elimination is in progress. The justification of program elimination because of financial need loses force and legitimacy if new expenditures are made while older expenditures are eliminated. Although not a hard-and-fast rule, it would be well to make no new appointments in other departments, *even if needed,* for at last a year after discharging tenured professors as part of program reduction or elimination. Temporary part-time appointments can typically be made in time to staff needed classes, and this seems preferable to making new regular appointments while eliminating others.

Reducing Faculty Costs

Obviously, there are some institutions in very poor financial health that have not yet reduced faculty. And the chances are that some of these may continue to live precariously well into the future. There are liberal arts colleges that have struggled at the end of every month for over twenty years to obtain the funds to meet the monthly payroll and that have never failed to meet each of those payrolls. But it is the thesis argued here that the 1980s will represent a new situation in which older ways of solving fiscal problems will no longer suffice.

During the 1930s and 1940s, institutions could in fact survive because faculty remuneration was kept low and because some of the more expensive activities that emerged in the late 1950s were not present. And during the 1960s, the general expansionism of higher education allowed steady increases in cash—for example, doubling tuition and enrollments within a decade furnished the resources to solve, or at least alleviate, every fiscal problem. But neither of those options are really available today. Faculty salaries will remain high or will increase for no other reason than that inflation will force them up. But tuitions, especially in the private sector in all save the most distinguished institutions, are likely to reach definite limits. This will be more a matter of emotional rather than rational buyer resistance. It can be shown rationally that, compared with consumer disposable income, tuitions of $6,000 in 1979 are no greater than tuitions of $3,600 ten years earlier, or $800 thirty years earlier. Yet students and parents faced with anticipated tuitions of $6,000 to $8,000 during the 1980s are likely to balk, especially if the economic value of a college degree continues to decline, as seems likely.

One major way of increasing the chances of institutional survival in a stable or deteriorating situation is by cutting back on faculty costs, which represent such a large proportion of an institutional budget. For example, a liberal arts college with 1,000 students, a faculty of fifty, and an operating budget of $4 million, will expend one fourth of that budget on direct faculty compensation. Dropping ten faculty positions would eliminate an annual operating deficit of $200,000 or would compensate for a sudden drop of sixty FTE students paying full tuition. Replacing twenty-five full professors at average salaries of $25,000 with twenty-five assistant professors at average salaries of $15,000 would save $250,000. The elimination of one fully tenured professor would free $750,000 from endowment or commitment of operating budget funds. Even granting early retirement to a fifty-eight-year-old professor whose total compensation (including fringe benefits) was $36,000 at 80 percent of his or her base pay would save the institution $12,000 since it would save both a portion of the base salary and fringe benefits, or 40 percent of the base salary of $30,000.

Reducing faculty costs substantially enough to affect institutional survival is radical surgery, but it is assumed that an institution considering it has already taken the easier first steps of deferred plant maintenance, reduction in expense money, reduction in staff support services, and other nonlethal economies. Although each institution must decide when the time has come to consider a serious reduction in faculty costs, several criteria can be suggested:

1. When almost continuous operating deficits have depleted reserves and threatened endowment and seem likly to continue
2. When the rate of increase of expenditure exceeds the rate of increase in income
3. When a rate of increase in tuition equal to that at similar institutions fails to generate enough income to permit increases in faculty salaries at least equal to those granted at similar institutions
4. When short-term loans to cover normal cash flow are usually necessary sixty or fewer days after each tuition payment period
5. When FTE student/faculty ratio falls below the average for similar institutions and stays low despite normal faculty attrition
6. When the cost of recruiting new students consumes an ever increasing percentage of tuition income

Institutions that must reduce faculty costs in order to maintain themselves are urged to follow a sequence of steps. If enrollment increases are possible, maintaining current faculty staffing levels can increase student–faculty ratios, which in time can bring relative faculty costs into line. The most direct way of reducing faculty costs is to increase the student–faculty ratio so that the cost per unit of credit is reduced. This can be accomplished by increasing the number of students who pay tuition or for whom legislature makes specific appropriations. If enrollment increases are not possible, or do not proceed rapidly enough, the next step is to allow normal attrition to operate through a policy of not filling positions as they came open, or of replacing tenure positions with part-time appointments. Depending on the kind of institution, this can produce a shrinkage of faculty of between 4 and 8 percent a year. In theory, faculty shrinkage could also be accomplished through early retirement. For most institutions however, experience indicates that this will not produce the needed savings. Thus, only a few quite affluent institutions should look to this technique. If the need persists for still further reduction of faculty, then a different plan for retrenchment should be developed along the lines presented earlier in this chapter. After a faculty of viable size has been reached, faculty policies should be reviewed in order to maintain that viability. Chapter Nine indicates what some of those policies might be.

Reduction Through Attrition

Draconian procedures regarding faculty have been advanced on the premise that financial problems appeared rather suddenly and that the institution was forced into action. However, it is possible for institutions to anticipate the picture a bit better and to accomplish the same ends (reduction in the number of faculty) in a more gradual way. This requires the development of a faculty planning model, based on historical practices within the institution, that will allow study of the effects of various changes in personnel policy. The University of Southern California has developed a model that can be used rather quickly by institutions of various types and that allows for consideration of various faculty alternatives such as increasing or decreasing the proportion of nontenured faculty who will be granted tenure (Linnell, 1976, pp. 22–26).

The U.S.C. Faculty Model is a computer-based simulation that will rapidly provide detailed predictions of faculty characteristics for future dates (usually year by year for the next five to twenty years), given a current faculty data base, specific policies, and other planning input. The faculty data required are birthday, rank, tenure status (and if nontenured, year of tenure decision), sex, ethnicity, salary, department, and full- or part-time employment. Policies and practices which may be studied are as follows:

1. Salary scales and changes with time.

2. Retirement policies.

3. Length of probation period and percent of nontenured faculty to be awarded tenure.

4. Promotion policies (distributions of rank, salary, tenure or nontenure status, tenure or nontenure track, full-time and/or part-time).

5. Annual resignation rates.

6. Total number of faculty.

7. Affirmative action planning.

The model permits rapid evaluation of current proposed policies and practices for their impact on the future academic and fiscal viability of the faculty. It can be used to develop realistic affirmative action plans and to make policy and practice changes consistent with college goals. As an educational tool, the model may be used by trustees, administrators, and faculty to make better decisions which are vital to the continuing strength of academic programs.

Initial uses of the U.S.C. model with selected institutions have revealed the little recognized phenomenon that the proportion of faculty vacancies coming available each year, even in the stabilizing years of the early seventies, was considerably higher than had been realized. Including resignations, retirements, deaths, and terminations, somewhere between 6 and 8 percent of a faculty leaves each year. This means that if an institution were to anticipate a need for retrenchment five years ahead, failure to fill those normal vacancies would allow a 30 to 40 percent reduction by the end of five years. Of course, those vacancies would include some positions that must be filled to maintain institutional mission, but some of the vacant positions might not be absolutely essential and some could be filled with acting or part-time faculty, especially in undergraduate teaching institutions. This would allow time to anticipate changing student demands, which would then determine the sorts of longer-term appointments that should be made. Obtaining more flexible use of 40 percent of a faculty in a five-year period could produce a radically reoriented institution in a very short time. In institutions that experienced extremely rapid growth during the 1960s, the opportunities for such a radical transformation will be even greater during the 1980s as the senior appointments of the sixties begin to retire.

Early Retirement

When institutions first realized the likelihood of faculty over-supply, provisions for early retirement were widely touted as a quick and easy way to reduce faculty and to replace high-salaried seniors with lower-priced juniors. In practice, however, the technique did not prove to be effective. The ability to provide an attractive plan (for example, 80 percent of base salary, elimination of fringe benefits and institutional contributions to retirement for faculty aged sixty to sixty-four) limited the number of institutions to the few institutions with considerable and flexible financial resources. In effect, it requires money to make money from this technique. In addition, almost simultaneously with the advent of the idea, unpredictably large and rapid inflation appeared, the course of which made individual financial planning with a fixed income extremely hazardous. At the same time, as one more element of the national mood concerning discrimination (this time discrimination against the elderly), there emerged a serious challenge to the idea of forced retirement.

Generally, universities best able to mount early retirement programs opted for one of several types of plans. The first is just accepting normal retirement earlier. This has long been available to faculty but rarely used because of the unfavorable economic consequences for most faculty members who have little or no outside income. In a few cases where retirement contributions are quite high, the net economic loss might be tolerable. A second method is one in which the institution makes a direct contribution that, when combined with retirement income and an end-of-retirement contribution, can make the net early retirement income approximate the net preretirement income. Only reasonably affluent institutions could mount this effort on any substantial scale. Variations on this plan, such as continuation of university contributions to health or retirement plans, make this form of early retirement more desirable but more expensive. (See Fincher, 1975, for further discussion.)

The record of attempts to generate early retirement has been mixed. Those plans that are large enough to encourage substantial numbers of faculty members to elect the early option require strict limitations on those eligible to retire in order to limit excessive drain on budgets. Less desirable plans simply do not attract faculty interest or participation. If the early retirement plan is designed to reduce faculty size with no replacement appointed, and the plan is attractive, it can effect budget reductions. If, however, the plan is designed to replace senior with junior appointments and is a desirable plan, the long-range effect will be a total increase in salary expenditures. As a general rule, early retirement does not appear to be a valid means for budget reduction. For institutions that can afford it, early retirement plans can be regarded as one more fringe benefit for those faculty members who wish to avail themselves of it. However, early retirement plans may be viewed as a desirable alternative to pay cuts or layoffs. Early retirement may also be a useful tool in phasing out programs.

By way of summary, all institutions should try to plan as best they can what enrollments will likely be five to ten years in advance and what programs and courses will be needed and demanded. This may sound like a truism of little practical import, except for the fact that, in the past, institutions have not used data wisely to plan for the future. Data were available, for example, predictive of a decline in demand for Ph.D.'s as early as 1966–67, yet were disregarded until the oversupply was actually clear to all.

Not that anticipating the future will guarantee that better decisions are made. That is an art form in and of itself. Nor can anticipation of enrollments or program demand be exact. Too many accidents of history will take place. But birthrates and school enrollments can be studied; shifts in the population of a state or region can be observed; and patterns of indexes within institutions can be examined to suggest a possible future. The invisible college characterized by enrollment decline, budget deficit, and increased dropout rate for nine of the past ten years is foolish if it uses the one year that was the exception as the basis for plans and decisions.

New federal and state retirement legislation will affect institutional plans in this area. Overly simplified, the Federal Employment Act of 1967 was modified in 1977 to change the age of mandatory retirement from sixty-five to seventy. Tenured faculty are exempted from the legislation until July 1, 1982, but after that time colleges and universities cannot mandate retirement until age seventy. This could very well place an additional enormous burden on institutions already facing serious financial conditions. For example, in one professional school having a full time faculty of thirty-five, thirteen full professors had been expected to retire between 1979 and 1983. At an average total compensation in 1978 of $40,000 for full professors, these thirteen cost $520,000 a year. Had retirement continued to take place as scheduled and the new replacement appointments been made at the assistant professor level ($18,300 total compensation), $282,100 could have been saved—a not inconsiderable amount even for a relatively affluent university. Now the institution may have to plan for at least five more years at the higher cost level.

A variety of ways of coping with this situation have been suggested. One is to end tenure at age sixty-five, thus allowing different ground rules for terminating appointments. This seems to be fraught with such potential legal complexities as to make it unworkable. A second suggestion for the future would be to replace tenure appointments with reasonably long-term contracts. But this would likely face a similar objection. In these times, given the ambiguities of evaluation of faculty performance and the casual quality of typical faculty record systems, establishing a case for termination of appointment after perhaps fifteen years of service would likely only improve the financial health of lawyers. Encouraging early retirement has already been shown to be ineffective for all save the most affluent institutions.

There are, however, some steps that can be taken to reduce the financial burden somewhat. First, institutional policy can state that the normal, expected age of retirement is sixty-five, and that although professors may not be required to retire at that age, they can be encouraged to do so. Institutions can also establish that after the normal expected age of retirement, certain institutional contributions will end. These would include contributions to retirement plans, medical plans, term life insurance, and the like. Second, various patterns of part-time appointments can be developed that would allow individuals to retire but to teach one fourth, one third, or half of the time. These individuals could maintain offices and contact with students and colleagues and could have an income close to or even greater than their take-home pay for full appointment. Consider the following situation:

- *Full-time appointment*
  $35,000 salary
  $ 4,200 retirement contribution
  $ 8,750 income tax
  $ 1,070 Social Security contribution
  _____
  $20,980 after-tax income
- *One-third appointment after retirement*
  $16,000 retirement pension
  $11,660 salary
  $ 4,733 income tax
  _____
  $22,927 after-tax income

And the institution has saved $8,334 in salary, based on $15,000 salary for replacement, and $1,666 in staff benefits—or a total of $10,000. In the professional school cited earlier, this would yield $130,000 in savings. (These issues are discussed at length in Corwin and others, 1978.)

Termination of Appointment

For those institutions facing real enrollment declines for any of a variety of reasons—cost, competition, or declining state or regional population—and unable to cut costs adequately through faculty attrition or early retirement and other measures, reducing faculty through termination is perhaps the only option. Termination of appointments of individuals requires delicate administrative skills. There are a few broad principles to be applied, involving timing, fair play, approximation of due process, examination of alternatives, consistency, impersonality of decision, judgment of peers, confidentiality, other placement assistance, and, if at all possible, some financial assistance to help individuals relocate. At the same time, several other factors should not be binding, such as length of service, judgments of comparative merit, changes in status because of merit, membership in the existing oligarchy, age, sex, race, or rank, with the exception of possession of tenure.

Difficulties in termination of appointments have typically emerged from unintentional violation of these principles. Thus, informing a faculty member in May that he or she will not be employed the following September is too sudden. Informing a faculty member by letter of nonreappointment and not providing an opportunity to discuss the matter before final decision violates both fair play and good procedure. Similarly, terminating without examining with the individual other possibilities within the institution or discussing other possibilities violates fair play and could result in litigation—if, for example, there were an unretrenched role for which the individual was prepared. Terminating one person while retaining another doing substantially the same work—for example, members of an English department or language department, each teaching basic skills courses—violates the principle of impersonality. In such a situation, decision by lot would be preferable to a substantive decision. An actual decision to terminate a faculty member made by a dean or president violates the principle of decision by peers. Each department or division, after careful and impersonal consideration of program needs, should decide one who is to be terminated.

It can be argued that the crisis might have been avoided had the growing deficits been taken seriously earlier, and this is true. Unfortunately however, in many institutions, the mentality of the 1960s distorted perceptions of the significance of deficits in the 1970s. There seemed to be a widespread belief that things were bound to improve. For example, at one established institution, authorities were inclined to discount the significance of an anticipated deficit, feeling that such an institution could well survive even several years of deficit spending. Now, eight years later, that institution is still running deficits and has finally been ordered by its board to eliminate them, even at the cost of radical program modification.

Decisions on where to make cuts in faculty should always be based upon the most objective data available. Only in the presence of persuasive data can charges of dismissal because of political beliefs or for other irrelevant concerns be avoided, or at least answered. Terminating faculty appointments, whether tenured or nontenured is almost always an unpleasant and difficult task. It is rarely done well and even more rarely well received. As it seems likely to become an increasingly frequent phenomenon during the eighties, there is need for some overall rationale and for some procedures that will safeguard individual and institutional interests.

Were it not for the principles of equity, justice, and tenure, faculty terminated for financial reasons would always be—except in the case of high-prestige institutions whose reputations are based on particular faculty members—the older and more senior members. This would seem to be the best move from the standpoint of institutional good. It can be argued that there is no persuasive evidence that age and experience are positively related to enhanced educational quality. And the higher salaries and possession of tenure of senior faculty members do limit the flexibility of institutions. Younger faculty members not only are paid less but, when not tenured, can also be terminated much more quickly if the need arises. Fortunately, however, collegiate institutions tend to be humanitarian with respect to personnel policies and to act on motives other than sheer economic concern. Thus, the entire matter of faculty termination should be undertaken with real concern for individuals and their rights and feelings, as well as the financial and programmatic needs of the institution.

Once the areas in which faculty reduction should be made have been established, termination of nontenured professors will usually be undertaken first. This is far from a rational policy. A case could be made that a tenured professor whose indexes of productivity have declined significantly should be terminated before a nontenured, but highly productive junior professor. But because of the tenure tradition, reinforced by some state law and some union contracts, it would seem prudent to eliminate nontenured professors first. As to procedures, several seem absolutely essential. First among these is that the department or professional school in larger institutions, the division or department in smaller institutions, and a committee representing the faculty as a whole in the quite small institution should be the bodies that recommend which specific individuals should be terminated. Discussions on this matter should be held as far in advance of the date for action as possible—certainly, except in cases of extreme emergency, a full twelve months before termination must take effect. The group considering the matter should be provided with all relevant information about institutional finances and about the performance of departments and individuals within departments. They *should not* be given specific recommendations by the administration concerning individuals, although representatives of the group may solicit specific comment about an individual which would become part of the record and would be available to the individual recommended for termination. The group should be given a specific charge (in writing) and a specific guarantee of actions to be taken once recommendations are made. The charge would give the details of the rationale, the number of positions to be terminated, and the date by which recommendations were required. The charge would also give assurance that recommendations made would not be summarily rejected. If the chief executive had reservations about the specific recommendation, he or she would return the recommendation and reservations to the group for reconsideration. The chief executive would terminate no one who was not recommended by the relevant group, so long as it abided by the charge to recommend someone. The group's refusal to accept and act on its charge would free the chief executive to act on his or her own.

Formal termination actions should conform to the terms of the appointment of the individual and, in general, the AAUP guidelines concerning notification. For this purpose, the AAUP contention is specifically rejected that service at other institutions should count toward receiving tenure at the end of six years of successful service. In general, instructors (where the rank is still in use) and assistant professors should be given an initial three-year appointment with notification required before December 1 of the third year as to whether or not reappointment will be made. Similarly, notification should be given by December 1 of the third year of the second appointment as to whether tenure will be granted or the individual terminated. Only at those two dates should actual termination notices be given, unless the institution can establish that only premature termination of contracts can prevent bankruptcy.

It is sound personnel policy and absolutely essential in a time requiring difficult decisions that a review procedure be specified. The procedure should indicate what steps the individual should take, which officer or unit will conduct the review, and which matters may or may not be considered. In cases of termination for institutional financial reasons, for example, the issue of professional effectiveness or ineffectiveness should not be adjudicated. When that is at issue, a different set of procedures should be used. A typical scenario for retrenchment of faculty for economic reasons would be for the chief executive officer to ask the involved departments or units to recommend concerning termination sometime between December and May of the academic year before notifications must be issued. Each unit would use whatever procedures it elects, with the proviso that the procedures must exhibit fair play and approximate due process. Recommendations would normally be forwarded to the chief executive officer and to the affected individuals not later than October 1 prior to December 1 when notification letters must be sent. If the affected individuals ask for a review, the chief executive officer should appoint a review agency or use an established one and ask it to determine the answers to these questions: (1) Is there a real financial condition that will be improved by the termination? (2) Were all possible candidates for termination considered and judged by the same criteria? (3) Did the procedures used exhibit fair play and approximate due process? Each institution should, of course, develop its own written statement of procedures following the general outline presented here. However, prudence would suggest that they should be reviewed and discussed by all relevant constituencies and by legal counsel before formal adoption by the board of trustees.

The termination of tenured faculty will in general follow

the same procedures. However, the proceedings should indicate that there are no comparable nontenured faculty members who could be considered for termination. Also, the deliberation and subsequent review, if asked for, should be done only by tenured faculty members. The possible conflict of interest if a nontenured faculty member were to judge a tenured faculty member is simply too great. When it appears likely that tenured appointments will be terminated, a number of cautions should be observed by the institution's administration:

1. The likelihood of need for faculty retrenchment should be announced well in advance of initiating any procedures, citing the reasons for it and the procedures to be followed. No sudden actions should be taken. Timing is all important. Administration should be in such close contact with the institution's fiscal condition that enough time can be allowed for acceptance of the problem and the solution.

2. At every major step in the process of retrenchment, all relevant constituencies should be informed in writing—safeguarding, of course, each individual's right to privacy and confidentiality. A poorly informed institution should not be tolerated.

3. The announcement of likely retrenchment should indicate that this process will be applied to all parts of the institution. The faculty must not develop suspicions that administration is asking them to bear the brunt of retrenchment while it continues to expand.

4. If there are identifiable centers of likely serious resentment or opposition because of ideology or personal animosity (a local chapter of AAUP or a group out to get the president or a faculty caucus), these must be specifically informed of all proceedings in scheduled meetings. Although such meetings may not end the opposition, they may serve to relieve some tensions and build a needed sense of openness and responsiveness.

5. In all institutions, there is an oligarchy of faculty that has a great deal to say about what decisions will be made. It is essential that this group be kept constantly informed and assured that due process is being followed.

6. When tenured faculty are likely to be terminated, it is best that

no advancement to tenure take place for several years after the terminations. A one-year additional appointment may be used, which indicates the option (for the individuals concerned) of considering the additional year as terminal or the beginning of what could be several years of annual reappointments until financial conditions change to allow tenured appointments. It is important to stress that a tenured appointment is a financial commitment of over a half million dollars. But it is also important to let the individual decide whether or not to allow the institution to deviate from the accepted operation of its tenure system. The general expectation is that, at the end of six years, a nontenured person will either be granted tenure or will be terminated. The institution should say it will follow this procedure unless an individual accepts, in writing, continuing annual appointments in the hope of eventually receiving tenure.

7. Above all, procedures used for termination due to financial exigency should be kept apart from procedures used to terminate for cause. The entire process must be seen as an unfortunate necessity.

Anticipating Financial Difficulty

A question arises as to whether institutions can be more sensitive than they have been concerning their financial condition. And the obvious answer is yes. However, there can also be considerable difference of opinion as to what those indexes might be.

In Chapter Four, several criteria were suggested to establish the existence of serious financial difficulty. Those were conservative criteria and are included in a list of indexes that should regularly be maintained to keep track of the financial condition of institutions. For institutions starting to develop a system of indexes and because 1968 seems to have been a turning point in American higher education, it is suggested that data for 1968 be collected and used as a base point for the following critical indexes:

1. Number of applications of first-year students
2. Ratios of applications to admissions of first-year students
3. Actual enrollment of first-year students

4. Ratios between fall-to-fall enrollments of second-, third-, and fourth-year students

5. Average difference between stated tuition and fees and student financial support provided, including institutionally provided work

6. Annual gift income and the percentage used for operating expenses

7. Dates and amounts of short-term loans obtained to cover immediate cash-flow problems

8. Annual operating deficits or surpluses compared with changes in reserves, endowment, and physical plant value

9. Number of courses actually offered each year by departments, average class size, and FTE student–faculty ratios

10. Changes in faculty salaries

If these data can be collected accurately, they might well be distributed to all key administrative officers so that there is a general awareness of the financial situation.

Further Readings

Controlling costs is an imperative, especially in a time of increasing inflation. But it becomes enormously difficult, particularly after the obvious cuts in expenditures have been made, such as reduction in travel and secretarial help and deferred plant maintenance. The existing literature offers many suggestions but there is little published that demonstrates, over time, what does and does not work. The few items cited here indicate the conventional wisdom, and the suggestions are worth examining. It will take five to ten years before the evidence is in to show how effective these approaches have been.

ALM, K. G., EHRLE, E. B., AND WEBSTER, B. R. "Managing Faculty Reductions." *Journal of Higher Education*, 1977, *48*, 153–163.

BOWEN, H. R., AND DOUGLASS, G. K. *Efficiency in Liberal Education: A Study of Comparative Instructional Costs for Different Ways of Organizing Teaching–Learning in a Liberal Arts College.* New York: McGraw-Hill, 1971.

BOWEN, W. G. *The Economics of the Major Private Universities.* Berkeley, Calif.: Carnegie Commission on Higher Education, 1968.

Carnegie Commission on Higher Education. *The More Effective Use of Resources: An Imperative for Higher Education.* New York: McGraw-Hill, 1972.

CHEIT, E. F. *The New Depression in Higher Education.* New York: McGraw-Hill, 1971.

CHEIT, E. F. *The New Depression in Higher Education—Two Years Later.* Berkeley, Calif.: Carnegie Commission on Higher Education, 1973.

COOMBS, P. H., AND HALLAK, J. *Managing Educational Costs.* New York: Oxford University Press, 1972.

JELLEMA, W. W. *From Red to Black?: The Financial Status of Private Colleges and Universities.* San Francisco: Jossey-Bass, 1973.

JENNY, H. H., AND WYNN, G. R. *The Golden Years.* Wooster, Ohio: College of Wooster Press, 1970.

JENNY, H. H., AND WYNN, G. R. *The Turning Point.* Wooster, Ohio: College of Wooster Press, 1972.

TOOMBS, W. *Productivity: Burden of Success.* Washington, D.C.: American Association for Higher Education, 1973.

Chapter 11

ﾒﾒﾒﾒﾌﾌﾌﾌ

Implementing
Survival Strategies

The prescription for collegiate institutional good health during the 1980s and 1990s should involve, for the most part, undramatic applications of a number of principles and practices, most of which have long been used in some institutions, with the addition of a few more recently developed ones. It is becoming clear that suggestions for radical changes from traditional practices are likely to prove counterproductive in the long run. Thus, the rapid entry into many new programs for many new kinds of students may help a college prosper for a time, but may then gradually erode the image of the institution and its long-term resources. The adoption of a complex new curriculum, such as a competency-based curriculum requiring major modification in how faculty members use their time, may

290

generate off-campus interest and even considerable foundation support but, at the same time, leave both faculty members and students confused and with sharply mixed feelings. Similarly, creating a complicated, new institution that focuses, say, on the environment and employs new nomenclature to establish a break with tradition may attract international attention and applications from unique kinds of individuals but fail to attract those students the institution was created to serve. Radical shifts in administration and governance—such as eliminating departments, asking the total faculty to decide in detail such complex matters as faculty retrenchment policy, or adopting a stylized, complex system of planning—may have visual appeal yet break down because people are not able to assume new roles for which their background and experience have not prepared them.

Cases for Consideration

The following case histories of two actual colleges will illustrate the application of some basic principles for institutional survival.

The first institution to be considered is a small, private liberal arts college in a Midwestern city, which has long served students from the city and from nearby areas. As a church-related college, it has stressed a degree of piety and supervision of student life, in addition to teacher preparation, athletics, and other traditional college offerings. Now in serious financial difficulties, it is tempted to seek a new mission but unwilling to attempt radical change.

During the early 1960s, this college was able to increase enrollments to about 800 students. It built new residence halls and a new science building with borrowed federal funds. It added faculty and allowed members to drift into tenure with little oversight. And it planned to continue to grow to at least double its enrollment. However, the state in which it is located has over a dozen private liberal arts colleges, two state universities, some regional state colleges, and some junior colleges and area vocational schools. Furthermore, the state has experienced a rather steady population decline, and the pool of prospective students began to shrink there a decade before the phenomenon was expected to take on national proportions.

In that situation, the college went into a classic condition of decline. Applications and enrollments declined and attrition rates mounted, so that by 1977 it had only about 400 students. The loss of tuition produced annual operating deficits of such magnitude that by 1977 the accumulated deficits were nearly equal to the total endowment, much of which could not be liquidated. Because of loss of enrollments, residence hall spaces were unfilled and the college was unable to pay on the principal of the federal loans used to construct the residence halls.

The steps used to solve the financial problem were also almost classic. Plant maintenance was deferred and one residence hall was closed and allowed to deteriorate. Increases in faculty compensation were eliminated and eventually discontinuation of fringe benefits was seriously considered. Cash flow was maintained through more and more frequent short-term borrowing. The size of the support staff was reduced and full-time staff were replaced by part-time student help, which, while less expensive, was also less effective. To attract students, operating income was used to pay scholarships and tuition was kept so low that it failed to generate the income needed just to keep pace with inflation. In addition, the faculty was encouraged to create a new curriculum that might be appealing to students, various changes in administrative structure were made, and the college joined a consortium in the hopes that an enriched program could be produced, increased enrollment generated, and perhaps some economies accomplished. Outside consultants were brought in and they made rather typical recommendations, such as improving the quality of campus life and putting the financial house in order. But still decline continued.

Throughout this period of decline, there were also manifest serious examples of mismanagement. The business office allowed accounts receivable to accumulate while, at the same time, no effective control was exercised over faculty expenditure of funds. The admissions staff was not supervised and, during especially critical periods, no admissions people were available to generate new enrollments. Administration responsibilities were changed frequently so that neither students, faculty, nor even administrative officers knew how to get things done. Recruitment of new faculty, when essential, was handled rather casually, with the typical appointment being the one who could be obtained least expensively and who would most resemble the faculty already in place.

Ultimately, the institution commissioned an evaluation of its administrative and management structure. The evaluators made a number of recommendations regarding governance but also addressed themselves to the more fundamental question of institutional survival. While they were not sanguine as to the future of the institution, they presented several alternatives for consideration. The first of these noted the success of some conservative, evangelical church-related colleges and suggested that one direction might be the adoption of a conservative posture regarding religion, personal behavior, and social life. If the college could appear as a good place for conservative parents to send their children, it might develop a constituency that would provide income and new students essential for institutional survival. Such a decision might alienate some faculty and administrators who were somewhat more liberal theologically and socially, but those might be replaced with more conservative individuals.

A second possibility noted the increase in accredited institutions that offer a variety of off-campus courses to adults who want degrees but who cannot spare the time or money to attend college as regular students. By using part-time faculty who could be employed at cheaper rates, expecting students living in out-of-the-way places to work largely through independent study, and assigning considerable academic credit for life experience, the institution could charge a reasonable but not excessive tuition that would generate enough revenue to support the program and yield a profit. The essence of this scheme is to shorten the time needed to earn a degree, so that a student pays a $2,000 tuition for one year to acquire a bachelor's degree that would cost $8,000 to $10,000 in tuition alone if taken in a more orthodox way. Several California institutions have eliminated million dollar annual budget deficits through such programs.

A third alternative suggested by the evaluators was that the institution cut its ties with the church and become a secular private college. There is the possibility that there are enough people in the state who would like a private education but one without religious overtones that a new clientele might be created. This shift might be linked to a curricular change that might attract students. An example would be a three-year bachelor's degree program that could save students about $8,000 (tuition, room and board, and forgone income) over a four-year period.

Before turning to the factors that should be taken into account by the leaders of this college in evaluating these consultant recommendations, consider the problems facing a somewhat more secure college: a private women's college in the East that is in strong financial condition but that foresees serious difficulties in the near future.

The tranquil hillside campus of this college, given character by nineteenth-century former estates of the elite of its city, can attend Janus-like either inwardly or out to the metropolitan richness that surrounds it. Despite its tranquillity, it has a history filled with episodes of enrollment crises and financial peril. Its most recent past president left the college, after an eighteen-year tenure, with a gemlike physical plant, a $15 million endowment, reserves of $700,000, a history of deficit-free operation, several attractive new programs whose soft-money support would soon end, a firm conviction as to the value of women's colleges, and a faculty that has come to expect the annual miracle of a balanced budget to allow it to stress the liberal arts and sciences. The enrollment outlook, however, is precarious.

The new president must now increase enrollment toward an optimum of 600 FTE students, cultivate annual unrestricted benefaction, reduce slowly rising attrition rates, produce an integrated curriculum of both occupational and liberal elements, create an administrative style and structure to enable her to lead, and find ways to use an expensive campus more effectively. Of the two essential problems of this college, one is the historically small-sized applicant pool, reduced as tuition has risen, and the sensed need to compensate for the rise in tuition with substantial and increasing financial aid to students. The other problem is that even with a maximum enrollment, which that pool allows, of about 750 students (full and part time), tuition and endowment income will not cover the full operation of the campus. In the past, the difference has been made up through various categorical grants such as foundation term support for new programs. There are other problems, but they are of the sort any institution is likely to encounter from time to time and can quickly be eliminated if the core problems are solved. These problems range from better articulation of various student services to improving the physical education program.

The new president has made her intentions clear. Increased budget support will be given initially only to those activities likely to generate adequate financial yield. Thus, the admissions staff will be enlarged and strengthened, the position of vice-president for development will be restored, and a study of the causes for attrition will be undertaken, attending especially to departments losing students and to those gaining them. Funds will also be used to conduct a market study to find out more about the college's appeal or lack of appeal. At the same time, the president is seeking ways to reduce expenditures without adversely affecting faculty morale or the essential program in the liberal arts and sciences.

In the 1960s, this college reaffirmed its unique mission of offering a liberal education for women. At that time, it successfully exploited foundations for money to start new and innovative programs needed to be responsive to the education of women in changing times. Almost two decades later, it continues to feel that if it can be true to its mission, it can solve most other problems. It is in complete agreement with the conventional wisdom well expressed by Earl McGrath (1975, p. 27): "If the colleges of liberal arts have the nerve to retrieve their independence and reestablish their traditional function of preparing youth to live an informed life committed to personal and civic fulfillment, they can restore values to a central position in undergraduate education and, at the same time, elevate the quality of our national life." The college is using marketing techniques to find the right consumers and to sell them on the values of this particular kind of education, and it is investigating limited new markets, such as older women. Clearly, this college is more viable than the Midwestern liberal arts college discussed earlier, but even its survival will be tested during the 1980s.

Overview of Survival Techniques

For both of these imperiled institutions and for hundreds of others like them, what advice can be offered? In this book, four elements emerge as central to institutional health.

Retaining Traditional Identity. Perhaps the first and most important prescription is that what institutions do should be clearly consistent with their traditions and their strengths. If an institution has historically served middle-ability level students, a sudden shift in emphasis either to high-ability level students or low-ability level students will likely fail and, at the same time, jeopardize its ability to deal with traditional clients. A major entry into off-campus graduate programs by a residential undergraduate college may produce increased revenue for a time but may very well erode the heart of the institution—the undergraduate program. Some major shifts can be made, such as from a single-sex institution to a coeducational one, but the transcendent educational tradition of residential undergraduate liberal arts education must be retained. A scenario for disaster would be for a residential liberal arts college for young women to become coeducational and, at the same time, seek to serve major new clientele, such as adults, the poor, minority group members, and the counterculture. The exemplar of healthy evolution would be Stanford's entry into high selectivity and national prominence built on, rather than violating, its traditions of being a residential university emphasizing science, technology, and professional education. Gettysburg, Bowdoin, and Colorado College all made significant changes in curricular structure or student body, yet retained their traditional identities. Collegiate institutions do, over time, evolve a saga, a charter, or a distinct identity that communicates to the world what they are. To violate such a charge should not be undertaken lightly.

Improving Administration. Second, the basic administrative structure that has developed in American colleges and universities through the years appears to be best suited to cope with the changed conditions anticipated for the 1980s and 1990s. There can and should be modification and refinement, but the basic elements and their relationships seem sound. Those elements are: (1) a strong board of trustees as steward of the institution and a check on administration; (2) a line administrative structure from president through deans down to and including department heads, which retains the essential prerogatives of finance, agenda setting, appointing power for administrative offices, and a legitimating and veto power over faculty appointments; (3) a faculty organization with delegated powers and a specific organization but with its ultimate responsibility to the president, who may approve or disapprove every action; (4) a detailed and structured communication system that ensures that everyone can know if they desire to know and, at the same time, facilitates a great deal of informal communication; and (5) a definite system of checks and balances to ensure monitoring of the activities of every constituency of the institution.

Such a structure has evolved over time to prevent serious error and misjudgment. A strong board and a strong faculty can prevent a president from overextending the institution or allowing deficits to accumulate. A strong president can similarly check the activities of his or her deans and can veto ill-advised faculty actions. And a strong and well-understood faculty organization can ensure that faculty thought and influence will be used to solve institutional problems.

The one major change that should be made in this traditional administrative structure is to decentralize much planning and administrative activity, but in a systematic way. Through much of the history of American higher education, the critical decisions regarding such matters as budget and program objectives were made by the president and his or her chief associates—sometimes, but not always, after informal consultation with others on campus. That worked reasonably well for relatively small institutions that were growing slowly. It even worked reasonably well during time of affluence and rapid expansion, although the system did break down when unanticipated crises developed, as during the student protest movement. Today, however, as institutions must plan carefully to use finite resources wisely, a different style is required. That style calls for each administrative unit—department, library, institute, and the like—to be responsible for developing clear objectives and, when appropriations are made, to have the resources to achieve those objectives. Thus, each subordinate unit develops its own objective and indicates the resources needed. These are aggregated and refined at each higher level and become, at the highest level, overall institutional program and fiscal policy. In essence, this style is what is called management by objectives.

There are several problems inherent in this style, as well as several strengths. First, it does clearly place departments in adversary relationship with each other as they set objectives and claim resources. As the plans are reviewed at higher levels, there must be ways of deciding on the allocation of resources. However, the arguments from each separate unit should be required to indicate priorities, which should help the review. And since the arguments present program objectives, various programs can be compared with each other and total institutional program priorities agreed upon. Further, the adversarial process can educate faculty and administration as to the direction an institution seems likely to take and can eventually produce a workable consensus.

When program objectives, programs, and requested resources are finally aggregated at the central administrative level, some may require substantial modification and some may even be eliminated, especially during times of potential retrenchment. Review prior to those decisions should obviously be thorough, but the decision should finally be made at the level of the governing board. Some institutions have tried to have an all-institutional faculty committee make those decisions—with disastrous results. Faculty voice should best be heard within operating units, and the faculty should be concerned with objectives, programs, and requested resources. Decisions about alternatives at the institutional level should have the benefit of faculty advice but not of faculty decision.

To the definite administrative structure and an approximation of management by objectives should be added the use of appropriate information and a definite system of management that can monitor events and take action when events start to drift out of control. The sophistication and complexity of management information and management techniques will obviously vary with the size, complexity, and resources of the institution. However, it is stressed that informed managerial monitoring and control exercised in a properly balanced administrative structure provides a strong context in which wise decisions can be made.

Rethinking the Curriculum and Instruction. The third central element is the educational program. In spite of claims to the contrary, the essence of the vast majority of collegiate institutions is the undergraduate educational program. It is quite appropriate for institutions to undertake, within definite constraints, some programs and activities peripheral to the central task. But when they begin to outweigh the central mission, they are headed for trouble. It is the tuition or tuition-based appropriation from the core undergraduate programs that maintains the financial integrity of the institution. It is the style of the undergraduate program, including both curricular and extracurricular activities, that contributes most to the institution's saga or charter and exerts the continuing attraction of the institution over generations.

Now, stressing that undergraduate core involves several different concerns. The first of these is the curriculum, which, regardless of course pattern, should be a limited curriculum deriving from the strengths of the faculty and the traditions of the institution and should involve both liberal arts and sciences and vocational courses. It is contended that institutions should refrain from asking faculty to create programs in areas in which they are clearly not expert (although the temptation to do so may be great). And it is further argued that hiring part-time faculty to develop programs concerning which the regular faculty and administration have no expertise is also questionable. Although a popular new field might well attract student enrollments and for a time be financially rewarding, the dangers of loss of quality and of changing institutional character are too great if long-range institutional vitality is a goal. It should be stressed that academic quality is best maintained through the pervasive interaction of many different individuals who are present on campus: those who know a subject or field, those who hear from students what takes place in classrooms, those who observe each other as they do or do not follow standard academic routines, those who observe patterns of student course enrollments, and those who constantly informally evaluate each other's intellectual strengths and weaknesses. That sort of constant quality control is not possible if no one on campus understands a field, nor is it possible if the courses and programs are offered at a considerable distance from the campus. There is no question but that adherence to the rule of limiting programs to actual faculty competence is one of the hallmarks of strong institutions.

Relatedly, the institution should not be overly concerned about the particular formal curricular structure. Especially in times of difficulty, time and energy should not be spent on elaborate curricular revisions, except as a device to revitalize the entire institution. It begins to appear that the impact of college derives primarily from a generic sort of concept of college as the various elements interact. Thus, what seems to be more important than the form of general education requirements is the interaction of a student with counselors, faculty, administration, and peers, and his or her involvement in registration procedures, cultural and recreational events, athletics, formal classes, and informal classes called "bull" or "rap" sessions.

It is with the purpose of enriching the total impact of such an environment that educational and curriculum innovation should be viewed. Although at some time in the future, some dramatic new curricular and instructional change may take place—comparable to the initiation of the case method for the study of law or the division of the medical curriculum into two years of basic science and two years of clinical work—the expectation of finding a major new method is not important. What is important is that experiments and innovations can make the institution more interesting and the faculty member doing the experiments more interesting. Whether team teaching, new uses of language laboratories, or computer-aided instruction last or not is, for the most part, immaterial compared to the likely improvement of the environment just because something new is taking place. Institutions properly should use whatever resources can be made available to stimulate innovation, but use of resources to find a curricular panacea to an institution's problems should be avoided. The same cautions apply to improvement of instruction. Helping faculty members improve whatever techniques they feel most comfortable using and experimenting with some new devices should be seen chiefly as matters that make the total campus milieu more vital and interesting—and this should be encouraged, so long as per-unit costs do not drift out of line in either direction. In essence, however, no institution in trouble is likely to survive because it reorganized its curriculum or encouraged educational innovation.

Clearly implied by this concentration on undergraduate education as the central institutional concern is the fact that efforts should also concentrate on recruitment and retention of undergraduates. It is argued that long-term institutional health will better be ensured by concentrating on that clientele than by searching for many new clientele. There is a fine point to be made here. As was indicated earlier, there can be no objection to limited programs for new kinds of students if they conform to institutional strengths and if they can be developed with relative ease. It should also be recognized that the financial plight of some institutions may be so precarious that the temptation is irresistible to do almost anything to generate new tuition income. Following such a course may be the only option open and may save an institution's life, but the odds are that it will result typically in institutional death.

Revitalizing the Faculty. The fourth element in this concentrated effort to retain or regain institutional health is the faculty. It seems essential that many institutions reduce the size of their faculties in the 1980s; this fact should be recognized and planned for. In addition, the steady increases in instructional costs must be slowed and even reversed. Thus, better utilization of faculty is necessary chiefly through modification of the student–faculty ratio and the course-teaching loads. And, although the phenomenon may be brief—lasting perhaps a decade—it seems likely that the faculty in many institutions will be an aging one and that these institutions will have to attend to faculty development so as to make faculty members more interesting people with whom students can interrelate. This is premised on the belief that—assuming some reasonable ability to communicate and understand student needs—when a professor teaches something that excites him or her, it is of more educational consequence than whether the course fits into some particular curricular design. The essence of formal undergraduate education is the interaction of young men and women with each other and with some significant teacher through words, numbers, and concepts in the belief that such interactions will produce changes in how they view themselves and the world. The particular subjects may change over time, as do some of the techniques of interaction—thus, drill and recitation in Latin produced the same results as lecture discussion of the humanities at a different time and as formal, self-paced study under guidance of biology still more recently—but education is both a simple and a mysteriously complex activity that can take place in a wide variety of ways.

In effect, education is not unlike liturgy—it is an act of faith. But this belief precludes neither serious discussion of ideals nor educational research and experimentation. Thus, periodically and especially when facing changed situations such as will come during the 1980s, faculties should be encouraged to ponder the curriculum, the purposes of education, and the possibility of educational reform. Such activities stress the ideals of human betterment and probably make the institution a more humane place. The necessary discussions also help socialize people into that particular setting. And a major review of an educational program loosens conditions so that changes, very likely already under way, can be tried out and given legitimacy.

A proper question here is, What emphasis should be given to such educational discussion by an institution facing serious trouble and possibly death? The answer is far from simple. In previous chapters, it has been urged that such institutions concentrate all energies on those matters most essential for survival: student recruitment, reduction of expenditure, and obtaining new capital. And for the moments of extreme crisis, this seems valid. But there may be room for organized serious discussion of educational goals and institutional destiny just for the sake of morale. Just as people in time of war need to feel that sacrifice and effort are for a noble cause, faculties and administrators need to feel they are embarked on a cosmic mission. Changing from semesters to a quarter system is really a mechanical sort of thing having no great educational significance, but seriously debating the issue in ideal terms may be educational for faculty and administrators as well as for students— and result tangentially in something important. As for institutional use of the growing reforming literature, within reason its existence should be recognized and, on occasion, some of it made the basis for serious discussion. In a similar vein, consultants or visiting scholars can be used to stimulate conversation and thought, which contributes to the socialization of faculty and administration and may encourage someone to do something new and interesting. But none of the formulations available can be used as a blueprint for institutional change.

A Final Word

The overwhelming factor that emerges from this analysis of institutional vitality is that it is accomplished not by heroic measures and the initiation of major new departures but through the wise use of some limited techniques and human talents in the presence of considerable luck. The small Bible college will rarely make it as an academically demanding liberal arts college, nor will the small liberal arts college experienced in training teachers be able to become a multicampus university. The best base for continued vitality is to continue to serve a traditional mission but with greater attention to details and refinement of technique.

Given that continuity with the past, the first and greatest need is to avoid error. In virtually every troubled situation can be found significant and avoidable error. There is the error of not determining the real circumstances of a major gift, or of making unrealistic assumptions of the amounts of gift income to be included in budgets. There is the error of a financial statement's not revealing actual conditions. There is the error of assuming but not knowing the size of a potential new market. There is the error of not monitoring expenditures. And there are the errors of making poor administrative appointments, alienating faculty or students, not using a board of trustees effectively, or not insisting upon good information.

As to how to avoid error, the best technique is broad and continuous consultation with all important constituencies and especially with those having special and relevant information. There is no substitute for a strong and involved board of trustees, vigorous and independent-minded administrative officers, and competent and concerned faculty members. When a president puts an issue before such groups, in a spirit of openness and willingness to explore rather than merely to seek legitimation, the odds increase for avoidance of error. But to that consultation must be added the other important element—information that can answer real questions rather than confuse and conceal. There need not be computer printouts of masses of data, but data so organized as to answer questions of costs, enrollments, and resources, and to offer alternative explanations of events. This is urged with the understanding that complete data are never possible and that decisions must nonetheless be made. For the most part, decisions represent an acceptance of probabilities. The odds can be lowered with incomplete data but never eliminated.

Next in importance to the avoidance of error is the need for administrators to have mastery of a wide variety of technical skills and abilities. Presidents should know in some detail how admissions works, what the roles and duties of various administrative officers are, how income is achieved and expenditures are made, how to read budgets and financial statements in detail, how to evaluate the credentials of faculty and the advice of experts, what it takes to acquire books for a library, how to evaluate construction costs, and what the various provisions of relevant state and federal legislation are. In addition, a chief administrator should be able to do the following reasonably well: call and chair meetings; write letters, memoranda, and reports; speak to large and small groups; elicit advice from individuals and groups; synthesize the views of many different people; seek funds; argue a case for his or her institution; delegate responsibility and hold others responsible; coordinate a staff and use its advice; enlist the aid of friend and foe alike; and, above all, identify the crucial elements of a problem. This last ability is the one most difficult to develop in people and the one most valuable when developed.

Two myths have grown up about collegiate administrators—that they are unprepared for their jobs and that if they would adopt newer techniques of management, institutions would be better run. It is true that a few presidents have been unprepared—especially those who entered the presidency from the ministry—but those who entered after ten to fourteen years as academics have generally socialized to understand an academic institution and have had the opportunity, through serving on committees and in minor administrative posts, to develop the essential skills. In office, they need to perfect those skills and to guard against error. New techniques of management can merely provide better information and suggest alternatives and their consequences. Ultimately, whether the action be that of appointing a new dean, embracing the concept of marketing, deciding to defer maintenance, determining tuition level, or authorizing new programs, the essential act is one of human judgment—it is to be hoped, informed human judgment. Institutional vitality, in large measure but far from absolute measure, will depend on that judgment.

Part of the unexplained success or failure of an institution is the matter of luck and of how well good luck can be exploited and bad luck contained. The examples are legion. It was good luck that gave John Hanna of Michigan State College two residence halls, owned free and clear, which he could parlay into a system of residence halls. It was bad luck that sent the cost of energy into orbit during the 1970's at the same time that the stock market turned down. In a sense, the essentials of the problems of the 1970s were produced by the accidents of earlier high birthrates and the subsequent enrollment growth of the 1960s and the equally unpredictable downturn in birthrates and the impact of that on college enrollments. It might be good administrative doctrine always to expect the unexpected and, over time, to develop the reserves needed for re-creation.

Further Readings

In a sense, all previously cited documents are also germane to this last chapter. However, a few additional statements are especially to the point. In *More Than Survival*, a definite agenda for institutional health is set forth, and in *The Third Century*, the anticipated conditions are variously enunciated.

BRATTON, D. L. "Life or Existence?" *Liberal Education*, 1976, *62* (4), 527–530.

Carnegie Foundation for the Advancement of Teaching. *More Than Survival: Prospects for Higher Education in a Period of Uncertainty*. San Francisco: Jossey-Bass, 1975.

Change Magazine. *The Third Century*. New Rochelle, N.Y.: Change Magazine Press, 1977.

HEATH, D. H. "Prescription for Collegiate Survival: Return to Liberally Educating Today's Youth." *Liberal Education*, 1977, *63* (2), 338–349.

MOOD, A. M. *The Future of Higher Education: Some Speculations and Suggestions*. New York: McGraw-Hill, 1973.

STEWART, C. T., AND HARVEY, T. R. (Eds.) *New Directions for Higher Education: Strategies for Significant Survival*, no. 12. San Francisco: Jossey-Bass, 1975.

TRITES, D. G. *New Directions for Higher Education: Planning the Future of the Undergraduate College*, no. 9. San Francisco: Jossey-Bass, 1975.

Appendix

𝕬𝕬𝕬𝕬𝕬𝕬𝕬𝕬

Increasing Income

Tuition and Student Fees

1. Raising tuition
2. Recruiting new students more actively
3. Admitting more transfer students
4. Raising out-of-state student fees at public institutions to equal state resident fees plus state tax support
5. Requiring larger advance deposits on tuition from students
6. Collecting full tuition, room, board, and fees at the beginning of the year to reduce billing costs and enhance short-term investment income
7. Increasing proportion of tuition charged for a dropped course or for withdrawal during the semester

Note: This material is reproduced with permission of the Management Division, Academy for Educational Development, Washington, D.C.

8. Making nonrefundable all advanced deposits from admitted students
9. Raising academic fees, particularly late registration, graduation, thesis, and so on
10. Reducing rebate for not using room and board plan
11. Charging fees for use of library by organizations not related to the university and by scholars and students from other institutions
12. Hiring a collection agency or appointing a collection agent for obtaining payment of student charges, instead of dropping students
13. Charging standard commercial rate of 1.5 percent per month on all tuition, fees, room and board owed the university
14. Increasing dormitory charges

Investments, Plant, and Facilities

15. Investing cash balances in short-term securities
16. Short-term investment of amounts usually held as balances in checking accounts (if properly handled, the normal delay in cashing checks will prevent overdrafts)
17. Investing cash over the weekend—into the market Friday afternoon, out of the market Monday morning
18. Putting new endowment gifts into high-yielding bonds instead of low-yielding growth stocks
19. Splitting portfolio between two independent managers—a bank and private financial consultants—to encourage competition and improve returns (telling both managers the minimum income needed each year and then giving each discretionary authority to proceed)
20. Using some of the appreciation on endowment for current expenses
21. Investing part of endowment in operating businesses and oil properties for higher return
22. Loaning securities in endowment portfolios to brokers for a fee
23. Selling off nonproductive properties
24. Selling two university buildings, three off-campus apartment houses, and a forty-six-acre lot near campus

25. Selling college-owned faculty housing facilities to faculty members occupying them
26. Renegotiating long-term leases on investment property to bring in more current income
27. At a state institution: Picking up monthly subsidy payments by messenger at state treasurer's office to save days in transit and make remittance available earlier for short-term investment
28. Raising rentals charged on university-owned property to cover full cost and a fair return on investment
29. Renting out empty dormitory space to another college
30. Renting space to other institutions and groups for classes
31. Renting computer, duplicating, and printing facilities, auditoriums, meeting rooms, and dorm facilities to outside groups or agencies (for example, for summer programs for the disadvantaged)
32. Offering "package deal" conferences in university facilities, using university-owned motel to accommodate participants
33. Charging bookstore full overhead cost for space and utilities used
34. Renting "airspace" on campus property (for example, building noncampus-related apartments on the top of new campus facilities)
35. Converting old trunk rooms, storage rooms, and lounge space in dormitories into rentable space

Other Income-Producing Activities

36. Increasing the number of concession businesses on campus and charging them more
37. Requiring a commission on sales by privately owned vending machines on campus
38. Filing claims with federal agencies for full overhead reimbursement on government grants
39. Charging a management fee for running off-campus programs for credit for governmental organizations and industry
40. Increasing the number of government-supported training programs (for example, training paraprofessional personnel for city school systems and for medical and public health organizations)

41. Obtaining operating money for the medical school from the state government or the federal government
42. Increasing charges for sports, cultural, and other campus events
43. Charging for press box seating
44. Increasing charges for parking
45. Installing parking meters for all visitor parking on campus
46. Charging a fee for both employee and student parking
47. Increasing fees for reading and speech clinics
48. Increasing fees for clinic or dispensary services
49. Charging students full cost for psychiatric or psychological services
50. Conducting telephone solicitation campaign (using students) to raise $42,0000
51. Door-to-door canvassing by students to raise $35,000
52. Raffling off a scholarship
53. Challenging students to raise $100 each, which they did by conducting letter-writing fund drives, giving blood, conducting "the world's largest garage sale," and so on
54. Soliciting funds on television, radio, billboards, bus signs, and so on
55. Establishing a new donors program that gives special recognition to those pledging $10,000 over a ten-year period
56. Promoting events on campus that are certain money-makers (for example, rock concerts)
57. Presenting free concerts featuring students, with contributions requested in return for choice seats
58. Conducting more summer conferences and other activities at a profit
59. Conducting more adult education programs at a profit
60. Charging more for community services that in the past have been offered free or at a nominal price
61. Charging for check-cashing services
62. Using students to persuade district voters to approve tax rate increase
63. Charging full cost of overhead for all special projects on campus
64. Lending endowment funds to students at interest rate lower than bank rate instead of at no interest

65. Offering a fifth-year master's program to a new student market without increasing faculty, library, or other expenses
66. Offering more evening master's programs to employed persons who do not require student aid
67. Charging for copies of college catalogues; limiting free distribution to general information brochures
68. Pushing book and record sales in campus bookstore
69. Selling college-owned artifacts, antiques, and art objects

Decreasing Expenditures

Faculty and Personnel

70. Reducing the number of nontenured faculty, adjunct or part-time faculty, consultants, research assistants, and teaching assistants
71. Using specialized faculty as guest lecturers in courses other than their own
72. Making greater use of adjunct faculty
73. Replacing faculty who leave or retire with lower-ranked staff or teaching assistants
74. Encouraging early retirement of tenured faculty
75. Strictly enforcing retirement schedule
76. Eliminating visiting professorships
77. Eliminating academic chairs as they become vacant
78. Leaving vacancies unfilled
79. Being more careful on tenure decisions
80. Issuing conditional contracts, mainly to faculty for summer school, night school, or adult education courses; then canceling classes if too few students enroll
81. Employing more part-time evening faculty who are not entitled to fringe benefits
82. Cutting back on high salaries paid distinguished scholars or other high-priced faculty members, artists, poets, or musicians in residence; sharing such people with other institutions
83. Freezing salaries
84. Establishing new salary schedule for administrative staff and faculty, beginning at one increment lower than previous schedule

85. Using a salary increase as an incentive for the faculty to permit increased student-teacher ratios

86. Increasing student contact hours per faculty member rather than increasing the number of faculty

87. Increasing faculty load in individual instruction and in the supervision of theses

88. Specifying that full-time faculty members spend a minimum number of hours in the classroom each week—fifteen hours in community college, twelve hours in undergraduate colleges, and nine hours in graduate schools

89. Requiring faculty to be available on campus for a full seven- or eight-hour day when not in the classroom

90. Reducing staff in office of coordinator of research since federal funds are now more limited

91. Reducing faculty time allowed for sponsored and departmental research

92. Cutting back on research allowances given to the faculty

93. Dropping foreign student advisors

94. Turning a senior division headed by a dean into a service department with only a director

95. Phasing out the dean of continuing education

96. Merging small departments and assigning administrators to some teaching duties

97. Reducing the number of vice-presidents

98. Purchasing packaged instructional units instead of hiring a new faculty member

99. Cutting back on the number and extent of sabbaticals given to the faculty

100. Reducing released time given faculty for administrative and committee assignments

101. Reducing the number of faculty committees or determining the cost of such committees and then requiring greater output to justify cost

102. Requiring prospective faculty and staff to pay their own job interview expenses (travel and so on)

103. Limiting support of association memberships for faculty and staff

104. Limiting attendance of faculty and staff at conferences away from campus

105. Requiring faculty and staff to pay their own expenses for professional meetings

106. Abolishing the Administrative Intern Program, the Office of Survey Research and Statistical Studies, and the Office of Legal Counsel

107. Maintaining all salaries in special grant projects at the amounts specified in the grant

108. Eliminating the use of temporary personnel

109. Using temporary personnel in offices with peak periods, such as admissions; cutting down on permanent staff in such offices

110. Reducing the number of administrative people, guidance counselors, placement counselors, testing personnel, and so on

111. Reducing campus health care staff by using community hospitals, clinics, and physicians

112. Lengthening the working day without providing additional compensation

113. Reducing the number of secretaries and clerks

114. Using secretarial or clerical pools and installing automated typing equipment for form letters

General Administration

115. Cutting back financial aid to amount provided by government funds, endowment, and private gifts made specifically for scholarship purposes

116. Reducing number of athletic scholarships

117. Actively recruiting students who are eligible for scholarships from state or private sources

118. Obtaining a state program of instructional grants to attract underprivileged students and to take the sting out of increased student fees

119. Recruiting students from affluent areas to reduce the number of scholarship applicants

120. Eliminating scholarships for honors work not based on financial need

121. Imposing a quota at a public institution on the number of out-of-state students admitted when their tuition does not cover costs

122. Developing a consortium for some managerial activities, such as servicing student loans
123. Establishing a planning office with a primary emphasis on cutting costs
124. Automating routine tasks wherever possible
125. Computerizing wherever possible to cut staff costs
126. Stretching out large expenditures (such as those for the installation of a computer system) over a longer period than previously planned
127. Simplifying admissions procedures, registration, record keeping; reducing the number of forms and documents required
128. Instituting paperwork control to eliminate old admissions and other records and save filing space and staff time
129. Simplifying procedures for student payment of tuition and fees; installing Master Charge credit card system for this purpose
130. Changing from quarter to semester system to elimate one registration and one grade recording per year
131. Making accident and health insurance optional for students and eliminating the subsidy previously provided
132. Merging with an adjacent or nearby college to cut down on administrative overhead, size of faculty, and number of small classes; also to increase property investment
133. Consolidating administrative offices operating separately at a sister institution; centralizing such functions as admissions, job placement, financial aid, housing, and counseling
134. Shifting responsibility for the operation of the computer facility and its budget from the mathematics department to a larger, merged division of science and engineering
135. Consolidating computerized functions of central administration, biomedical network, and research foundation into one system
136. Using the computer to prepare classroom rolls that will fit easily into a standard binder
137. Converting some scholarships into long-term loans
138. Establishing in next year's budget the upper limit of spending for each budget center on campus
139. Requiring the head of each budget center to project his plans within fixed limits for each of the next five years

140. Reducing the university chapel budget
141. Providing in-service training on budget preparation for department chairmen and deans
142. Involving department heads in considering the problem of "needs" versus "resources"; soliciting proposals from department heads to reduce administrative costs by 10 percent
143. Starting the budgeting process earlier and completing the budget earlier than in the past
144. Using only one format for submitting budget requests to the state central agency and the legislative committee
145. At a state college: having all checks and withholding tax forms prepared by the state accounting office that now prepares the payroll for other state employees
146. Building sabbatical programs around overseas contracts with government agencies or private firms
147. Reducing the number of federal grants accepted in which there is "cost sharing"
148. Returning grants for which matching or overhead funds cannot be found
149. Avoiding the establishment of a community college approved by the legislature where population does not justify it; establishing instead an extension center operated by the state's land-grant college (which already has professional staff in the area to be served)
150. Eliminating technical services to private industry unless fully self-supporting
151. Eliminating overtime pay
152. Scaling down or eliminating inaugural ceremonies, commencement activities, convocations, and other academic pageants
153. Reducing the number of conferences operated at a deficit on campus
154. Investigating pool and consortium approaches to saving on insurance costs
155. Increasing deductibles on insurance policies
156. Buying catastrophe insurance only
157. Self-insuring (where permitted) for workman's compensation
158. Reducing space and personnel subsidy to college presses and

to professional journals, associations, and outside professional societies using campus facilities

159. Contracting out the warehousing and distribution details of a university press to a commercial firm to eliminate most personnel costs in these areas

160. Cutting back on instructional services and office/laboratory space previously offered free to postdoctoral students

161. Providing less tuition reimbursement for faculty children

162. Abolishing inventory of inexpensive office and maintenance items when the inventory cost is greater than the value of the items

163. Eliminating all charge accounts in the campus bookstore

164. Eliminating annual contributions to neighborhood social service agency

165. Planning space utilization and architectural design for new construction at the same time

166. Eliminating football

167. Eliminating basketball and field and track

168. Eliminating all spectator sports that are costly

169. Utilizing space more economically in order to reduce rented space and the need for new construction

170. Constructing classrooms of varying sizes in order to reduce vacant seats in occupied classrooms

Maintenance and Security

171. Bolting typewriters, adding machines, and so on to desks in order to reduce theft and replacement costs

172. Organizing security measures with neighboring institutions and community organizations in a cooperative-type arrangement

173. Using students in security department

174. Using closed-circuit TV cameras to reduce personnel needed for security purposes

175. Using citizens' band radio sending and receiving units for police and traffic officers, night watchmen, and for communication with maintenance and repair forces on campus

176. Using mobile repair units to move from task to task on campus

177. Improving supervision of maintenance activities to increase efficiency

178. Putting janitorial services on night shift only
179. Reducing janitorial services from five to three nights a week
180. Reducing dormitory cleaning services to once every other week
181. Reducing office cleaning except of wastepaper baskets to once a week
182. Banning tobacco smoking except in lounges to reduce janitorial expense
183. Discontinuing maid service in dormitories
184. Discontinuing provision of cooking utensils, sheets, pillows, and blankets to residence halls
185. Using disposable bath towels in locker rooms instead of laundering cloth towels
186. Repainting less often
187. Cutting back on building maintenance expenses, refurbishing, and repairs
188. Halting all building renovations
189. Ending the employment of professional interior decorators for new college buildings
190. Calling in outside specialists to review power plant efficiency
191. Closing entire buildings at night or on weekends to save heat, light, and so on; closing lounges at 10 P.M.
192. Instructing personnel not to turn off fluorescent lights unless the lights will be left off more than two to three hours
193. Installing electronic devices to control light, heat, air conditioning, locking of buildings, and so on from central office, thus reducing the costs of utilities and personnel servicing campus buildings
194. Turning air conditioning down at night
195. Switching from fuel oil to natural gas for heating when cost is lower
196. Cutting off heat previously provided in hockey area
197. Closing a road on campus to save maintenance money
198. Banning autos for underclassmen to save outlays for parking lots and paving
199. Closing a campus-owned recreational park
200. Transferring a state university-owned arboretum to the State Department of Parks and Recreation
201. Closing a college operated farm

202. Deferring a tree care program
203. Replacing flower beds with grass or bushes
204. Installing artificial turf in heavily trafficked areas that had to be resodded each year
205. Installing automatic sprinkler irrigation system, using untreated water to reduce labor costs and water charges
206. Running environment campaign to keep campus clean

Office Expenses

207. Reducing the quality and quantity of office supplies (no more two-color printed stationery)
208. Using only one printing company and one style of type for all printing
209. Using one all-university letterhead with college, department, division, or office information typed in
210. Sending fewer catalogues, financial reports, and other printed reports by first-class mail
211. Cutting size of catalogues, reducing course descriptions, eliminating nonessential information and printing on cheaper paper; this also cuts mailing cost
212. Dividing the catalogue into sections, printing each section in the number of copies needed; not sending prospective freshmen the course descriptions for advanced courses (which they do not need)
213. Sending out supplements to catalogues, bulletins, and so on, rather than printing a whole new publication
214. Postponing publication of new catalogues for one or two years
215. Using stickers to indicate changes in the catalogue, rather than reprinting part or all of it
216. Redirecting advertising so that it goes mainly to potential students, rather than using scattered mailing lists
217. Cleaning up mailing lists; following up on nondeliveries, old addresses, unwanted communications
218. Cutting down on public relations, glossy-type publications, alumni materials, and so on
219. Minimizing costly publicity programs for campus productions; using local newspapers to publicize evening and cultural events, thereby saving most of the printing and postage costs

220. Giving up the publication of a quarterly scholarly journal
221. Cutting down on the numbers and sizes of college newspaper and magazine issues
222. Cutting back on number of private office telephones on campus

Purchasing, Equipment Rental, and Leasing

223. Using a purchasing cooperative
224. Getting more bids than previously on larger items
225. Requesting discounts for immediate payment
226. Using campus centralized purchasing
227. Using central state purchasing for standard equipment items, such as automobiles, typewriters, office equipment, and so on
228. Negotiating to allow private colleges and universities to purchase through state contract
229. Increasing control of purchasing near the end of a budget period
230. Buying government surplus property whenever possible to save money
231. Cutting back or eliminating purchase of new equipment
232. Buying cheaper equipment
233. Buying used equipment, particularly from industry (where some might be contributed)
234. Cutting down or eliminating rental of equipment
235. Changing to cheaper copying equipment
236. Establishing tighter control on use of Xerox machines and other duplicating facilities
237. Eliminating all automobile purchases except for maintenance equipment
238. Renting time on a computer instead of buying one
239. Delaying two years in expanding the use and capacity of present computer
240. Changing to a cheaper computer
241. Purchasing rather than renting computer equipment (as opposed to federal policy that frequently prefers rental to purchase)
242. Leasing apartment buildings to house students (the number of which may be at peak levels) rather than building additional dorms

Travel Expenses

243. Reducing or eliminating university-financed out-of-state travel by faculty and administration; in some cases, eliminating all travel subsidies
244. Requiring coach instead of first-class tickets
245. Cutting down on number of university-owned automobiles and limiting their use more rigidly
246. Disposing of university aircraft used less than 300 hours a year
247. Cutting down travel by admissions office to areas of marginal productivity
248. Paying closer attention to items included in travel expense accounts
249. Requiring new employees to pay their own moving expenses previously provided by the university
250. Cutting out free limousine service between two campuses
251. Discontinuing shuttle bus service on the campus of a large university

Food Services

252. Eliminating *all* food services
253. Eliminating all sit-down, served meals
254. Closing dining services during vacation periods
255. Reducing subsidy on faculty and administration dining rooms
256. Closing faculty dining rooms
257. Eliminating free guest meals or guest catering in dining facilities
258. Establishing commissary-type food service in conjunction with neighboring institutions: joint purchasing and preparation with delivery to participating institutions
259. Combining nine food service units into central facility
260. Using a "super snack bar," designed along the lines of a supermarket, where food is prepared and delivered in bulk, and arranged on racks to cut labor costs
261. Converting cafeteria to vending machine service
262. Establishing campus bakery to produce baked goods at a lower cost than regular purchase price
263. Directing more careful attention to menu planning and to size of portions served in dining hall

264. Cutting the deficit of faculty club in half by catering for meetings of local service clubs

Departments, Schools, Programs, Courses

265. Abolishing departments or academic programs that have too few students to justify continuation
266. Eliminating course sections with fewer than fifteen students except for required courses
267. Increasing the size of regular classes and lecture sections
268. Closing down School of Education—too few students and too costly
269. Discontinuing laboratory school in School of Education
270. Cutting back services and activities in Campus School; maintaining only clearly defined experimental programs
271. Discontinuing communication arts and computer science departments
272. Eliminating theater department and dramatic arts productions
273. Offering more of the advanced courses in alternate years
274. Operating an alternate degree program or interim term during the summer to utilize staff and facilities more fully
275. Offering required courses in only two of three quarters, even though it delays graduation of some students
276. Providing accelerated degrees, external degrees, and credit by examination, independent study, and work-study instead of required courses
277. Abolishing language requirements; ultimately abolishing language departments with too few students
278. Cutting out physical education requirement
279. Sharing students with a consortium to allow a reduction in the number of courses offered
280. Reducing degree programs: offering a single undergraduate program and degree in the field of engineering instead of a variety of specialized undergraduate degrees; eliminating master's degree program in science and mathematics
281. Cutting some Ph.D. programs to permit lower faculty and library costs
282. Requiring the faculty to defend every single academic program now being offered

283. Dropping a summer theatre and a summer language program (both had been subsidized)
284. Reducing the number of public concerts and extent of the lecture series
285. Dropping those research projects that require substantial university support
286. Refusing to begin any new academic projects without special funding
287. Using restricted funds for current programs rather than new ones
288. Allowing a department to create a new course only by dropping an old course
289. Using only a language laboratory for foreign language courses in lieu of instructors
290. Using senior undergraduate students to teach freshman language courses
291. Negotiating arrangements with a foreign university so that students can study abroad at an institution where tuition and air travel combined is less expensive than regular tuition
292. Curtailing the study abroad program even though the program costs the state less per student than on-campus study
293. Using less expensive materials, less equipment, and fewer supplies for laboratory experiments
294. Using audiotapes for language drill and for prerecorded lectures
295. Using auto-tutorial programs for teaching electronic technology, nursing, foreign languages, and biology
296. Using individually prescribed instruction in engineering courses
297. Using closed-circuit two-way telephones for statewide adult education courses
298. Combining upperclass and graduate courses that duplicate each other
299. Combining undergraduate schools that overlap each other
300. Reducing the extent of continuing education, agricultural research, and extension programs
301. Building a core program that all first-year students must take
302. Using core program for both freshmen and sophomores

Library

303. Cutting down number of subscriptions to periodicals and newspapers
304. Reducing acquisition of special collections, such as manuscripts and rare books
305. Buying microfilm copies of magazines and journals instead of binding issues
306. Postponing binding periodicals
307. Cutting down book purchases; buying microcards, microfilm, microfiche instead
308. Buying used books instead of new editions
309. Cutting noncurrent book purchases by 50 percent this year; maybe 100 percent next year
310. Dividing up library acquisition areas with neighboring institutions; organizing an interlibrary loan system
311. Consolidating library collections and departmental libraries to eliminate need for some library personnel
312. Developing one periodical library for several large neighboring universities to handle subscriptions, binding, and storing
313. Discarding obsolete library books and records to save space, shelves, file cabinets, and handling costs
314. Renting less expensive storage space for rarely used books
315. Tightening up on the number of books and journals ordered by faculty and charged to the college
316. Reducing multiple-copy book acquisitions by faculty
317. Reducing standing orders to major university presses
318. Reducing the hours of library service; closing the library Friday and Saturday nights
319. Opening stacks to all graduate and undergraduate students to reduce library staff

References

❀❀❀❀❀❀❀❀

AAUP/AAC Commission on Academic Tenure. *Faculty Tenure: A Report and Recommendations.* San Francisco: Jossey-Bass, 1973.

ALM, K. G., EHRLE, E. B., AND WEBSTER, B. R. "Managing Faculty Reductions." *Journal of Higher Education,* 1977, *48,* 153–163.

American Alumni Council. *Educational Fund Raising Manual.* Washington, D.C.: American Alumni Council, 1972.

ANDERSON, C. A., BOWAN, M. J., AND TINTO, V. *Where Colleges Are and Who Attends: Effects of Accessibility on College Attendance.* New York: McGraw-Hill, 1972.

ANDREW, L. D., AND FRIEDMAN, B. D. *A Study of the Causes for the Demise of Certain Small Private Liberal Arts Colleges in the United States.* Blacksburg: Virginia Polytechnic Institute and State University, 1976.

ANGELL, G. W., KELLY, E. P., JR., AND ASSOCIATES. *Handbook of Faculty Bargaining: Asserting Administration Leadership for Institutional Progress by Preparing for Bargaining, Negotiating, and Administering Contracts, and Improving the Bargaining Process.* San Francisco: Jossey-Bass, 1977.

ASKEW, T. A. *The Small College: A Bibliographic Handbook.* Washington, D.C.: Council for the Advancement of Small Colleges, n.d.

ASTIN, A. W. *Who Goes Where to College?* Chicago: Science Research Associates, 1965.

ASTIN, A. W. "College Dropouts: A National Profile." *American Council on Education Research Reports,* 1972a, 7 (1).

ASTIN, A. W. "Undergraduate Achievement and Institutional Excellence." In K. Feldman, *College and Student.* Elmsford, New York: Pergamon Press, 1972b.

ASTIN, A. W. *Preventing Students from Dropping Out.* San Francisco: Jossey-Bass, 1975.

ASTIN, A. W. *Four Critical Years: Effects of College on Beliefs, Attitudes, and Knowledge.* San Francisco: Jossey-Bass, 1977.

BAIRD, L. L., AND RICHARDS, J. M., JR. *The Effects of Selecting College Students by Various Kinds of High School Achievement.* ACT Research Report No. 23. Iowa City, Iowa: American College Testing Program, 1968.

BALDERSTON, F. E. *Managing Today's University.* San Francisco: Jossey-Bass, 1974.

BALDRIDGE, J. V., AND OTHERS. *Policy Making and Effective Leadership: A National Study of Academic Management.* San Francisco: Jossey-Bass, 1978.

BALDRIDGE, J. V., AND TIERNEY, M. L. *New Approaches to Management: Creating Practical Systems of Management Information and Management by Objectives.* San Francisco: Jossey-Bass, 1979.

BENNIS, W. *The Leaning Ivory Tower.* San Francisco: Jossey-Bass, 1973.

BERDAHL, R. O. *Statewide Coordination of Higher Education.* Washington, D.C.: American Council on Education, 1971.

BERDAHL, R. O. (Ed.). *New Directions for Institutional Research: Evaluating Statewide Boards,* no. 5. San Francisco: Jossey-Bass, 1975.

BERQUIST, W. H., AND PHILLIPS, S. R. "Components of an Effective

Faculty Development Program." *Journal of Higher Education,* 1975, *46,* 177–211.

BLACKBURN, R., AND OTHERS. *Changing Practices in Undergraduate Education.* Berkeley, Calif.: Carnegie Council on Policy Studies in Higher Education, 1976.

BLAU, P. *The Organization of Academic Work.* New York: Wiley, 1973.

BLOOM, B. S., AND PETERS, F. R. *The Use of Academic Prediction Scales.* New York: Free Press, 1961.

BOLEN, J. G. *Management Information for College Administrators.* Athens, Ga.: Institute of Higher Education, 1971.

BOWEN, H. R. *Investment in Learning: The Individual and Social Value of American Higher Education.* San Francisco: Jossey-Bass, 1977.

BOWEN, H. R., AND DOUGLASS, G. K. *Efficiency in Liberal Education: A Study of Comparative Instructional Costs for Different Ways of Organizing Teaching–Learning in a Liberal Arts College.* New York: McGraw-Hill, 1971.

BOWEN, H. R., AND MINTER, W. J. *Private Higher Education.* Washington, D.C.: Association of American Colleges, 1976.

BOWEN, W. G. *The Economics of The Major Private Universities.* Berkeley, Ca.: Carnegie Commission on Higher Education, 1968.

BOYD, J. E., AND SCHIETINGER, E. F. *Faculty Evaluation Procedures in Southern Colleges and Universities.* Atlanta, Ga.: Southern Regional Education Board, 1976.

BRADY, J. J. "Strategies for Grant Development." In A. W. Rowland (Ed.), *Handbook of Institutional Advancement.* San Francisco: Jossey-Bass, 1977.

BRATTON, D. L. "Life or Existence?" *Liberal Education,* 1976, *62* (4), 527–530.

BRENEMAN, D. W., AND FINN, C. E., JR. (Eds.). *Public Policy and Private Higher Education.* Washington, D.C.: Brookings Institution, 1978.

BROWN, J. D. *The Liberal University.* New York: McGraw-Hill, 1969.

BUCKLIN, R., AND BUCKLIN, M. C. *The Psychological Characteristics of the College Persistor and Leaver: A Review.* Washington, D.C.: U.S. Office of Education, 1970.

BUDIG, G. A. *Dollars and Sense: Budgeting for Today's Campus.* Chicago: College and University Business Press, 1972.

Carnegie Commission on Higher Education. *New Students and New Places.* New York: McGraw-Hill, 1971b.

Carnegie Commission on Higher Education. *Papers on Efficiency in Management of Higher Education.* New York: McGraw-Hill, 1972a.

Carnegie Commission on Higher Education. *The More Effective Use of Resources: An Imperative for Higher Education.* New York: McGraw-Hill, 1972b.

Carnegie Commission on Higher Education. *Governance of Higher Education: Six Priority Problems.* New York: McGraw-Hill, 1973.

Carnegie Council on Policy Studies in Higher Education. *The States and Private Higher Education: Problems and Policies in a New Era.* San Francisco: Jossey-Bass, 1977.

Carnegie Foundation for the Advancement of Teaching. *More Than Survival: Prospects for Higher Education in a Period of Uncertainty.* San Francisco: Jossey-Bass, 1975.

Carnegie Foundation for the Advancement of Teaching. *Missions of the College Curriculum: A Contemporary Review with Suggestions.* San Francisco: Jossey-Bass, 1977.

CENTRA, J. A. *Strategies for Improving College Teaching.* ERIC/ Higher Education Research Report No. 8. Washington, D.C.: American Association for Higher Education, 1972.

CENTRA, J. A. *Faculty Development Practices in U.S. Colleges and Universities.* Princeton, N.J.: Education Testing Service, 1976.

Change Magazine. *The Third Century.* New Rochelle, N.Y.: Change Magazine Press, 1977.

CHEIT, E. F. *The New Depression in Higher Education.* New York: McGraw-Hill, 1971.

CHEIT, E. F. *The New Depression in Higher Education—Two Years Later.* Berkeley, Calif.: Carnegie Commission on Higher Education, 1973.

CHEIT, E. F., AND LOBMAN, T. E., III. "Private Philanthropy and Higher Education: History, Current Impact, and Public Policy Considerations." In Commission on Private Philanthropy and Public Needs, *Research Papers: II.* Washington, D.C.: U.S. Department of the Treasury, 1977.

CLARK, B. R. *The Distinctive College: Antioch, Reed, and Swarthmore.* Chicago: Aldine, 1970.

COHEN, A. M. (Ed.). *New Directions for Community Colleges: Toward a Professional Faculty,* no. 1. San Francisco: Jossey-Bass, 1973.

COHEN, M. D., AND MARCH, J. G. *Leadership and Ambiguity.* New York: McGraw-Hill, 1974.

COLEMAN, J. S. "The Principle of Symmetry in College Choice." *College Board Review,* 1969, *73,* 5–10.

Commission on Private Philanthropy and Public Needs. *Research Papers: II.* Washington, D.C.: U.S. Department of the Treasury, 1977.

Committee on Economic Development. *The Management and Financing of Colleges.* New York: Committee on Economic Development, 1973.

COOLEY, C. A. *Fund Raising for the Private School: The Alumni Fund.* Boston: Independent School Consultants, 1962.

COOMBS, P. H., AND HALLAK, J. *Managing Educational Costs.* New York: Oxford University Press, 1972.

CORNELL, C. D. "Staffing the Small College Development Office." *Techniques,* 1970, *5* (1), 11–13.

CORSON, J. J. *Governance of Colleges and Universities.* (rev. ed.) New York: McGraw-Hill, 1975.

CORWIN, T. M., AND OTHERS. *Changing Retirement Policies.* Washington, D.C.: American Association for Higher Education, 1978.

CRAY, E. "The University of Southern California: Avis on the Pacific." *Change,* May 1977.

CROSS, K. P., VALLEY, J. R., AND ASSOCIATES. *Planning Non-Traditional Programs: An Analysis of the Issues for Postsecondary Education.* San Francisco: Jossey-Bass, 1974.

DAVIS, R. E. "Reflections on the Passing of a College." Unpublished paper prepared for the Commissioner of Education for the Commonwealth of Pennsylvania, 1978.

DEEGAN, A. X., AND FRITZ, R. *MBO Goes to College.* Boulder, Colo.: Division of Continuing Education, Bureau of Indpendent Study, 1975.

DILL, D. D. *Case Studies in University Governance.* Washington, D.C.: National Association of State Universities and Land Grant Colleges, 1971.

DODDS, H. W. *The Academic President—Educator or Caretaker.* New York: McGraw-Hill, 1962.

DOERMANN, H. *Crosscurrents in College Admissions.* New York: Teachers College Press, 1968.

DRESCH, S. P. "A Critique of Planning Models for Postsecondary Education: Current Feasibility, Potential Relevance and Prospectus for Future Research." *Journal of Higher Education,* 1974, *46* (3), 245–286.

DRESSEL, P. L. *College and University Curriculum.* Berkeley, Calif.: McCutchan, 1971.

DRESSEL, P. L. *Handbook of Academic Evaluation: Assessing Institutional Effectiveness, Student Progress, and Professional Performance for Decision Making in Higher Education.* San Francisco: Jossey-Bass, 1976.

DRESSEL, P. L., AND ASSOCIATES. *Institutional Research in the University: A Handbook.* San Francisco: Jossey-Bass, 1971.

DRESSEL, P. L., AND FARICY, W. H. *Return to Responsibility: Constraints on Autonomy in Higher Education.* San Francisco: Jossey-Bass, 1972.

DURYEA, E. D., FISK, R. S., AND ASSOCIATES. *Faculty Unions and Collective Bargaining.* San Francisco: Jossey-Bass, 1973.

DYKES, A. R. *Faculty Participation in Academic Decision Making.* Washington, D.C.: American Council on Education, 1968.

EBLE, K. E. *The Art of Administration: A Guide for Academic Administrators.* San Francisco: Jossey-Bass, 1978.

FIFE, J. D. *Applying the Goals of Student Financial Aid.* Washington, D.C.: American Association for Higher Education, 1975.

FINCHER, V. *Early Retirement Plans in Higher Education.* Pasadena, Calif.: University of Southern California Press, 1975.

FORD, D. H., AND URBAN, H. B. "College Dropouts: Successes and Failures." In L. A. Pervin, L. E. Reik, and W. Dalrymple (Eds.), *The College Dropout and the Utilization of Talent.* Princeton, N.J.: Princeton University Press, 1966.

FROOMKIN, J. *Needed: A New Federal Policy for Higher Education.* Washington, D.C.: Institute for Educational Leadership, 1978.

GAFF, J. G. *Toward Faculty Renewal: Advances in Faculty, Instructional, and Organizational Development.* San Francisco: Jossey-Bass, 1975.

GOLLATTSHECK, J. F., AND OTHERS. *College Leadership for Community Renewal: Beyond Community-Based Education.* San Francisco: Jossey-Bass, 1976.

GREEN, J. L., JR. *A New Approach to Budgeting in Higher Education.* Detroit, Mich.: Business and Finance Office, Wayne State University, 1972.

GRINOLD, R. C., HOPKINS, D. S. P., AND MASSY, W. F. "A Model for Long-Range University Budget Planning Under Uncertainty." *Bell Journal of Economics,* 1978, 9 (2).

Group for Human Development in Higher Education. *Faculty Development in a Time of Retrenchment.* New Rochelle, N.Y.: Change Magazine Press, 1974.

HAMMONS, J. O., AND WALLACE, T. H. S. "Sixteen Ways to Kill a Faculty Development Program." *Educational Technology,* 1976, *16,* 16–20.

HARKNESS, C. A. *College Staff Personnel Administration.* Urbana, Ill.: College and University Personnel Association, 1965.

"Harvard's Report on the 'Core Curriculum'." *Chronicle of Higher Education,* March 6, 1978, pp. 15–19.

HEATH, D. H. "Prescription for Collegiate Survival: Return to Liberally Educating Today's Youth." *Liberal Education,* 1977, *63* (2), 338–349.

HEATON, C. P. (Ed.). *Management by Objectives in Higher Education.* Durham, N.C.: National Laboratory for Higher Education, 1975.

HEILBRON, L. H. *The College and University Trustee: A View from the Board Room.* San Francisco: Jossey-Bass, 1973.

HELSABECK, R. E. *The Compound System: A Conceptual Framework for Effective Decision Making in Colleges and Universities.* Berkeley: Center for Research and Development in Higher Education, University of California, 1973.

Higher Education Research Institute. *National Conference on Academic Planning.* Los Angeles: Higher Education Research Institute, 1978.

HODGKINSON, H. L. *How Much Change for a Dollar: A Look at Title III.* Washington, D.C.: American Association for Higher Education, 1974.

HOPKINS, D. S. P. *Analysis of Faculty Appointment, Promotion and Retirement Policies.* Academic Planning Office Report No. 73-2. Stanford, Calif.: Academic Planning Office, 1973.

HUDSPETH, D. R. *A Long-Range Planning Tool for Education: The Focused Delphi.* Albany: New York State Education Department, 1970.

IFFERT, R. E. *Retention and Withdrawal of College Students.* DHEW Bulletin No. 1. Washington, D.C.: U.S. Government Printing Office, 1957.

IHLANFELDT, W. "A Management Approach to the Buyer's Market." *College Board Review,* 1975, *96.*

IVANCEVICH, J. M. "Longitudinal Assessment of Management by Objectives." *Administrative Science Quarterly,* 1972, *17* (1), 126–138.

JACKSON, G. A. "Financial Aid to Students and the Demand for Postsecondary Education." Unpublished doctoral dissertation, Harvard University, 1977.

JACOB, P. *Changing Values in College.* New York: Harper & Row, 1957.

JELLEMA, W. W. (Ed.). *Efficient College Management.* San Francisco: Jossey-Bass, 1972.

JELLEMA, W. W. *From Red to Black?: The Financial Status of Private Colleges and Universities.* San Francisco: Jossey-Bass, 1973.

JENNY, H. H., AND ALLAN, M. A. "Philanthropy in Higher Education: Its Magnitude, Its Nature and Its Influence on College and University Finance." In Commission on Private Philanthropy and Public Needs, *Research Papers: II.* Washington, D.C.: U.S. Department of the Treasury, 1977.

JENNY, H. H., AND WYNN, G. R. *The Golden Years.* Wooster, Ohio: College of Wooster Press, 1970.

JENNY, H. H., AND WYNN, G. R. *The Turning Point.* Wooster, Ohio: College of Wooster Press, 1972.

JONSEN, R. W. *Small Liberal Arts Colleges: Diversity at the Crossroads.* Washington, D.C.: American Association for Higher Education, 1978.

KATZ, J., AND ASSOCIATES. *No Time for Youth: Growth and Constraint in College Students.* San Francisco: Jossey-Bass, 1968.

KAUFFMAN, J. F. *The Selection of College and University Presidents.* Washington, D.C.: Association of American Colleges, 1974.

KEETON, M. T. *Models and Mavericks: A Profile of Private Liberal Arts Colleges.* New York: McGraw-Hill, 1971.

KEMENY, J. G. "The First Five Years—A Report by the Thirteenth President." *The Dartmouth Alumni Magazine,* 1975.

KEMERER, F. R., AND BALDRIDGE, J. V. *Unions on Campus: A National Study of the Consequences of Faculty Bargaining.* San Francisco: Jossey-Bass, 1975.

KLINGELHOFER, E., AND HOLLANDER, L. *Educational Characteristics and Needs of New Students: A Review of the Literature.* Berkeley: Center for Research and Development in Higher Education, University of California, 1973.

KNOWLES, A. S. (Ed.). *Handbook of College and University Administration.* New York: McGraw-Hill, 1970.

KOTLER, P. "Applying Marketing Theory to College Admissions." In *A Role for Marketing in College Admissions.* New York: College Entrance Examination Board, 1976.

LAHTI, R. E. *Innovative College Management: Implementing Proven Organizational Practice.* San Francisco: Jossey-Bass, 1973.

LAWRENCE, B. G., AND SEVICE, A. L. *Quantitative Approaches to Higher Education Management.* Washington, D.C.: American Association for Higher Education, 1977.

LEE, E. C., AND BOWEN, F. M. *The Multicampus University.* New York: McGraw-Hill, 1971.

LESLIE, L. L., AND FIFE, J. D. "The College Student Grant Study: The Enrollment and Attendance Impacts of Student Grant and Scholarship Programs." *Journal of Higher Education,* 1974, *45* (9), 651–671.

LEVINE, A. *Handbook on Undergraduate Curriculum: Prepared for the Carnegie Council on Policy Studies in Higher Education.* San Francisco: Jossey-Bass, 1978.

LEVINE, A., AND WEINGART, J. *Reform of Undergraduate Education.* San Francisco: Jossey-Bass, 1973.

LINNELL, R. H. "The USC Faculty Planning Model." *AGB Reports,* November/December 1976, pp. 22–26.

LIPSETT, S. M., AND LADD, E. C., JR. *Professors, Unions and American Higher Education.* Berkeley, Calif.: Carnegie Commission on Higher Education, 1973.

MC CONNELL, T. R. *The Redistribution of Power in Higher Education.* Berkeley, Calif.: Center for Research and Development in Higher Education, 1971.

MAC DONALD, D. S. *Alternative Tuition Systems.* Washington, D.C.: American Association for Higher Education, 1977.

MC GRATH, E. J. *Memo to a College Faculty.* New York: Teachers College Press, 1961.

MC GRATH, E. J. *Values, Liberal Education and National Destiny.* Indianapolis, Ind.: Lilly Endowments, 1975.

MC HENRY, D. E., AND ASSOCIATES. *Academic Departments: Problems, Variations, and Alternatives.* San Francisco: Jossey-Bass, 1977.

MC KEACHIE, W. J. *Teaching Tips: A Guidebook for the Beginning College Teacher.* (6th ed.) Lexington, Mass.: Heath, 1969.

MC KENNA, D. L. "Ethics for Earthquakes and Other Emergencies: Moral Responsibility of Admissions Counselors." *Journal of the National Association of College Admissions Counselors,* 1978, *21,* 27–28.

MAGARRELL, J. "Part-time Professors on the Increase." *Chronicle of Higher Education,* January 16, 1978.

MARCH, J. G. *Leadership and Ambiguity.* New York: McGraw-Hill, 1974.

MAYHEW, L. B. (Ed.). *Educational Leadership and Declining Enrollments.* Berkeley, Calif.: McCutchan, 1974.

MAYHEW, L. B. *Legacy of the Seventies: Experiment, Economy, Equality, and Expediency in American Higher Education.* San Francisco: Jossey-Bass, 1977.

MEYER, J. W. "The Charter: Conditions of Diffuse Socialization in Schools." In W. R. Scott (Ed.), *Social Processes and Social Structures.* New York: Holt, Rinehart and Winston, 1970.

MEYER, J. W. "The Effects of the Institutionalization of Colleges in Society." In K. A. Feldman (Ed.), *College and Student: A Sourcebook in the Social Psychology of Education.* New York: Pergamon Press, 1972.

MEYER, J. W., AND ROWAN, B. "Notes on the Structure of Educational Organizations." Unpublished paper, Stanford University, 1975.

MICHALAK, C. L. (Ed.). *Managing Tomorrow's University.* Proceedings of the University of California Academic Business Officers Conference, Berkeley, September 1977.

MILLER, R. I. *Evaluating Faculty Performance.* San Francisco: Jossey-Bass, 1972.

MILLER, R. I. *Developing Programs for Faculty Evaluation: A Sourcebook for Higher Education.* San Francisco: Jossey-Bass, 1974.

MILLER, W. F. "Institutional Policy Setting—A Dynamic View." Unpublished paper, Stanford University, 1978.

MILLETT, J. D. *Allocation Decisions in Higher Education.* New York: Academy for Educational Development, n.d.

MILLETT, J. D. "Higher Education Management Versus Business Management." *Educational Record,* 1975, 56, 221.

MILLETT, J. D. *The Multiple Roles of College and University Presidents.* Washington, D.C.: American Council on Education, 1976.

MILLETT, J. D. *Planning in Higher Education.* Washington, D.C.: Academy for Educational Development, 1977.

MILLETT, J. D. *New Structures of Campus Power: Success and Failures of Emerging Forms of Institutional Governance.* San Francisco: Jossey-Bass, 1978.

MINTER, W. J., AND BOWEN, H. R. *Independent Higher Education.* Washington, D.C.: National Association of Independent Colleges and Universities, 1978.

MIX, M. M. *Tenure and Termination in Financial Exigency.* Washington, D.C.: American Association for Higher Education, 1978.

MOOD, A. M. *The Future of Higher Education: Some Speculations and Suggestions.* New York: McGraw-Hill, 1973.

MORTIMER, K. P. (Ed.). *Faculty Bargaining, State Government and Campus Autonomy: The Experience in Eight States.* Denver, Colo.: Education Commission of the States, 1976.

MORTIMER, K. P., AND MC CONNELL, T. R. *Sharing Authority Effectively: Participation, Interaction, and Discretion.* San Francisco: Jossey-Bass, 1978.

MORTIMER, K. P., AND RICHARDSON, R. C., JR. *Governance in Institutions With Collective Bargaining: Six Case Studies.* University

Park: Center for the Study of Higher Education, Pennsylvania State University, 1977.

MURPHY, P. E., AND MC GARRITY, B. A. "Marketing Universities: A Survey of Student Recruitment Activities." *College and University*, 1978, *53* (3), 249–261.

NASON, J. W. *The Future of Trusteeship*. Washington, D.C.: Association of Governing Boards of Universities and Colleges, 1974.

National Association of College and University Business Officers. *College & University Business Administration*. (3rd ed.) Washington, D.C.: National Association of College and University Business Officers, 1974.

NESS, F. W. *An Uncertain Glory: Letters of Cautious but Sound Advice to Stanley, a Dean-in-Waiting, from C. F. Coltswood, a President-at-Large*. San Francisco: Jossey-Bass, 1971.

ODIORNE, G. S. *Personnel Administration by Objective*. Homewood, Ill.: Irwin, 1971.

Organization for Economic Cooperation and Development. *Methods and Statistical Needs for Educational Planning*. Washington, D.C.: Organization for Economic Cooperation and Development, 1967a.

Organization for Economic Cooperation and Development. *Social Objectives in Educational Planning*. Washington, D.C.: Organization for Economic Cooperation and Development, 1967b.

ORWIG, M. D., JONES, P. K., AND LENNING, O. T. *Enrollment Projection Models for Institutional Planning*. ACT Research Report No. 48. Iowa City, Iowa: American College Testing Program, 1972.

PALOLA, E. G., LEHMANN, T., AND BLESCHKE, W. R. *Higher Education by Design: The Sociology of Planning*. Berkeley: Center for Research and Development in Higher Education, University of California, 1970.

PALOLA, E. G., AND PADGETT, W. *Planning for Self Renewal: A New Approach to Planned Organizational Change*. Berkeley: Center for Research and Development in Higher Education, University of California, 1971.

PANTAGES, T. "Studies of College Attrition: 1950–1975." *Review of Educational Research*, 1978, *48*, 49–101.

PATON, G. J. "Determinants of Voluntary Support to Private Liberal

Arts Colleges." Unpublished doctoral dissertation proposal, Stanford University, 1979.

PERKINS, J. A., AND ISRAEL, B. B. (Eds.). *Higher Education: From Autonomy to Systems.* New York: International Council for Educational Development, 1972.

PERVIN, L. A., REIK, L. E., AND DALRYMPLE, W. (Eds.). *The College Dropout and the Utilization of Talent.* Princeton, N.J.: Princeton University Press, 1966.

POLLARD, J. A. *Fundraising for Higher Education.* New York: Harper & Row, 1954.

RAIA, A. P. *Management by Objectives.* Glenview, Ill.: Scott, Foresman, 1974.

RICHMAN, B. M., AND FARMER, R. N. *Leadership, Goals, and Power in Higher Education: A Contingency and Open-Systems Approach to Effective Management.* San Francisco: Jossey-Bass, 1974.

ROWLAND, A. W. (Ed.). *Handbook of Institutional Advancement: A Practical Guide to College and University Relations, Fund Raising, Alumni Relations, Government Relations, Publications, and Executive Management for Continued Advancement.* San Francisco: Jossey-Bass, 1977.

SANDIN, R. T. *Power and Purpose in Collegiate Government: Role of the Faculty in Academic Planning.* Toledo, Ohio: Center for the Study of Higher Education, University of Toledo, 1969.

SCOTT, R. A. *Lords, Squires and Yeomen: Collegiate Middle Managers and Their Organization.* Washington, D.C.: American Association for Higher Education, 1978.

SELZNICK, D. *Leadership in Administration.* New York: Harper & Row, 1957.

SEYMOUR, H. J. *Designs for Fund Raising.* New York: McGraw-Hill, 1966.

SHULMAN, C. H. *Employment of Nontenured Faculty: Some Implications of Roth Sinderman.* Washington, D.C.: American Association for Higher Education, 1973.

SHULMAN, C. H. *Private Colleges: Present Conditions and Future Prospects.* Washington, D.C.: American Association for Higher Education, 1974.

SHULMAN, C. H. *University Admissions: Dilemmas on Potential.*

Washington, D.C.: American Association for Higher Education, 1977.

SMART, J. C., AND MONTGOMERY, J. R. (Eds.). *New Directions for Institutional Research: Examining Departmental Management*, no. 10. San Francisco: Jossey-Bass, 1976.

SMITH, A. B. *Faculty Development and Evaluation in Higher Education*. ERIC/Higher Education Research Report No. 8. Washington, D.C.: American Association of Higher Education, 1976.

SMITH, B. L., AND ASSOCIATES. *The Tenure Debate*. San Francisco: Jossey-Bass, 1973.

SOSDIAN, C. P. *External Degrees: Program and Student Characteristics*. Washington, D.C.: National Institute of Education, 1978.

Southern Regional Education Board. *Faculty Development Centers in Southern Universities*. Atlanta, Ga.: Southern Regional Education Board, 1976.

STECKLEIN, J. E. *How to Measure Faculty Work Load*. Washington, D.C.: American Council on Education, 1961.

STEWART, C. T., AND HARVEY, T. R. (Eds.). *New Directions for Higher Education: Strategies for Significant Survival*, no. 12. San Francisco: Jossey-Bass, 1975.

STROUP, H. *Bureaucracy in Higher Education*. New York: Free Press, 1966.

SUMMERSKILL, J. "Dropouts From College." In N. Sanford (Ed.), *The American College*. New York: Wiley, 1962.

THRESHER, B. A. *College Admissions and the Public Interest*. New York: College Entrance Examination Board, 1966.

TICE, T. N. (Ed.). *Faculty Bargaining in the Seventies*. Ann Arbor: Institute for Continuing Legal Education, University of Michigan, 1973.

TINTO, V. "Dropout from Higher Education: A Theoretical Synthesis of Recent Research." *Review of Educational Research*, 1975, *45* (1).

TOOMBS, W. *Productivity: Burden of Success*. Washington, D.C.: American Association for Higher Education, 1973.

TRENT, J. W., AND MEDSKER, L. L. *Beyond High School: A Psychosociological Study of 10,000 High School Graduates*. San Francisco: Jossey-Bass, 1968.

TRITES, D. G. (Ed.). *New Directions for Higher Education: Plan-*

ning the Future of the Undergraduate College, no. 9. San Francisco: Jossey-Bass, 1975.

WEATHERSBY, G. B., AND JACOBS, F. *Institutional Goals and Student Costs.* Washington, D.C.: American Association for Higher Education, 1977.

WEATHERSBY, G. B., AND WEINSTEIN, M. C. "A Structural Comparison of Analytic Models for University Planning." Berkeley: Ford Foundation Program for Research in University Administration, University of California, 1970.

WEICK, K. E. "Enactment Processes in Organizations." In B. M. Stow and G. R. Salanik (Eds.), *New Directions in Organizational Behavior.* Chicago: St. Clair Press, 1977.

WILLIAMS, H. *Planning for Effective Resource Allocation in Universities.* Washington, D.C.: American Council on Education, 1966.

WING, C. W., JR., AND WALLACH, M. A. *College Admissions and the Psychology of Talent.* New York: Holt, Rinehart and Winston, 1971.

WITHEY, S. B. *A Degree and What Else?* New York: McGraw-Hill, 1971.

WOOD, L., AND DAVIS, B. G. *Designing and Evaluating Higher Education Curricula.* Washington, D.C.: American Association for Higher Education, 1978.

WORMLEY, W. M. "Factors Related to the Ability of Certain Small Private Liberal Arts Colleges to Cope with the New Depression in Higher Education." Unpublished doctoral dissertation, Stanford University, 1978.

YOUNG, D. P. "Registrar, the Admissions Officer and Academic Consumerism." *College and University,* 1978, *53,* 153–163.

YUKER, H. E. *Faculty Workload: Facts, Myths and Commentary.* ERIC/Higher Education Research Report No. 6. Washington, D.C.: American Association of Higher Education, 1974.

Index

$\lessgtr\lessgtr\lessgtr\lessgtr\lessgtr\lessgtr\lessgtr\lessgtr\lessgtr$

A

Academic deans: and crisis management, 86; and faculty committees, 46

Academic planning and budgeting, process of, 107-108

Academic vice-president: and faculty mental health, 244; and program cuts, 273

Academy for Educational Development, Management Division of, 268, 306n

Accreditation: and crisis management, 88, 89; and vulnerability of unique institutions, 6-7

Administration: analysis of structure and policies for, 32-62; authority of, centralized, 33-34, 297-298; and boards of trustees, 37, 42-43; budget decentralization in, 51-53; cabinet system of, 44-46; communication confused in, 34-35; consultation rights of, in union contract, 258-259; as contributor to failure, 73-74; decentralization of, 33-34, 297-298; decreasing expenditures for, 312-315; duties clarified for, 53-55, 239-240; effectiveness of, 30; environment difficult for, 64-66; faculty participation in, 46-51; and faculty senate, 35, 43, 46-47; improving, and survival, 296-298; leadership by, 63-83; leadership needed in, 27-28; legitimacy for, from faculty, 225-226; misalignment of, 34; mismanagement by, types of, 74; overload of, 35-36; policies for, written, 59-60; poorly organized, case of, 37-41; position control by, 246-248; positions necessary for, 57; positions unnecessary for, 58-59; preparation for, inadequate, 36; principles of, 41, 50-51, 56, 60-61; program and budget responsibilities uncoordinated in, 36-37; skills needed for, 36; staff limitation for, 55-59; structure needed for, 27, 296; termination responsibility of, 286-287; and unionism, 254-255, 259-262; unitary system of, 41-44; weaknesses in, 33-37. *See also* Management; President Administrative units: and budget decentralization, 51-53, 268-269; and reducing expenditures, 320-321; responsibility of, 297-298; self supporting, 249-250; and termination decisions, 282, 284

Admissions: attrition related to, 197-198; likelihood of, and college choice, 158; staff for, 172-173. *See also* Recruitment

Admissions director: and crisis management, 85-86; and direct reporting to president, 34; and recruitment, 169-170; role for, 173-174

Adulthood, striving toward, as reason for attending college, 156

Advising: and admissions, 174; system for, and attrition, 198-200

Advocacy, administrative responsibility for, 54

Affirmative action, and tenure, 253

ALLAN, M. A., 330

ALM, K. G., 288, 323

American Alumni Council, 323

American Association of University Professors (AAUP), 39, 79, 251, 258, 261, 263, 284, 286, 323

American Council on Education, 109

American Federation of Teachers (AFT), 257, 258

Amherst College, intellectual stimulation at, 235

ANDERSON, C. A., 189, 323

ANDREW, L. D., 31, 323

ANGELL, G. W., 261, 263, 323-324

Antioch College: curriculum of, 203; diversification by, 72; mission of, 148-149, 162; position of, 177

Antioch Law School, dual administrative system at, 42

Arkansas, high school students' perceptions in, 206

ASKEW, T. A., 31, 324

Association of American Colleges (AAC), 263, 323

ASTIN, A. W., 189, 196, 204, 222, 324

Attrition: achievement related to, 194-196; admissions related to, 197-198; and advising system, 198-200; analysis of reducing, 192-200; of faculty, 276-278; and financial aid, 196; and institutional environment, 196-197; reasons for, 192-193

B

BAIRD, L. L., 189-190, 324

BALDERSTON, F. E., 109, 324

BALDRIDGE, J. V., 61, 97, 109, 264, 324, 331

Baptist Institute for Christian Workers, 88-91

BENNIS, W., 83, 324

BERDAHL, R. O., 83, 324

Berea College, mission of, 135

BERGQUIST, W. H., 263, 324-325

BLACKBURN, R., 207, 325

BLAU, P., 61, 325

BLESCHKE, W. R., 134, 334

BLOOM, B. S., 190, 325

Boards of trustees. *See* Trustees, boards of

BOLEN, J. G., 109, 325

Boston College, mission of, 154

Boston University: College of Basic Studies at, 218; effective leadership at, 75-81; mission of, 154, 171, 189; reason for attending, 161; regional nature of, 23

BOWAN, M. J., 189, 323

Bowdoin College: identity of, 296; successful survival of, 8-13

BOWEN, F. M., 83, 331

BOWEN, H. R., 31, 113, 172, 204, 216, 288, 325, 333

BOWEN, W. G., 289, 325

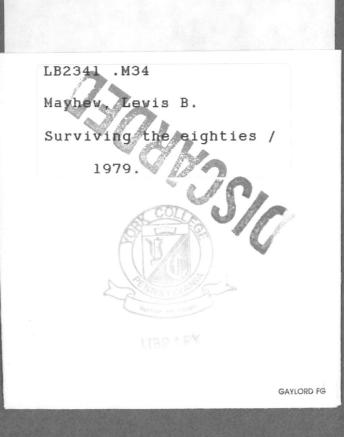